John Codman Ropes

The First Napoleon

A Sketch

John Codman Ropes

The First Napoleon
A Sketch

ISBN/EAN: 9783337350178

Printed in Europe, USA, Canada, Australia, Japan

Cover: Foto ©Thomas Meinert / pixelio.de

More available books at **www.hansebooks.com**

THE FIRST NAPOLEON

A SKETCH, POLITICAL AND MILITARY

BY

JOHN CODMAN ROPES

MEMBER OF THE MASSACHUSETTS HISTORICAL SOCIETY, THE MILITARY HISTORICAL
SOCIETY OF MASSACHUSETTS, THE HARVARD HISTORICAL SOCIETY; FELLOW
OF THE AMERICAN ACADEMY OF ARTS AND SCIENCES; AUTHOR OF
"THE ARMY UNDER POPE," IN THE SCRIBNER SERIES OF
"CAMPAIGNS OF THE CIVIL WAR"

BOSTON AND NEW YORK
HOUGHTON, MIFFLIN AND COMPANY
The Riverside Press, Cambridge

PREFACE TO THE TWELFTH EDITION.

I READILY embrace the opportunity afforded me by the printing of this edition, to make a few corrections in my account of the campaign of Waterloo. Since the book was first published, in 1885, I have had occasion to make a careful study of this campaign, the results of which I have embodied in a separate work. The changes I have made in this edition, while not numerous, are of some importance.

I have (on page 249) stated my present belief that Napoleon did, on the afternoon of the 15th of June, order Marshal Ney to seize Quatre Bras that evening. I have (on pp. 250, 251, 260) shown why the Duke of Wellington delayed ordering the assembling of his army at Quatre Bras, and have stated that his orders for this movement were given about or soon after midnight of the 15th, and not when he arrived at Quatre Bras the next forenoon.

I state (on page 257) that it was the bearer of the two P. M. order to Marshal Ney, who took it upon himself to order d'Erlon's corps toward St. Amand. I have also given (on page 263) what I have now no doubt was the real reason of Napoleon's dictating the famous Bertrand order, namely, that the news, — which arrived after he had given Grouchy the verbal orders, — that a Prussian corps had been seen at Gembloux, made the Emperor think it by no means unlikely that Blücher meant to join the English and fight another battle.

Lastly, I have rectified (on pp. 281, 282) the account of the last charge and repulse of the Imperial Guard.

The portrait of Napoleon which is prefixed to this volume is from a sketch in india ink taken in 1814. It once belonged to a large collection of likenesses of the Emperor made by the widow of General de Billy, who was killed at the battle of Jena, in 1806. It is attributed either to the Count de Waldeck or his daughter, both of whom were portrait painters of some reputation under the Empire. Other sketches of Napoleon, which once belonged to the same collection, are in the Library of the Military Historical Society of Massachusetts, where is also an account of the collection, and of the acquisition of a portion of it by the Society. The resemblance between this portrait of Napoleon and that in Meissonier's picture entitled 1814 is striking.

JOHN C. ROPES.

99 MOUNT VERNON STREET,
    10th January, 1895.

INTRODUCTION.

THE Lectures which are published in this volume were delivered in Boston, under the auspices of the Lowell Institute, in March, 1885. They are now submitted to the public without substantial alteration. A few appendices are added.

So much has been written about Napoleon that the publication of another book on his life and work may seem to some to require a few words of explanation. Let me, then, say, that in the sketch which I have given of Napoleon's foreign and domestic policy, I have chiefly proposed to point out what I conceive to have been the real nature of the contest in which he played so prominent a part, and the actual political capacity at that time of the peoples over whom he ruled or whose institutions he shaped. I have not undertaken to write a new history, but simply to indicate the lines upon which a new history might be written. The task of rectifying the fundamental notions with which nearly all historians have approached the study of the epoch of Napoleon is the task which I proposed to myself.

I have, therefore, endeavored to point out clearly the distinction between the extension of personal liberty, the removal of abuses, the abolition of privileges and disabilities, and the like legal and social changes, on the one hand, and the acquisition and enjoyment of political power by the people, on the other. These results are very often confounded, but they are really very different things.

I have also called attention to the fact that, where political rights are conferred upon populations whose previous political experience has in no wise fitted them for the exercise of those rights, they will continue, in spite of the most advanced constitutions and laws, to be subject to somebody or other, as completely as before such rights were conferred.

Accordingly, I have endeavored to show that the task of the French Revolution was a very different one from what it has been generally supposed to be by historians and writers of the liberal school. The Revolution undoubtedly did abolish the great and crying abuses, and it introduced important improvements in legislation. It gave, in fact, to the populations of the west of Europe much better administrative governments than any they had ever enjoyed before. But, suddenly to transform those populations, whether by its convulsions or its enactments, into self-governing communities, to confer in a moment upon the bourgeois and peasant of the continent the political capacity inherited by the English freeholder and the American farmer, was, in the nature of things, impossible. Once let a clear-headed man get hold of this distinction, and he will see that very many of the criticisms which have been levelled at Napoleon's government of France and her dependencies are entirely misdirected. He will also, I think, be inclined to regard it as a very fair question whether Napoleon did not understand the political needs and capacities of his generation far better than any of his critics.

The real character of the Napoleonic wars cannot be mistaken. It was no soldier's ambition that carried the great conqueror from Madrid to Moscow. At the bottom of the twenty years' strife was the " irrepressible conflict " between liberty and equality on the one hand, and privilege and despotism on the other. What the ruling classes had always enjoyed they defended by the sword; what the people had gained they maintained at the point of the bayonet. Add to this, that Napoleon saw in the alliance of Russia, Austria, and Prussia a menace and a danger to the more liberal and progressive civilization of western Europe. Much of what he foresaw has actually happened. The weight of this alliance now presses heavily against France herself. There is now no western Germany. That there is now an Italy is mainly due to the enlightened sagacity of another Napoleon. But the three emperors to-day control the affairs of the continent. Napoleon's aim — the establishment of a sort of federative union, under the protection of France, of the states lying west of the Elbe, the Tyrol, and the Adriatic, which should accept the modern ideas of equality and toleration, and which were thenceforth to be free to mould their institutions in accordance with the views of an enlightened policy accommodated to the growing political capacity of the populations, free from the dictation of Berlin, St. Petersburg, or Vienna — will never be carried out now. But it was to accomplish this end, to bring it about that the three great reactionary monarchies should be powerless to interfere with or encroach upon the progressive states of the West, that French and German soldiers fought the Austrian Kaiser at Wagram and the Russian Czar at Borodino. Opinions may differ as to the desirability of this aim, but when it is once clearly conceived as a project for the location of the centre of political power in the more enlightened western states of the continent, the foreign policy of Napoleon — so far, that is, as it was initiated by him, and not forced upon him — becomes intelligible and well worthy the most careful consideration. The truth is, that Napoleon was not aiming at the conquest of Europe, as has been so often said, but at such an adjustment of the balance of political power in Europe as would definitively relieve the freer and more progressive states of the West from the aggressions and the predominant influence of the three great military monarchies of the East.

It will be seen that there are many incidents in the career of Napoleon to which I have not adverted; many, and some of them, very likely, important, events in the history of the times of which I have not even spoken. While some of these omissions are no doubt accidental, by far the greater part are deliberately made. I have not attempted to write a history, even an abridged history. I have confined myself strictly to presenting what appear to me to be the more important and characteristic features of the period, and to pointing out what seems to be their true political significance.

It is hoped that the few military narratives and discussions in the following pages will not prove unacceptable. Knowing the much greater familiarity of the general public with the details of the campaign of 1815, I have thought that a somewhat extended examination of it would be interesting. Much national, and, of late years, political, prejudice has entered into the discussion of this subject in Europe, but it would seem that it ought to be possible for Americans to arrive at an impartial estimate of the credit and blame which should attach to the chief actors in that famous drama.

J. C. R.

99 MOUNT VERNON STREET,
BOSTON, *October* 1, 1885.

TABLE OF CONTENTS

LECTURE I.

TOULON AND ITALY.

	PAGE
Our general knowledge of the Napoleonic epoch; and of the various views about it	1
Our difficulties in arriving at conclusions	1
State of things in Europe in 1789	2
Divine right of kings	2
Oppressive privileges of the favored classes	3
Different countries	3
Russia	3
Prussia	3
Austria	3
France	4
Italy	4
General improvement in the preceding century	5
Backwardness of Spain	5
No such thing as government by the people possible anywhere	5
Practical reform, not assertion of rights, the need of the times	5
The American Revolution a wholly different matter	6
Assertion of the rights of man by the French Revolutionists accompanied by despotic government	7
Cause of this anomaly	8
The French people did not exercise political rights, but gained liberty and equality	9
The losses of the privileged classes occasioned by the reforms of the Revolution	9
Their hostility to the new system	10

TABLE OF CONTENTS.

Fierce and aggressive character of the Revolution	10
Alarm of the privileged classes throughout Europe	11
"Irrepressible conflict" between the principles of the Revolution and those underlying existing European society	11
War everywhere	11
The volunteers and regular army of France	12
First appearance of Napoleon Bonaparte	12
His character as a soldier	12
His studies	12
His attention to detail	13
Anecdote	13
The Siege of Toulon	14
Appointed general, and serves with the army of Italy	15
His aversion to cruel measures	15
His alleged indifference to the evils of war	16
The 9th of Thermidor, 1794	18
Changes in public opinion	18
The Constitution of 1795	18
Provisions ensuring continuance of Republican rule	19
Revolt of the Sections, 13th Vendémiaire, 1795	19
Bonaparte's marriage to Madame Beauharnais	20
Her character	20
Bonaparte appointed to the command of the Army of Italy	21
Sketch of the campaigns of 1796 and 1797	23
Bonaparte's dealings with the Italian states	25
Growth of his reputation as a general	26
Augereau, Masséna, Lannes	28
The 18th of Fructidor, 1797	29
Character of the new government	30
The expedition to Egypt	30
Nature of the contest in Europe	32
Illustrated by the revolution in Naples	34
The side of France the side of progress	34
Suppression of the Parthenopæan Republic	36
Lord Nelson sets aside the capitulation	36
And has Caraccioli hanged	37
Reverses of the French in Italy and on the sea	38
Unpopularity of the Directory	39
It is felt to be a mere temporary expedient	39
Return of Bonaparte from Egypt	41

LECTURE II.

THE CONSULATE.

Weakness of the Directory	42
Popularity of Bonaparte	42
The 18th of Brumaire, 1799	43
The French people of that time unable to govern themselves	43
What the Revolution could and what it could not accomplish	44
Danger of a return of the Bourbons	45
Necessity of a change in the form of government	45
The *coup d'état* followed by no proscriptions	46
And generally acceptable to all classes	46
The three Consuls	47
Amnesty to the emigrants	47
Bonaparte's efforts for peace fail	48
Return of the French army from Egypt	49
The war with Austria resumed	49
Campaign of General Moreau in Germany	50
Campaign of the First Consul in Italy	51
His plan	52
His army	52
He crosses the Alps	53
Marches upon Milan	54
Then turns to seek the Austrians	54
Difficulties of the Austrian situation	55
Battle of Marengo	56
Effect of the victory	57
The campaign discussed : —	
Its completeness of design	57
Its audacity	58
Napoleon's peculiar characteristics as a general	59
He frequently takes unjustifiable risks	59
Comparison between him and Moreau	59
Lanfrey's criticism too severe	60
Napoleon's fault very common in men of affairs	61
Peace concluded with England and Austria	62
The Jacobins oppose the Consular government	63
But have no following among the people	63
The Royalists are supported by the British government	64

TABLE OF CONTENTS.

The Infernal Machine of December, 1800	65
The conspiracy of Georges Cadoudal	66
Character of Georges	66
His plan is openly to murder Bonaparte in the streets	66
His devotion to the cause of legitimacy	67
His plan is favored by the Comte d'Artois	67
And assisted by the British government	68
Strength of the Legitimist prejudice	68
Citation from Scott's Life of Napoleon	69
Excitement in Paris on the discovery of the plot	70
The Duc d'Enghien suspected of complicity with it	71
He is arrested at Ettenheim in Baden	72
And tried by court-martial at Vincennes and shot	72
Charges against Bonaparte	72
General principles applicable to a case of this nature	73
The arrest clearly justifiable	74
The doings of the court-martial	75
Constitution of the court	75
The original records lost	75
Savary's statement of the Duke's reply to the court	76
The court really had no option but to condemn him	77
The real question was, Why was he tried?	78
Bonaparte's reasons	78
The Duke's papers seized at Ettenheim	78
His anxiety about them	79
Bonaparte examines them	80
He frames questions out of their contents	80
Probable contents of the papers	81
Miot de Melito's statements	82
The Duke's anxiety to see the First Consul	82
Responsibility for the promptitude of the execution	85
Savary probably not responsible	86
Bonaparte certainly not	86
It was most likely a mistake of the Judge Advocate	86
Summary of the case	87

LECTURE III.

NAPOLEON IN GERMANY.

Suppression of the conspiracy of Georges	88
Reforms of the Consular government	89
Lanfrey's perverse criticisms	89

TABLE OF CONTENTS. xv

Cause of Lanfrey's animosity against Napoleon	90
The Code Napoleon	91
Napoleon's share in this great work	91
Its great utility	93
The Concordat	94
Establishment of the Empire	96
Demanded by public opinion	97
Dilemma of the Republican theorists	97
The Empire really a change for the better	98
The Peace of Lunéville and its consequences	99
French influence in Germany	100
Its wholesome character	100
Opposing view of German nationalists	100
Stein and the Knights of the Empire	101
Fyffe's objections to French interference examined	103
Necessity for these changes in Germany	104
No national feeling then existent in Germany	105
The course of the West German States justified	106
Italy becomes a kingdom	107
Causes of the coalition of 1805	108
The projected invasion of England	108
Its probable fate, if it had been attempted	110
Battle of Trafalgar	110
The campaign of 1805 in Germany	111
German allies of France	111
Capture of Ulm and entry into Vienna	112
The French advance into Moravia	112
Danger of Napoleon's situation	112
Hostile demonstration of Prussia	113
Battle of Austerlitz	114
Causes of his great success on this occasion	115
A different policy should have been followed by the allies	116
Peace of Presbourg	117
What we should look at in these conflicts	118
The result of the war a benefit to Europe	119
The Confederation of the Rhine established	120
Continuance of the war by England	121
Her attitude towards France not unlike her attitude towards the United States in the late Civil War	121
The policy of Prussia vacillating	123
The war party finally prevail	124
Great age of the leading Prussian generals	126

The campaign of Jéna 126
Manœuvres prior to the battle 127
Battles of Jéna and Auerstädt 127
The Emperor rewards Davout 128
Conquest of Prussia 128
Battles of Eylau and Friedland 129
Peace of Tilsit 129

LECTURE IV.

TILSIT TO MOSCOW.

Peace of Tilsit 130
Establishment of the Grand Duchy of Warsaw . . . 130
And of the Kingdom of Westphalia 130
Its new Constitution 131
Its characteristic features 131
Napoleon's letter to Jerome 132
Napoleon's views of the needs of the western states of
    Europe 133
His treatment of the Neapolitan Bourbons and of the Span-
    ish Bourbons 135
His mistaken view of the Spanish people . . . 136
What he tried to do for Spain 137
Spain rejects the new system 139
Napoleon invades and leaves Spain 140
Austria declares war without provocation . . . 141
The campaign opens at Abensberg and Eckmühl . . 142
Battle of Aspern 143
Battle of Wagram 145
Remarks on this battle 149
The Peace of Vienna 149
Beneficial changes effected throughout the Empire . 150
The continental system 152
The stability of the Empire dependent on Napoleon's life 152
The divorce of the Empress Josephine 154
Causes of the continuance of the wars 156
The fundamental difference between the old and the new
    systems 156
The aggrandizement of the Empire of Napoleon . . 157
War impending between France and Russia . . . 158
Its general causes 158
The Polish question: Russia's plans 159

Russia hopes to break the power of Napoleon . . . 161
Napoleon hopes to reëstablish Poland 162
His preparations and armies 163
He crosses the Niemen 163
Position of the Russian armies 164
Napoleon succeeds in separating them . . . 165
But fails in forcing Barclay de Tolly to fight alone . . 166
Operations about Smolensk 167
Junot's inaction at Valoutina 169
Napoleon's situation at Smolensk 169
He determines to advance on Moscow . . . 171
Battle of Borodino 172
His mistake in not putting in the Guard . . . 174
He arrives at Moscow 175

LECTURE V.

MOSCOW TO ELBA.

Condition of the French army at Moscow . . . 176
The city is burnt 177
Retreat unavoidable 178
Napoleon's inexcusable delay 180
Possibility of effecting a safe retreat . . . 180
Activity of the Russian armies 181
The discipline of the Grand Army impaired . . 182
Battle of Malo-Jaroslawetz 183
The retreat commenced 184
Arrival at Smolensk. The cold begins . . . 184
Terrible losses 184
The different corps retreat separately on Krasnoi . . 184
Battle of Krasnoi 185
Heroic conduct of Ney 186
The weather moderates 186
Reorganization of the army at Orcha . . . 186
Mistake of Koutousof 187
The crossing of the Beresina 188
Criticism on Napoleon's conduct 189
The retreat continued to Wilna 191
Severity of the cold 192
Napoleon leaves the army 192
Sir Robert Wilson's opinion of this step . . . 192
The army falls back to Kowno and thence into Prussia . 193

Losses of the campaign 193
Partly due to preventable causes 194
Sufferings of the Russians 195
The French army practically dissolved 195
Disgraceful conduct of General Yorck 195
Retreat of the Austrian contingent 198
Russia gains the Grand Duchy of Warsaw . . . 198
The Czar aims at the "Deliverance of Europe" . . . 198
The attitude of Prussia and Austria 199
Awakening of the Legitimist party throughout Europe . 202
Great efforts of France and her allies for the coming campaign 202
Prussia joins the coalition 203
Liberal promises of the allies 203
They appeal to the sentiment of German nationality . 204
The real state of the countries forming the French Empire 205
Napoleon obstinately persists in the Spanish war . . 207
And in keeping up the continental system . . . 207
The new Grand Army and its faults 208
Opening of the campaign of 1813 209
Battles of Lützen and Bautzen . . . 210
Austria exacts terms for her neutrality 211
Napoleon refuses to yield anything 211
His folly in so doing 213
Austria joins the coalition 214
Battle of Leipsic 215
Napoleon's terrible mistake in not concentrating his armies 215
He refuses reasonable terms of peace 217
His obstinate and reckless persistence in continuing the war 219
Campaign of 1814 and fall of Paris 219

LECTURE VI.

THE RETURN FROM ELBA.

State of France in 1814 220
Unpopularity of Napoleon 221
But there existed no desire to return to the old régime . 221
The allies refuse to treat with Napoleon . . . 222
Folly of this course 222
And of restoring the Bourbons 223
Napoleon exiled to Elba 224

Louis XVIII. on the throne	225
His difficulties	226
Discontent in the army	227
The Judiciary interfered with	228
The fanaticism of the returned emigrants	228
The Constitution of Louis XVIII.	229
It avails the king but little	229
Hard terms exacted from France	231
Depression of manufactures	231
Napoleon not held responsible for these troubles	232
He leaves Elba and lands near Cannes	233
His unopposed march to Paris	234
League against him of all the European Powers	235
Folly and injustice of this course	236
The liberal party in France	237
They alone are lukewarm	238
The several courses open to Napoleon	239
State of Italy and western Germany	241
Occupation of Belgium by the allies	241
Armies of Wellington and Blücher	242
Napoleon's plan of campaign	242
His army and its chiefs	243
Napoleon and Davout	244
Soult takes the place of Berthier	246
Condition of Wellington's army	247
And of that of Blücher	247
Napoleon crosses the Sambre	248
Ney and Quatre Bras	249
The Prussians concentrate on Ligny	250
Wellington fears that Napoleon will turn his right	250
Concentration of the French at Frasnes and Fleurus	252
Napoleon resolves to attack the Prussians	253
Battle of Ligny	253
Ney's partial concentration at Frasnes	255
The first corps under d'Erlon march towards Saint Amand	255
Battle of Quatre Bras	256
The staff-officer's error	256
Result of the battle of Quatre Bras	257
Consequences of d'Erlon's not being engaged	257
Criticism on Blücher and Wellington	258

LECTURE VII.

WATERLOO AND SAINT HELENA.

The morning of the 17th of June	261
No sufficient reconnoissances made	261
Careless confidence of Napoleon	262
He detaches Grouchy in pursuit of Blücher	263
The Bertrand order	263
The Emperor marches on Quatre Bras, and Grouchy on Gembloux	264
Criticism of the Emperor for not attacking the English at Quatre Bras	265
Blücher retires on Wavre	266
Grouchy's letter of ten P. M. of the 17th	266
Grouchy ascertains that the Prussians have fallen back on Wavre	268
His true course	268
His delay in starting on the 18th	269
He declines to march to the sound of the cannon	270
Situation of the two armies at Waterloo	271
Wellington's position	272
Delay of Napoleon in commencing the action	272
Battle of Waterloo	273
Attack upon Hougoumont	273
D'Erlon's attack and its failure	274
Losses of the English. Death of Picton	274
The Prussians seen approaching	275
The sixth corps detached to resist them	276
Inadequate force of infantry in the front	276
The cavalry put in	276
Failure of the cavalry attacks	276
Losses of the English from artillery and skirmishers	277
La Haye Sainte taken	278
Critical condition of Wellington's army	278
The action near Planchenoit	279
The sixth corps reinforced by a portion of the Guard	279
Napoleon determines to put in the Old Guard against the English	280
Arrival of the Prussians on the English left	281
A cessation of offensive operations the wiser course	280
Attack of the Imperial Guard and its failure	281

The Prussians defeat Lobau and carry Planchenoit . . 283
Rout of the French army 283
Great praise due to Wellington and Blücher . . . 284
Review of the campaign 285
Successes of the French on the 15th and 16th . . . 285
Fatal neglect in not ascertaining the direction of the Prussian retreat after Ligny 286
Napoleon's mistaken conjecture as to that direction . 286
His delay in starting Grouchy 286
Grouchy's duty on the 18th 286
The despatches sent Grouchy 287
Grouchy rejoins the wreck of the army 292
The situation in Paris after Waterloo 293
Napoleon's abdication 294
Efforts of the provisional government to obtain recognition 294
Convention of Paris 295
Louis XVIII. resumes the throne 295
Napoleon exiled to Saint Helena 295
His life there 296
His treatment by the English government 296
His commentaries on his wars 297
Absurd charges against him 298
His death and funeral 298
The Bourbons restored 299
Trial and execution of Ney 299
Indifference of Wellington 300
He allows his convention to be violated by the king . 301
The reaction on the continent 301
Erroneous view of Napoleon by liberal writers . . 303
Estimate of Napoleon and his work 304
Charge of selfishness 306
His character and his acts 307

APPENDICES.

APPENDIX I.
On Napoleon's occasional severities 309

APPENDIX II.
On Napoleon's hold upon his soldiers 310

APPENDIX III.

On Mr. Herbert Spencer's employment of the "Great Man Theory of History" in reference to Napoleon . . . 320

APPENDIX IV.

On the Polish question and the Russian war . . . 321

APPENDIX V.

On Marmont's criticism on Napoleon's tactics in his later campaigns 325

APPENDIX VI.

On the numbers engaged and on the losses in the war with Russia 326

APPENDIX VII.

On the Bertrand order 329

APPENDIX VIII.

On Ney's employment of the cavalry of the Guard at Waterloo 338

APPENDIX IX.

On Dr. Edward A. Freeman's continuing to use the name "Buonaparte" in his histories 338

LIST OF MAPS.

ITALIAN CAMPAIGN OF 1796	facing page 24
ITALIAN CAMPAIGN OF 1800	between pages 54, 55
BATTLE OF AUSTERLITZ	facing page 114
BATTLE OF WAGRAM	facing page 148
RUSSIA, WILNA TO SMOLENSK	between pages 166, 167
CAMPAIGN OF WATERLOO, *June 16, 1815, 9 A. M.*	facing page 250
THE SAME, *June 16, 1815, 5 P. M.*	facing page 256
THE SAME, *June 18, 1815, 4 A. M.*	facing page 268
BATTLE OF WATERLOO,[1] *June 18, 1815, 7.45 P. M.*	
	between pages 282, 283

[1] For this map the author is indebted to Captain Siborne's valuable Atlas.

THE FIRST NAPOLEON.

LECTURE I.

TOULON AND ITALY.

The career of Napoleon Bonaparte possesses an irresistible attraction for every one. We recognize the fascination of that wonderful story of brilliant achievement, steady toil, and unparalleled success, followed by defeat, abdication, exile. The great names, Marengo, Austerlitz, Jéna, Leipsic, Waterloo, St. Helena, are all familiar to our ears.

Moreover, we are all more or less acquainted with the various and frequently opposite opinions that have been held regarding Napoleon and his work. We know that Sir Walter Scott and Sir Archibald Alison give us the views of the nation that was always his most active and persistent foe; that Thiers, in his great work, tries as a patriotic Frenchman to do him full justice; that Lanfrey, in his recent biography, attacks his memory with all the virulence of political hate, caused by existing political controversies in which he has been himself a most active partisan.

We know, also, not only that we are three thousand miles away from the scene of Napoleon's activity, but that our country is separated by a great gulf, in laws, traditions, and social and political conditions, from the Europe of the First Napoleon. Doubtless many of us have seen the absurdity of instituting any comparison between him and Washington; no doubt we have recognized that there is no substantial resemblance between the French Revolution and our own. Very likely we have all felt the great difficulty of forming any conclusions in regard to Napoleon and his work in which we should ourselves place any very great confidence. Let us, however, make another trial.

And our first task must be to understand the character of the times.

Prior to the French Revolution the continent of Europe, with the exception of Switzerland, was ruled in the interest of privileged classes. The Emperor of Germany, the Kings of France, Prussia, Spain, and Portugal, the Czar of Russia, the Electors, Dukes, Margraves, Landgraves, and Archbishops who ruled over the smaller German States, the Senates of Venice and Genoa, all these princes and potentates governed their subjects, with greater or less attention to their needs to be sure, but with a uniform assumption of the "divine right of kings." But this was not all. Everywhere on the continent there were orders of nobility, ecclesiastical functionaries and the like, who were not amenable to the general laws of the land; who, many of them, were not liable to taxation; who in many cases possessed rights over their poorer neighbors that were extremely oppressive, vexatious, and burdensome.

While all this was universally true, there were distinctions. In Russia there existed an oriental despotism, modified, to be sure, by occasional assassination, but still hopelessly incapable of modification in the direction of progress. In Prussia there was the strictest of military systems, permeating entire society. The army was officered solely from the nobility. The serfs were tied to the soil. No doubt the Great Frederic had done much for his people, but Prussia, although an enlightened country in many ways, was wedded to a system of which the king, the army, the nobility, and the serfs were the chief and almost the only constituents. In Austria, and in the Catholic states of Germany, the situation was rendered more complicated by the great wealth of the Roman Catholic Church, its enormous political influence, and the comparative immunity of its large possessions from taxation. In fact, the army, the nobility, the church, and the peasantry, constituted throughout upper Germany almost the only components of the population, and from neither of these classes could important changes for the better be expected, at least within any reasonable time.

In France the situation was in some respects worse, and in some respects better than in Germany. The absenteeism and extravagance of the nobility were no doubt more pronounced than in Germany, and led to worse results. The peasants were ground down by agents, and their hard earnings were wasted in luxurious profligacy at Paris and Versailles. They were, besides, subject to numerous petty but extremely vexatious exactions in the way of labor, tithes, and the like, which added greatly to the misery of their situation. Moreover, France was heavily in debt; she had been for years recklessly straining her resources in foreign wars. Still, she possessed one element which the states of Germany did not possess, at least to anything like such an extent, and that was a large and prosperous and intelligent middle class. These people, though shut out from participation in the administration of the government, were often well educated and of real importance. Then the nobility and gentry of France contained very many men of enlightened views, who were determined to improve the condition of their country. The philosophical and political writings of Voltaire and Rousseau, and their coadjutors, which attacked the principles on which the old *régime* was based, found a large and influential audience.

Italy was, then as now, composed of various communities. The States of the Church and the Kingdom of Naples were misgoverned to such a degree that the wretchedness of the poorer classes in those countries has rarely been equalled. The Austrian provinces and Piedmont fared somewhat better. Italy also possessed a tolerably large educated class, and many public-spirited private citizens.

In all these countries there had been an improvement in the condition of the people since the beginning of the century, due partly, no doubt, to the well-intentioned efforts at reform of many of the rulers, but mostly to the growth of wealth, and the consequent enlightenment and social influence of the middle classes. But in Spain there had been little change. Here the old system of things existed in full force. Here was the most corrupt and bigoted of courts, the most unmitigated priestly despotism, and an almost entire separation from the ideas of modern Europe.

It is obvious from this brief review that in none of the countries of which we have spoken was there anything like government by the people. In fact, it is sufficiently clear, I think, that in most, if not all, of these countries anything of this sort was for the moment, at least, wholly impracticable. The first need of these countries was *better* government; to this, contentions regarding the *right* to govern might well be postponed. The evils under which the peoples of the continent were groaning in 1789 were real and not theoretical, and until they should be delivered from them, questions of theory must wait. It was no doubt a fair question for the freemen of Massachusetts and Virginia whether the King of England was entitled to levy taxes from them without their consent any more than from the freemen of York and Sussex; and it was equally within their competency to resist by force of arms a pretension, the burden of which they had actually never felt. They were already possessed of political power; they and their ancestors had enjoyed it for hundreds of years; the only question of 1776 regarded the extent of its exercise. But the Europe of the French Revolution stood in no such attitude as this to the problems of 1789. It was with the Europe of that day not a question of political power, except incidentally; the need, the all-absorbing need, was relief from intolerable oppression, gross and most exasperating inequalities in social and economical and political *status:* it was to undo the heavy burdens and to let the oppressed go free, and to break every yoke. Connected with this, an essential part of it, we may admit, was the participation of that portion of the people of each country who were fit for it in the tasks and privileges of government. But the first, the imperative, thing to do was to break down the power of the privileged classes, to subject the nobleman and the ecclesiastic to the penalties of the same law that bore upon the bourgeois and the peasant, and to impose the same taxes upon their property; and at the same time to give the humbler classes the same legal rights that belonged to their nobler and wealthier neighbors, to lift from them the burden of extortion, imposition, and injustice, and to open to them the chance of attaining the legitimate objects of human ambition. This done, and the possession and exercise of political power would come in good time.

Naturally enough, however, the French Revolutionists asserted the rights of man, and based their proceedings upon that assertion. Yet, as a matter of fact, at no time during the Revolution did the people of France govern themselves in the sense that we are to-day governing ourselves. The National Assembly, the Terrorists, the Committee of Public Safety, the Directory, governed France as despotically as ever had Louis the Fourteenth; nor can we wonder at it. Had they not done so, the tide of revolution would probably have gone backward. The masses of a people who have been rigidly governed for centuries, however true may be the statement that they possess the *right* to govern themselves, — a question I will not discuss here, — do not and cannot be expected all at once to exercise that right. Like many other arts in this world, the art of self-government is of slow growth, and neither the enactments of 1789 and 1790, nor the terrible tragedies of 1792 and

1793 were able to confer upon the masses of the French people the political aptitude for managing their own affairs, which was the inheritance of English and American freemen. Hence the harsh and searching despotism of the Reign of Terror, a despotism which had undoubtedly for its object to maintain the most advanced positions of the extreme party on the subject not only of liberty, but of the political rights of man. You observe the anomaly, but observe also the alleged necessity. Close students of the French Revolution assure us that it was more than once in danger of stopping, and of reaction: that is, the people, if left to themselves, would have receded from the claims put forward in their behalf, and have welcomed the return of the old order of things, with, of course, some important changes. To prevent this, the revolutionary party felt themselves obliged to take stringent measures; that is, the party which asserted the rights of man felt themselves obliged to refuse to those who differed from them the exercise of those rights. Singular position, indeed; but this is always the result of conferring political rights in advance of the fitness of the grantees to wield their new privileges. But what I want you to remember particularly here, is, that during the entire Revolution France was despotically governed; there was no local self-government to speak of; everything was done according to orders from Paris. True, this was done professedly in the interest of liberty, and was doubtless necessary, unless the people were to be left free to return to the monarchy; still it was done; even the French Revolution made no very general practical difference in respect to the *quantum* of political power actually exercised by the people.

But in respect to the *quantum* of liberty and equality enjoyed by the people it made a tremendous difference. All artificial distinctions were swept away; all unequal burdens were rectified; great monopolies were suppressed; all privileges were abolished; the burdens of taxation and military service were imposed alike on noble and peasant; the throne, the church, the nobility, were destroyed. A new era was fairly and hopefully begun. An enthusiasm for the rights of man, ardent and contagious, filled the air.

Revolutions, as we have often been told, are not made with rose-water; certainly the French Revolution was no exception to this rule. The changes of which we have been speaking, beneficial as they were to the many, were crushing blows to the few. Rank, privilege, office, emoluments, salary, perquisites, often the very means of subsistence, were ruthlessly and suddenly swept away. The destruction of the inequalities that weighed so grievously upon the poorer and middle classes was, in another aspect, nothing but the abolition without compensation of innumerable vested rights. To free slaves is to take away the property of masters. Hence, the great and beneficent reforms of the French Revolution, carried through as they were, not gradually and cautiously and mildly, but suddenly and violently and harshly, excited the implacable resentment of those who suffered by them and those whose lives were bound up with the old order of things. Many of them became traitors to their country, and stirred up against her the hostility of the other powers. Others excited insurrections at home, or carried on treasonable correspondence with the enemy. All this naturally and inevitably increased the revolutionary furor, and led to extreme measures of retaliation.

I need not dwell on this part of the subject. Every one knows the fierce and aggressive character which the Revolution assumed; the intolerance, the espionage, the despotism, of demagogues and of jacobin clubs; the terrible scenes of blood; the continuous and indiscriminate executions; the revolutionary furor, not only overspreading France, but burning to carry revolutionary principles and methods at the point of the bayonet and to the fierce music of the Marseillaise into all the respectable and conservative duchies and oligarchies and monarchies of Italy and Germany.

And the fact really was that the French Revolution was the beginning of a new order of things, of which the leading principle was the equality of all men before the law; and this principle was not only opposed to the theories entertained at that time by the great mass of the well-to-do and cultivated classes, but on the continent, at any rate, it actually threatened their material well being. Where was the French nobleman? An exile, if fortunate enough to be still alive. Where was the French gentleman, whose income, and often a slender one, was drawn from certain manorial or other rights or impositions, which lay like mortgages or ground rents on the lands of the neighboring farmers? His income wholly gone, teaching French for a living, very likely, in London or New York. Nothing like such a wholesale spoliation of the upper classes of a country had ever been seen or heard of before. No doubt imagination and terror added much to the natural hostility provoked by French principles, as they were called. But, in sober truth, the Revolution stood for a new and utterly antagonistic system: from the first moment there began between the Revolution and the established order of things in Europe what the late Mr. Seward would have termed "an irrepressible conflict." That this conflict should express itself in war was of course to be expected. In the same year that Louis XVI was guillotined, France was at war with all her neighbors from the Scheldt to the Pyrenees.

We have not time here to enter into the details of the war; we can only take a hasty glance at its general features. The raw volunteers which France sent in multitudes into the field were at first badly beaten. The organization of the old regular army had been broken up in great part by revolutionary proscription, and its discipline and efficiency greatly impaired; nevertheless it was these troops that saved France. After a while able men came upon the stage: Jourdan, Pichegru, Moreau, Hoche, appeared at the head of armies. And, second in command of the artillery at the siege of Toulon, then occupied by British troops, supported by a British fleet, a young major of artillery, by name Napoleon Bonaparte, made his mark for the first time. He saw at once, with the unerring eye of a great soldier, the key to the position, and when his advice had been taken and Toulon had fallen, he was a man of distinction.

Major Bonaparte was at this time twenty-four years of age. He was an officer of the old army, having been regularly educated at the military school at Brienne, and having served continuously from the time of his graduation. While at Brienne he was known for his intense application to his studies, and he left the school with a reputation for talent. Unlike most army officers, he found in the profession of arms a profession worthy of his utmost devotion. He read and studied the great campaigns of the world. He wrote for his own use commentaries and criticisms on Cæsar's operations in Gaul and Frederic's campaigns in Saxony and Silesia. Of every species of military knowledge he was a serious and accurate student. He was, moreover, as attentive to the dry details of the art as he was fond of studying its higher branches. No man in the army had a more sure eye for ground, could estimate more certainly what could and could not be effected by a battery placed here or placed there, whether a column of troops could or could not reach a given point by such or such a time. Nay, more than this, no captain of a company knew better than he whether the rations furnished to the men were what they should be or not; Napoleon to the end of his days was a good judge of the common soldier's soup and bread. Let me illustrate the care with which he would look after little things. Long after the time of which I am speaking, when he had become Emperor, he was one day inspecting the Invalides, the home for aged and disabled soldiers in Paris, and the matron was showing him the chests of drawers where the soldiers' linen was put. He bade her open a drawer: "I suppose you know," said he, "how to arrange these shirts when they come back from the wash." The good woman hesitated, and the Emperor then explained that the proper way was to put those newly washed at the bottom of the drawer, so that the same garments should not be worn and washed continually. I mention this to illustrate his love of detail and of exactness. Nothing was too small for him.

On the other hand, the promptitude with which he despatched the Toulon business showed not only the mind of the master, but the wide and careful study which takes the place of experience. Here, when he arrived, was a poor and small army, under poor generals, attempting a task entirely beyond its strength : that of laying siege to the large and strongly fortified city of Toulon. Bonaparte not only pointed out to the generals that with their present resources success in such an operation was wholly impracticable, but he showed them that there was no necessity of attempting it; that the defence of the place depended entirely on the presence of the fleet in the harbor, and that the capture of a certain promontory, l'Eguillette, would enable the French to compel the evacuation of the harbor. His counsel was followed, and the proper steps were taken to reduce the works which the English had erected to maintain their position. In the meanwhile the young major reformed the artillery service of the army and doubled its efficiency. When the time came, the French carried the English fort, Mulgrave, erected their batteries on l'Eguillette, and the British fleet sailed away. How long the siege might have lasted had not the major opportunely arrived, it is hard to tell. But every man in that army, and what was more important perhaps at that time to the major, the deputies of the Convention, who had come down from Paris to push the siege vigorously, felt that in Bonaparte they had an officer of great capacity, who thoroughly knew his profession. He became at once one of the men of mark, one of those to be relied on in circumstances of difficulty and danger. He was without delay appointed to the rank of general of brigade in the army which was operating near Nice, and he very soon, by his skilful manœuvres, enabled the French commander to turn the Austrian positions which he had been idly threatening for weeks, and to take up a new and much more advantageous situation.

At this time, the close of the year 1793 and the early part of the year 1794, Robespierre was at the head of France and governed her with a ruthless fanaticism, of which I need not to speak here. The fall of Toulon was followed by wholesale executions. With these atrocities Napoleon would have nothing to do. Even Lanfrey, who invariably makes the worst of the subject of his biography, admits frankly that all these harsh and barbarous doings were abhorrent to Napoleon's nature, and that he did what he could to shield those unfortunates who came under the suspicion of the authorities. As to this side of Napoleon's character, we may as well pause here a moment and consider it. In spite of all the battles that he fought, and all the death, wounds, sickness, and misery inseparable from such vast military operations as for twenty years he conducted, it may safely be affirmed that Napoleon was not a harsh, still less a cruel man. All the contemporary writers of any authority admit this in so many words, even though they may consider his comparative indifference to all this suffering almost as bad as cruelty or harshness, and even though they can point to some incidents in his career that certainly look like both.[1] But the popular accusation of Napoleon on this head proceeds on the mistaken notion that to conduct so many wars a man must have a very hard heart. A little reflection, however, will show that this need not be so at all. A statesman deciding on war may no doubt often be charged rightly with not having sufficiently considered the miseries which his decision must involve. But, culpable as this is, it does not show any unusual indifference to human suffering: it is merely the failure properly to bring these wretched incidents of war before the mind; it is a deficiency in imagination. Twenty odd years ago we were plunged into a great war; we may perhaps fairly hold that those who brought it about were in their intense political excitement inexcusably careless of the sufferings which a great war must occasion; but none of us ever accused any of them of being personally harsh or cruel people. Napoleon, bred in a military school, wrapped up in the military profession, undoubtedly considered war as the shortest and best way of settling all political disputes; and, very likely,

[1] See Appendix I.

as a military man, "a man of war from his youth," many of the incidents of a campaign which to the civilian mind are most distressing were so familiar that it never occurred to him to notice them. As the ruler of the French Empire he no doubt often resorted to war when any one in his place not a military man, and accustomed as he was to military methods, would have chosen some peaceful mode of action. When at the head of an army, careful as he undeniably was of his soldiers' welfare in all respects, he used them, as any general who expects to win a battle must use them, with a single eye to the success of the day, and without allowing the imagination to raise disturbing pictures of wounds and death. Just so, a surgeon, devoted to his profession, magnifying its importance, may resort to an operation when his professional brother, the physician, would have counselled milder treatment; and, when he is performing the operation, he must, if he is a good surgeon, use the knife unshrinkingly. Yet we all know that it would be very erroneous for us to attribute to such a surgeon any special harshness of temper or indifference to human suffering. Bearing these principles and keeping these analogies in mind, we shall understand, I think, pretty clearly what can and what cannot fairly be alleged against Napoleon in this regard. He was, as I have said, a soldier, born and bred; he was all his life in the army; he had a genius for war, and was skilful and successful beyond measure in military operations. If he sometimes engaged in a war when one more alive to its evils would have avoided it, he never countenanced unnecessary or purposeless fighting. With him, a battle was always a serious and a critical matter; the troops were spared as much as possible beforehand; it was always his plan to make the encounter a decisive one, and for this end he spared no pains. In his attention to the sick and wounded he has never been surpassed.

Let us now return to our story. Seven months after the fall of Toulon occurred the Revolution of the Ninth of Thermidor, by which Robespierre and his chief associates were brought to the block, to the immense relief of everybody. The Convention, freed from the tyranny of the Jacobin Club, resumed its authority. But the people had ceased to respect the Convention. The Reign of Terror had worked a great change in public opinion. The interests of property and of social order began to assert themselves. Moderate men saw that the experiment of governing France by a National Assembly had resulted in a government by factions, oppressive and iniquitous beyond example, and they demanded some security against a recurrence of similar evils. Even the partisans of the monarchy began to show their heads. It was clear that the government must undergo some transformation if France was to retain the benefits of the Revolution. In 1795, therefore, a new constitution was adopted, which gave the executive power to five Directors. In this and other respects the new arrangement was an advance towards a conservative solution of the revolutionary problem. But the republicans in the convention had no notion of running the risk of having their work undone by a royalist reaction. There were many signs of a widespread change in the popular feeling, and in such an inflammable country as France a sudden overthrow was among the possibilities to be guarded against. Accordingly it was provided in the new constitution that two thirds of the existing convention should be members of the new legislature, and that, after the first election, only one third of the members should annually go out of office. This device, so well calculated to ensure to the republicans the control of the country for some years at any rate, was unpopular with the reactionary party, who were foolish enough to try a resort to arms. Bonaparte was charged by the convention with the defence of the government. The "sections," as they were called, of Paris rose on the 13th of Vendémiaire, or the 4th of October, 1795; but, formidable as the insurrection had appeared, it was easily quelled. General Bonaparte had by great personal exertions collected a sufficient number of guns commanding all the approaches to the Tuileries, against which the attack was directed. His orders were explicit, his soldiers were steady, the guns did their work. The mob of Paris had at last met its match.

During the autumn of this year, 1795, General Bonaparte made the acquaintance of Madame Beauharnais, a lady somewhat older than himself, whose husband, an officer of rank, had perished in the Revolution; and early in 1796 they were married. She was a woman of uncommon wit and fascination, and of considerable beauty, and Bonaparte was devotedly attached to her. On her side there was unquestionably also a strong feeling of admiration for her husband, and of pride in his talents and character; and she loved him, it would seem, with an affection which, while it certainly was not as strong as his at the outset, increased as time went on. Josephine was well aware of her powers of fascination, and in the earlier part of their married life caused her husband great vexation, and even apprehension, by her course in society. She was also a most extravagant person, to whose mind the economy, order, and exactitude that Napoleon insisted on in the public service, and would gladly have carried into his household, were disagreeable, and in fact insupportable. She caused him great annoyance by her lavish expenditures, and frequently excited his anger by her foolish attempts at prevarication when interrogated as to the amount of her debts. Josephine was a good woman and a clever one, but she did not possess a well-informed mind, or a strong and deep nature, or a well-balanced character. Still she loved her husband, and assisted him to the best of her ability. At any rate she was the only woman whom Napoleon ever loved, in the strict sense of that word; and she always possessed great influence over him, an influence that, whatever may have been his occasional infidelities, was shared by no other woman; and their married life was undoubtedly a really happy one. In his letters to Josephine, and in all that he says about her, we see the best side of Napoleon's character; and no one familiar with the facts can fail to recognize the true affection and confidence that existed between them, despite occasional misunderstandings. Of the divorce, I must speak later; suffice it to say now, that, as every one knows, it was not the result of any disagreement between them.

Immediately after his marriage General Bonaparte took command of the Army of Italy, to which post he had just been appointed by the Directory. He arrived in Nice on the 27th of March, 1796. In this region the French armies had been for some two years or more opposing the troops of the King of Sardinia and the Emperor of Austria, but without achieving anything of great importance. The French forces were inferior in numbers, discipline, and equipment to those of the allies, but it was soon to be seen what a man of first-rate ability could accomplish against odds.

I shall not, of course, attempt to describe in any detail the campaigns of General Bonaparte in Italy. No military operations can be understood without close study, and those of 1796 and 1797 were often extremely complicated. It is not worth our while to follow them too closely. Let me, however, try to give you a general notion of the plan of Napoleon.

Many of you no doubt have been in Nice, and have made the journey from Nice to Genoa either by the Corniche road, which skirts the shore of the Mediterranean, or by the railroad, which pursues substantially the same route. You recollect, perhaps, how the Maritime Alps, which are a chain of mountains running generally parallel with the line of the coast, and sending out their spurs almost to the sea, shut off the Riviera di Ponente, with its lovely villages, Mentone, Ventimiglia, San Remo, Finale, Savona, and the others, from the rest of the world. The French Army of Italy was scattered along the Riviera from Nice almost as far as Genoa. Nice was its base of supplies. Behind the first ranges of mountains, in detachments occupying the mountain villages, in positions lying to the north of those occupied by the French, was the main body of the Sardinian or Piedmontese army, connecting on its left, that is at the easterly end of its line, and to the north or northeast of Savona, with the Austrian troops.

Napoleon's base of operations was, as I have

said, Nice; his communications were confined to the Corniche road, or rather to the path which then existed, such as it was, for the magnificent Corniche road was begun by him. The difficulties in undertaking operations in the neighborhood of Genoa, on account both of the distance from his base, and of the possibility of his single line of communication being imperilled by a descent from the English fleet, which was watching the coast of the Riviera for an opportunity to do mischief, were obvious. But he saw that the enemy's troops were also occupying a long line, and were much separated and scattered, and that a concentrated attack on an important part of that line, if successful, would lead to great results.

The thing to do was, if possible, to separate the two armies, to interpose between the Sardinian and Austrian forces, and to deal with each separately. To do this it was necessary to operate at a great distance from Nice, because the Austrian right was not advanced much beyond Genoa. The project was a most daring one, and it required all Napoleon's unerring skill and unceasing activity to give it a chance of success. But his temperament was hopeful; of two courses he invariably preferred the bolder, and the greater the risk, the more interest he always took in the game. He concentrated his army at or near Savona, pushed his troops up through the passes, overcame by the superiority of force which his greater military capacity procured for him the Austrian and Sardinian troops that attempted to bar his progress; crossed the Maritime Alps; interposed between the Sardinian and Austrian armies; and, holding the latter in check by skilfully manœuvring with a small fraction of his army, threw the bulk of his forces upon the Sardinians, defeated them again and again, and finally extorted a separate peace from the Sardinian government. Then, turning upon the Austrians, he outmanœuvred them in crossing the Po, and, after the gallant affair of the Bridge of Lodi, where he seized the opportunity of making his own personal courage known to his troops, he entered the city of Milan, the capital of Austrian Lombardy.

Nothing so striking and brilliant had been seen since the time of Charles XII. of Sweden. Europe was astonished, France elated beyond measure. Nor did his successes stop here. The Austrian government replaced their general, an octogenarian by the name of Beaulieu, by another brave old veteran, Wurmser, but he was beaten over and over again, and finally forced to take refuge in Mantua. Their next general, Alvinzi, though having the advantage of dealing with a force that had been seriously depleted, for the successes of the French had cost them dear, was no more fortunate than his predecessors; and though, during the terrible three days of fighting at the Bridge of Arcola, victory

ITALIAN CAMPAIGN OF 1796.

Situation of the Armies on the 15th. of April.

seemed undecided, the daring and skill of Bonaparte at last prevailed, and the brilliant action of Rivoli crowned a campaign which had been illustrated by desperate and persistent courage, as well as by wonderful fertility of resource. Finally, the great Archduke Charles himself, reputed the best general of the continent, was sent into Italy; but he soon found that with a discouraged and weakened army he was utterly unable to hold his own against the invaders. On the 18th of April, 1797, just a year from the crossing of the Maritime Alps, the preliminaries of peace were signed at Leoben, and were followed in six months by the treaty of Campo Formio.

During the progress of the war, the French had come into contact with nearly all the Italian states; with the Duchies of Parma, Modena, Tuscany; with the oligarchical republics of Genoa and Venice; and with the States of the Church. It would be tedious and unprofitable for me to attempt to give the facts in detail. All that it is necessary for us to take into account here is, that the advent of the French meant to these populations escape from the misgovernment under which they labored, and a participation in the grand movement toward equal rights and privileges inaugurated by France. The sentiment which welcomed the French existed chiefly in the middle and upper classes; the ignorant peasantry, led by their bigoted priests, were equally averse to foreign intervention and to new ideas. Bonaparte played skilfully the part he had to play; he recognized fully that all these little princes and potentates desired to see him beaten by the Austrians; he heard their mutterings whenever his luck seemed for the moment to fail; he knew that he owed them nothing; but he did the best he could for the populations. The city of Venice and its adjoining possessions he was compelled to resign to Austria as a necessary condition of peace; but Austrian Lombardy, with the states of Modena, Reggio, Bologna, and Ferrara, and a part of the Venetian territory were organized into a new state by the name of the Cisalpine Republic, which we may probably consider as the germ of the united Italy of to-day. This new republic received a democratic constitution, and though no doubt the work of organization was very hastily and very imperfectly done, yet the change was unquestionably a change for the better in all that constitutes liberal and just government. The objects of the war had been attained in forcing Austria to make peace, and in gaining such solid political benefits for the Italian neighbors of the French republic.

The war, too, had been the making of the successful general. His reputation was of a different kind from that of the other distinguished generals of the republic: it was not founded on a single great battle, like that of Jourdan, or on

a well conducted retreat, like that of Moreau,
nor on an almost unopposed, though skilfully
conducted invasion, like that of Pichegru. It
was far higher than any of these. Bonaparte
had been tried in his year of fighting in Italy in
every sort of way, and he had risen superior to
every obstacle. Difficulties of transportation and
communication, lack of siege equipage, of pontoon trains, of clothing and equipment, had all
been overcome. Again and again heavy numer-
ical odds had been encountered, and again and
again had his unwearied diligence and alertness,
his imperturbably clear head, and his hopeful
and daring courage extorted victory where escape even seemed well-nigh hopeless. Here in
these campaigns in Italy he laid the foundations
of that extraordinary hold which he always had
over the soldiers of his armies. He was ever
with them, seeing to everything himself, observ-
ing the enemy with his own eye, and several
times, at any rate, leading on his grenadiers
sword in hand. At Lodi he was the second man
across the bridge. At Arcola, where not even
his example could carry the men over, he was
in the *mêlée* forced off the causeway into the
marshes. Such a commander as this had never
been seen. He was the idol of the army.[1] The
soldiers believed in him implicitly. Many of
the men who fought at Lodi and Arcola and
Castiglione and Rivoli lived to see the sun of

[1] See Appendix II.

Austerlitz and the snows of Russia. Here too, in these Italian wars, were recognized for the first time some of the great generals of the period. Of these Augereau was perhaps the most distinguished at that time; but, following close on his steps, certainly, was a far abler soldier, Masséna, who was one of the two or three ablest of Napoleon's lieutenants, and of whom the Duke of Wellington used to say that he gave him more anxiety than any of those of Napoleon's marshals to whom he had ever been opposed. Masséna was a thorough soldier, a man very fertile in resources, very daring, and very resolute. Lannes, also, another man of first-rate ability, came under the eye of Napoleon in these campaigns.

It is time that we returned to France. While Bonaparte was settling the terms of the treaty with Austria, France was undergoing another constitutional change. Another movement, aimed, like that of the Sections of Paris in 1795, at weakening the extreme republican party, found its expression in the elections of 1797, and was favored by two of the five Directors. We find it impossible, with the very inadequate means at our command, to apportion praise or blame to the actors in these almost forgotten crises with any great certainty of being right in our award. Nor is it necessary for us to attempt this task. These crises seem to me to be the natural *sequelæ*, as the doctors would say, of a severe revolution. Astronomers tell us that the celestial bodies, from having once been in a state of high incandescence, have by degrees cooled down and become contracted in size, and that this process is attended by certain geological catastrophes. In like manner it was to be expected that France, in her cooling down from the white heat of her Revolution, must have her violent contractions and convulsive epochs of refrigeration. One of these was the 13th of Vendémiaire, 1795, when Bonaparte put down the rising of the Sections; one was the 18th of Fructidor, 1797, of which we are now speaking; another was the 18th of Brumaire, 1799, of which we shall speak soon. Of this crisis, then, which culminated in the revolution or *coup d'état* of the 18th of Fructidor, 1797, all that we need know is that the army, which was still untouched by the reactionary influence which had of late been quite perceptible in Paris, declared its intention of standing by the three Directors who were opposed to the Assembly; that Bonaparte sent Augereau to Paris with a division of troops; that the two Directors who were in sympathy with the Assembly were promptly disposed of; that a great many persons were proscribed, banished to the colonies, and imprisoned; and in short, that the three successful Directors ruled matters with a high hand.

It is important for us to take all this into account for one reason especially, and that is, that it was this republic, so called, this government of the 18th of Fructidor, 1797, which Bonaparte overthrew on the 18th of Brumaire, 1799, when he assumed control of the government. Many persons ignorantly talk about Napoleon's having enslaved France, destroyed free institutions, and so forth. Do not let us forget that what he destroyed in 1799 was the arbitrary and irresponsible rule of these three Directors. You will find that Lanfrey, speaking of this *coup d'état* of the 18th of Fructidor, 1797, calls the Directors "triumvirs," says that all liberty of the press was destroyed, that France was enslaved, and that all was ready for a military dictatorship; yet when this consistent and veracious writer comes to treat of the 18th of Brumaire, 1799, when Napoleon by another *coup d'état* put down this Directory, you would suppose, to judge from the way he speaks of the subject, that Bonaparte was pulling down a republic at least as orderly and constitutional as that of Massachusetts. But we are anticipating.

The winter of 1797 and 1798 was passed by General Bonaparte in Paris. During this period the expedition to Egypt was projected. It is difficult to assign a good reason for this unnecessary and hazardous undertaking. It seems quite probable that the Directory had their heads turned by the recent successes in Italy; they were eagerly launching out in every direction, and were evidently excited with the hope of gaining important acquisitions beyond the sea. And it is quite likely that Bonaparte himself, who possessed together with a clear and sound judgment on means and methods a very vivid and enterprising imagination, allowed himself to entertain great ideas about the conquest of the East. At any rate he always, to the end of his days, talked in this strain regarding this episode of his life. Viewed, however, from the standpoint of the needs and welfare of France, no undertaking could well be more preposterous than an expedition to Egypt. It is true that at that time there still existed a French fleet; but neither at that time nor at any other time were the French superior to the English on the seas. How absurd, then, was the project of sending a powerful French army to Egypt, whence its only possible communication with home must be by water! At this time, too, the political horizon was far from clear. Austria seemed on the brink of recommencing the struggle, and it looked as if the Czar Paul would throw his sword into the scale against the French republic and its young client republics. It was an act of absolute folly on the part of the Directory to embark in such a distant and uncalled-for and unprofitable venture.

The expedition to Egypt was, however, decided on, and it sailed in May, 1798. Taking Malta on the way, the French vessels arrived safely at Alexandria without the knowledge of the British fleet, which under Lord Nelson was flying hither and thither in hopes of intercepting them. It may show us how the world has gone ahead in some respects to recall the fact that this expedition, which left Toulon on the 18th of May, did not land at Alexandria till the last of June! Alexandria and Rosetta fell without a struggle, and the army set out for Cairo early in July. But it will not be worth our while to pursue the fortunes of the Egyptian expedition. It is so evidently an outside matter, so entirely disconnected with the march of events in Europe, that we had better leave the French army trudging through the sands along the banks of the Nile under the shadow of the pyramids, and return to Italy.

What I am particularly trying to direct your attention to in this investigation is the general character of the contest that was being waged between France and her dependencies, on the one hand, and the rest of Europe, on the other. It is represented by most English writers as a mere struggle for territory, for power, or even as a war of spoliation on the part of France. The sacred rights of nationality were, it is alleged, wantonly invaded and trampled on by the republicans. The resistance to the armies of France was inspired by the most sacred motives of patriotism.

Let us now examine these assertions with a little care. We will take an example. The king dom of Naples, over which ruled a branch of the house of Bourbon, may serve as our illustration. The court, the priests, and the lazzaroni constituted one party; the enlightened part of the upper class and the middle class formed the other. It would be impossible to say which were the more bigoted, cruel, or tyrannical: the king, or the church, or the mob. The government was an absolute despotism, and the despots were not only absolute, but, what is worse, they were cowardly, and they were cruel. On mere suspicion the most respectable men were sent to the loathsome jails, often never to be taken out even for examination. Spies and informers infested the homes and places of business of well-to-do citizens. People of education, of public spirit, of enlightenment, were suspected of favoring French principles, and were treated with a rigor wholly unjustifiable. In all this the court party were fully maintained by England. In fact, the wife of the English minister, the celebrated Lady Hamilton, was the bosom friend of Queen Caroline; and Admiral Lord Nelson, whose mistress she was, supported the government in every measure of severe repression.

From this intolerable state of things, respectable and intelligent people in Naples looked to France as to a deliverer from Middle Age barbarism. Accordingly, when Ferdinand, in an access of rage against French interference with the Papal territories, declared war against France, and his army, under the redoubtable Austrian general, Mack, whose career culminated several years later at Ulm, was defeated and dispersed in its encounters with the French army under Championnet, the French, when they entered Naples, were received by the better classes with the most sincere joy and relief, but by the lazzaroni, excited to fury by their bigoted priests, with fanatical hostility. You will find everything that I have said in all the accounts; I am not aware of having departed a jot from the standard authorities, — and I ask you the question, With which of these contesting parties is the cause of progress, of civil liberty, of enlightenment? Is it with the French invaders, or with the rabble of Naples? To my mind, there can be but one answer to the question. I am not concerned to consider whether or not according to the practice of civilized nations the doings of the French in Rome gave to Ferdinand a legitimate *casus belli*. I am free to say that I do not estimate the ignorant patriotism of the mob of Naples as a very important element in the solution of our problem. Those persons in Naples who were competent to form a judgment sided with the revolutionary party, and welcomed the assistance of the French; and I think they were right. The question of relief from intolerable misgovernment, bolstered up by foreign support, was the question of the day at Naples. And no heated declamation about patriotic resistance to

French invasion obscures this question in my mind.

Substantially, this was the nature of the contest in the rest of Europe, although nowhere, probably, was the precise character of the question made so clear as in Naples. But in the Papal territories, in Austrian Italy, in the smaller fiefs and duchies and principalities of western Germany, especially in Spain, the opposing sides were taken by very much the same classes of the population as we have seen favoring and opposing in Naples the advent of the French. No doubt the French often abused their successes; the continual wars were certainly a terrible drain on the population, and on the patience and temper of the people; moreover, the presence of the foreigner became in time well-nigh insupportable, even though he had originally been the bringer in of great reforms. Still, however true all this may be, it is a total perversion of the truth to represent France merely as a conquering nation, overrunning its neighbors solely from the vulgar greed of territory; or to dwell so fondly on the heroic and patriotic conduct of the most ignorant, bigoted, and prejudiced portions of the populations of these states in resisting stoutly the invaders of their soil. In point of fact, they were unwittingly the real enemies of their several countries; they did what they could to retard their development, to retain oppressive institutions, to keep up the reign of intolerance and of superstition, and to keep out humane legislation, equal rights, and religious freedom.

Let us follow the fortunes of the revolution in Naples a little farther. The French, as I have said, entered Naples, to the great relief of the better part of the people. The royal family fled to Sicily. A new government was organized, called the Parthenopæan Republic, which was supported by most of the best citizens, and by many of the most distinguished men of the kingdom. But the enterprise was, so far as the French were concerned, an ill-advised one. Bonaparte was in Egypt. The French arms met with reverses in the north of Italy, and Naples had to be abandoned. The peasantry under Cardinal Ruffo rose against the new republic. Naples could not be defended against these fanatical hordes, assisted as they were by British vessels of war in the harbor. A capitulation was signed, providing for the safety of the persons and property of all connected with the revolution, and an amnesty was proclaimed. For those who had been especially compromised, and who desired to go to France, passage was to be provided. Suddenly the British fleet, under Nelson himself, appeared. He at once of course assumed command of all the British vessels in the harbor. One of his ships carried Ferdinand and his Queen, and Sir William and Lady Hamilton. The whole capitulation and amnesty were set aside as a compact with traitors. The unfortunate prisoners were executed in great numbers. In vain the English captains who had signed the papers protested that the honor of the British flag was involved, that the well understood code of military law forbids the molestation of men who with arms in their hands have been allowed to surrender. To all these remonstrances Nelson was deaf. He was himself a fanatic on the subject of the divine right of kings; popular risings were abominations in his eyes; and the support of the whole abortive attempt by France aggravated his rage. Lady Hamilton, as I have said, was the intimate friend of the Queen, and the Queen was most implacable. Nelson went all lengths. He allowed officers of the republic included in the surrender to be tried by courts-martial held on board English vessels of war, and he disgraced the British flag by hanging at least one of them, and him the most distinguished, Admiral Caraccioli, from the yard-arm of an English frigate. I have many a time seen in Naples, in the Strada di Mergellina, a house bearing a tablet containing an inscription to the memory of this unfortunate man.

It is not at all with the view of attacking Lord Nelson that I have adverted to this painful theme. It is with the view of showing you by an unmistakable example that in all your study of this epoch you must expect to find things of this sort, when done by the party which finally succeeded, that is the reactionary party, passed over in comparative silence; and everything of the kind done by their opponents magnified and dwelt upon so as to distort the truth of history. I suppose there may be twenty people who have condemned Napoleon for the execution of the Duc d'Enghien, where there is one that has condemned Lord Nelson for the murder of Caraccioli. One reason of this certainly is that Nelson and his side were in the end successful, and Napoleon and his side were not. All I mean to say is that we must look out for this feature in the histories of this period, and make due allowance for it.

Returning now to our story. The war had broken out again in 1799, and Russia sent her celebrated general, Souvorof, into Italy to help the Austrians. The French were generally unsuccessful. Macdonald and Joubert were badly defeated; even Masséna was forced into Switzerland; and it looked at one time as though an invasion of France was a not impossible event. But Masséna proved himself more than a match for the Russian general, and in a series of severe actions near the Lake of Zurich, he forced Souvorof to retreat with great loss.

On the sea, too, the French had been most unfortunate. Nelson had destroyed the French fleet in the roads of Alexandria, in the celebrated action known as the Battle of the Nile, and thenceforward the French army in Egypt enjoyed only the most precarious means of communication with their own country.

At home the Directory was very unpopular. Not only had military events gone against public expectation in Italy, but elsewhere there was much to complain of. The government had provoked a causeless quarrel with the United States; French frigates and privateers had captured American merchantmen; and the tone assumed by the Directory in its negotiations with the American envoys was ill calculated to avoid an open rupture.

But the great cause of dissatisfaction with the existing government was that every one felt it to be a mere transitory phase of the revolutionary movement, and that, as a transitory phase, it had lasted about long enough. It was not, and did not pretend to be, a government by the people. It had in fact, in the *coup d'état* of the 18th of Fructidor, 1797, withstood by force of arms the effect of the popular vote, fearing lest, if the people were to be allowed freely to express their will, its own continuance in power might be endangered, and even a return of the monarchy brought about. Hence the Directory of 1799 was in a singular position. It stood for the Revolution as against the Reaction, undoubtedly; but it also did not hesitate to employ illegal methods, imprisonment, banishment, force, in short, to maintain its position. It was a creature of yesterday. No man on the Board of Directors was a specially eminent man. The world has put up with a good deal of tyranny from monarchs whose hereditary right to reign is claimed on the strength of a descent from a long line of kings. An oligarchy composed of great nobles, actually possessing political power, has often, as in Venice for instance, ruled for generations with the consent and general approval of the governed. But the position of the five men who constituted the French Directory was unlike anything of this nature. It was due not to their talents or services, but to political intrigues. Viewed separately, they were insignificant men. As an oligarchy, they ruled France in her internal and external relations with a despotic hand. Against this public opinion revolted. It was evident that another crisis, similar in some of its aspects to those of the 13th of Vendémiaire, 1795, and the 18th of Fructidor, 1797, another catastrophe of refrigeration or contraction, — to recur to my former simile, — was inevitably approaching. The present state of things satisfied no man's theoretical views; it did not succeed well as a practical scheme. It was felt to be merely one step in the progress of events which had begun in 1789. How long this provisional state of things would last, nobody could tell; what would come next, nobody could foresee. That the existing system had no hold upon the country, that it satisfied no one, that it must inevitably before long pass away, — all this was plain.

At this moment, when these opinions were most strongly felt, Bonaparte, on the 6th of October, 1799, returned from Egypt.

LECTURE II.

THE CONSULATE.

It did not take General Bonaparte long, after his arrival in Paris in 1799, to comprehend the political situation. The weakness of the Directory was evident; its unpopularity manifest. And, as I have substantially said before, it was not only that the members of the government were personally disliked. It was clear, by a thousand unmistakable signs, that the Directory as a form of government, as a phase of the revolutionary disease, or, if you please, convalescence, had served its purpose, and would soon be replaced by something else. It only needed some one who had the courage to push his shoulder against the wall; it was sure to tumble. The Directory, in fine, existed on sufferance.

Nor were signs wanting to Napoleon of his being the man to whom the nation looked as its leader, as the man whose mission it was to terminate this strife of revolutionary factions, to unite all Frenchmen, both at home and abroad, in a cordial support of the new flag, to become the head of a stable and settled order of things, which should nevertheless be founded on the great and beneficial reforms brought about by the Revolution.

In a very few weeks occurred the *coup d'état* of the 18th of Brumaire, 1799. I do not propose to take up your time with a narration of what took place. Suffice it to say, that by a skilful show of force, Bonaparte, without firing a shot, overturned the Directory, dispersed the legislature, and assumed the reins of government. But I do want you to remember that the government which he overthrew was not such a republican government as that under which we are living, here in Massachusetts, to-day. It was an arbitrary government; the Directors had themselves, only two years before, as we have seen in the last lecture, put down their constitutional opponents by force of arms, and punished them by banishment and imprisonment. The republic of 1799 need not be mourned.

We can go farther than this. We can safely say that a people, the masses of whom are in such a state of political inexperience and incapacity as were the French people in 1789, do not and cannot govern themselves. It is of no consequence what assertions as to their natural right to do so may be made on their behalf by political philosophers or by honest patriots. They cannot do so, because it is work to which they have never been in the least accustomed. Let no one think that in what I say I am speaking against the possibility of a people governing itself. Not at all. I am only saying that no nation in the state in which France was in 1789 could possibly be expected to govern itself. Such a nation requires an education in the art of self-government. The people have not the needed knowledge of affairs, or the moderation, or the sagacity in the selection of their rulers, nor do they possess the inherited political traditions which exist or have existed among all the populations that do or ever have governed themselves. And as matter of fact, France never had been more rigorously governed than since her entry upon the revolutionary epoch. The Assembly, the Terrorists, the Committee of Public Safety, the Directory, governed everything by decree from Paris. All this was what might have been expected. It was not only perfectly natural, but it was inevitable that it should be so. No laws, no changes in the form of government, no bestowals of power, no executions, no catastrophes, no victories, no declamations, could do for France more than what had been done for her. And what was that? To break the chains of unjust and unequal law; to raise the masses of her people to a legal equality with the better classes; to allow her the opportunity of establishing in her political and legal system the great principles of justice, equality, and humanity; and to put it within her power to enter on a course of political experience, if she chose so to do, which would result in the course of time in making her then ignorant and bigoted peasantry fit to exercise the franchise. More than this, no human power could have accomplished. This had been at least fairly and hopefully begun, and the task of Napoleon in his domestic administration was to carry it out thoroughly and wisely, and to establish it on a permanent and secure basis. This work of the Revolution was in 1799 in danger of being swept away in a returning tide of royalist reaction, for it was impossible, now that the revolutionary fervor had subsided, that property and all the other conservative elements in society should not reassert their customary influence, put a stop to the succession of revolutions and *coups d'état*, and establish in their stead a monarchy of some kind. Let the Bourbons return in 1799, and the good work of the last ten years would be undone with a vengeance. Yet it was either the Bourbons or Napoleon. A republic existing in a country where you cannot trust the people, where you have to annul the elections and send representatives to penal colonies, unless you are prepared to see the halls of a republican legislature filled with the partisans of monarchy,—and that was precisely the position of the French republic in 1799,—is indeed in a precarious situation. I should rather say, however, that such a republic is not a republic at all; it is really a kind of oligarchy; it is the case of a country in which monarchy has been abolished, and in which great and beneficial reforms have been introduced, being despotically ruled by a few obscure politicians, who, not owing their position to high birth or to great possessions, or to anything which appeals to the imagination, are the objects of universal jealousy and hostility. They cannot hold their position; it is time that they retire, and allow a man of real distinction to assume their part. No one is the worse for a change of this kind. The country in fact feels reassured in the conviction of the greater security of its newly gained liberties.

Napoleon, then, in the *coup d'état* of the 18th of Brumaire, 1799, did not destroy the liberties of France; I hope you all feel clear about this. What he put down was an irresponsible and arbitrary oligarchy; as for the liberties of France, they were soon to receive from him their grand and permanent embodiment in the Code Napoleon, without which, it is safe to say, they could not have resisted the assaults of the Restoration. Of this I shall speak in another lecture.

Two features illustrated the new *coup d'état*: the first, that it was followed by no political proscriptions; and the second, that it was hailed by all classes with joy and satisfaction. A revolution never was accomplished more happily than this. The truth is, everybody wanted it. Then, the surprise, and grateful surprise, of the good people of France, to find for the first time in ten years that they had a ruler who did not find it necessary to kill, banish, or imprison his political opponents, must have been a delightful feature in the new situation. All the accounts concur in representing the change as a most fortunate and auspicious one, welcomed by the conservative classes as putting an end to the Revolution, and giving sincere satisfaction to the masses, as assuring them that their newly acquired rights would now be entrusted to an efficient defender.

Bonaparte was the head of the new *régime* under the title of First Consul. The other Consuls, Cambacérès and Lebrun, were both good men of affairs. The new government at once went to work to reorganize all the departments of administration, which were in an extremely neglected condition. Bonaparte summoned to his aid the best talent, and the most honest and faithful public servants he could find. Royalist or republican, returned emigrant or regicide, it was all the same to the new chief, who recognized and made everybody feel that France had taken a new departure, and that "bygones must be bygones." One of the objects which the First Consul desired most ardently was to terminate the political strifes and animosities of the Revolution. He saw the great desirability of uniting all parties and all factions in France in a cordial support of an administration which, while it recognized and proceeded upon accomplished facts, was averse to radical changes in either direction. Besides, he desired sincerely the return to France of the *émigrés*, the royalists in exile, who, from being unable to accept the ruthless spoliation of the revolutionary epoch, or from a well-grounded fear that their lives were in danger if they remained in a community so given over as France was in the days of the Terror to suspicion and violence, had left their native country, to which they were now forbidden under severe penalties to return. To the great bulk of these classes he extended a complete amnesty.

Before, however, prosecuting further the work of internal reorganization, it was necessary for the First Consul to turn his attention to the foreign relations of France. Two powers, England and Austria, alone kept up the war; Russia had retired from the field. The First Consul determined to signalize his elevation to the chief power in the state by communicating personally with the Emperor and the King. He urged upon them the miseries of war, and the willingness of France to make peace. The Emperor Francis returned a civil, though unsatisfactory answer; but King George the Third replied through his minister for foreign affairs, Lord Grenville, that the best evidence France could give of the sincerity of her pacific intentions would be to recall the Bourbons. To such a haughty reception of her overtures France could, of course, make but one answer, — to prepare vigorously for war.

There was nothing to be done against England; the French fleet was too weak even to attempt to rescue the army in Egypt. The English sent there a considerable force under a gallant old soldier, Sir Ralph Abercromby. Unhappily for the French, Kléber, who was really an able man, had fallen by the hand of an assassin, and the army under the incompetent Menou was unable to make head against the English. A convention was finally concluded, and the veterans of Aboukir and Acre returned to France.

The war with Austria presented a wholly different aspect. Two great Austrian armies were threatening the French frontier: one, under Kray, on the Rhine; the other under Mélas, in Italy. The theatres of the operations of these armies were separated by Switzerland, and Switzerland was occupied by French troops. Its possession, therefore, gave to France a very great advantage in either campaign, for it was equally possible, by operating from Schaffhausen, to throw a force upon Kray's communications with Ulm, and by crossing the Great St. Bernard, to interpose between Mélas and his communications with Austria. Both these schemes Bonaparte resolved to attempt.

The French army of the Rhine was commanded by Moreau, an officer unquestionably of great merit, though not possessing genius. He was a rather cautious man, a man who trusted very little to the inspiration of the moment, a man of sober methodical ways, to whom the speculative character of Napoleon's mind was altogether foreign and distasteful. Hence, when Napoleon proposed to him to throw his whole army from Schaffhausen directly in rear of the Austrians, urging upon him the splendid and overwhelming triumph which success in such an operation would give him, Moreau's mind reverted to the certain difficulties of the project, and proposed on his side a plan by which the Austrian general should be induced, by demonstrations near Strasburg and Neu Brisach, to weaken his force opposite Schaffhausen, so that, although the French force crossing at Schaffhausen would be diminished by the detachments needed to make these demonstrations on the lower Rhine, it was certain that it would not be obliged to meet the entire Austrian army. After many conferences, Moreau was allowed, as he certainly should have been, to have his own way; and his campaign, for we may as well finish with it here, was very ably conducted. His crossing was successfully made; he drove the Austrians back upon Ulm in a series of actions in which he constantly maintained his superiority; he then forced the passage of the Danube below Ulm, and compelled its evacuation; and, finally, when Marshal Kray had been foolishly superseded by the Archduke John, he routed his antagonist in the famous battle of Hohenlinden, and was well on his way to Vienna, when his victorious course was arrested by the signing of the preliminaries of peace. Moreau was, in fact, a very skilful officer; probably his abilities have never received full recognition; his unfortunate subsequent course brought about his exile, and he was finally killed in battle, at Dresden, fighting against his country. But this campaign of his in 1800 seems to me fully to justify the high encomiums that his admirers have awarded him. If not equal in brilliancy and striking audacity to that of Napoleon in 1805, we should remember that Moreau was in a subordinate position, while the Emperor controlled all the resources of France and western Germany. Certain it is, that Napoleon, though he always adhered to his criticism on Moreau's plan for opening the campaign, nevertheless always spoke of its conduct in the highest terms.

But we must return to the other campaign proposed by the First Consul, that of a descent into Italy through the passes of the Alps. The Austrians, you will recollect, had during Bonaparte's absence in Egypt recovered Italy; they were now besieging Masséna in Genoa, and pressing the remnants of the French army of Italy into the Riviera. Sardinia had allied itself with Austria, or, rather, Austria had occupied and absorbed the dominions of the King of Sardinia.

Of course it was possible to repeat the manœuvres of 1796, to break from the Riviera through the Maritime Alps, and to emerge on the plains of Lombardy. But the First Consul had something far more effective and attractive than this in contemplation. He intended taking the almost unheard of step of crossing the Alps, — a step which he knew would never be anticipated, — and then to place himself boldly between Mélas and his base of operations.

There are three principal passes leading from Switzerland into Italy. The westernmost one, over the Mont Cenis, now pierced by a tunnel, lies almost due west of Turin; that by the Great St. Bernard lies northwest of Turin; lastly, there is that by Mont St. Gothard, which brings you out between the lakes of Como and Maggiore, almost due north of Milan. This latter pass was not in possession of France at the opening of the campaign, but as soon as Moreau's successes opened it to French troops, a strong force was carried through it; but this need not concern us at this moment.

The First Consul had given to Moreau the only large army that France possessed. For his own use he caused a corps insignificant in numbers to be collected at Dijon, which was called the Army of Reserve, and to which alone the attention of the Austrian spies was directed. To this were added such troops as could be collected from depots and garrisons. In this way the entire force which was to cross the Alps over the Great St. Bernard was made up to about 35,000 men. It was not a well organized army, in fact it can scarcely be said to have had any existence as an army at all, until it began to march. Among its generals, however, were counted Lannes, Victor, and Desaix, all excellent officers.

By a demonstration made near the pass of Mont Cenis, the attention of the enemy was attracted in that direction, and the road over the Great St. Bernard was left comparatively unguarded. Over this road, often difficult, but still passable for wagons and artillery, the First Consul led his army as speedily as possible until it reached the plains of Lombardy at Ivrea, a point nearly north of Turin. Mélas, not fearing an attack from this quarter, had scattered his forces. Part of his troops were besieging Masséna in Genoa; part were pushing Suchet towards Nice; part were near Turin watching the Mont Cenis pass. Napoleon could no doubt have marched upon Genoa, for the relief of Masséna, who was stoutly holding out to the last. Apart from the natural policy of such a movement, there would certainly have been a good chance of defeating the scattered forces of Mélas, if they should attempt to bar his progress. But, once at Genoa, the whole task of reducing Lombardy would still remain to be done. He would have to deal with an enemy superior in numbers, whose communications were unembarrassed. It would have been 1796 over again. It was not worth while to cross the Alps for this.

A bolder and far more brilliant plan was devised, one of those plans most characteristic of the man; he determined to possess himself first of Milan, the moral effect of which could not but be great; then to establish himself behind the Ticino and the Po, and shut Mélas up in the plains of Lombardy by placing the French army across his only communications with Austria.

Accordingly, after feigning to march on Turin, he directed his course east upon Milan and entered it. By this time Moreau had begun his movement on the Rhine, and a force of 15,000 or 20,000 men was, as had been agreed between them, detached from Moreau's army, and sent over the pass of St. Gothard to Milan. This increased Bonaparte's disposable force to at least 50,000 men. Leaving garrisons at all the important places, he commenced his march southward and westward, crossing the Po, and moving by way of Montebello towards Alessandria, keeping on the south side of the Po. Uncertain of the whereabouts of the enemy, the first news came in the form of a severe action at Montebello, where Lannes defeated the Austrians. Pursuing his march westward, and fearful lest Mélas should escape him, Bonaparte detached Desaix to the southward to get further information. Suddenly, in the plain of Marengo, the Austrians were encountered in force.

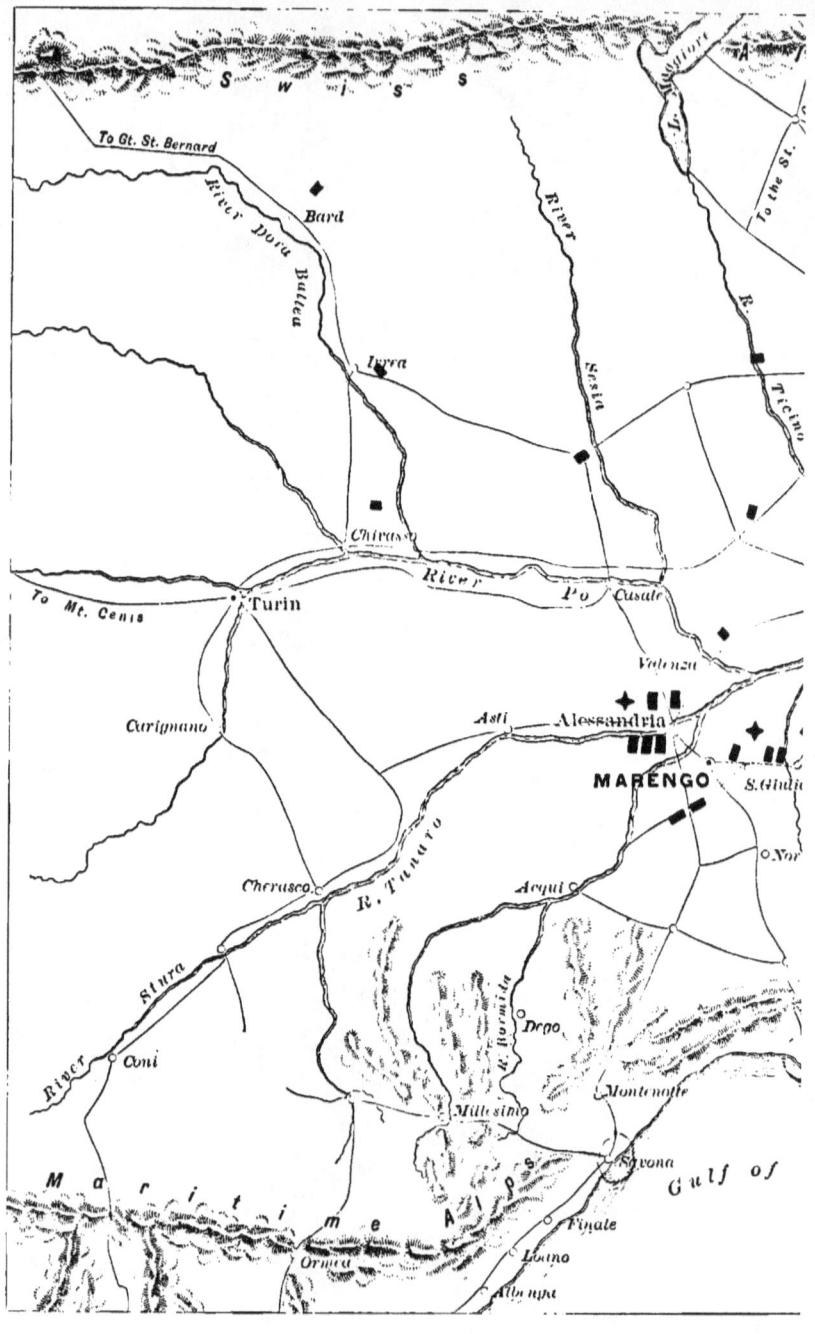

ITALIAN CAMPAIGN OF 1800.
Situation of the Armies on the 14th. of June,
the day of the Battle of Marengo.

Mélas, who, though a very old man, was still a capable and vigorous officer, had endeavored, since he heard of the crossing of the Alps by the French, to collect his scattered forces. But Ott, who was besieging Genoa, insisted on waiting until Masséna should be obliged to surrender, and that resolute soldier held out so long that Mélas could not effect the concentration of his army in time to make for the Po, and gain his lines of communication. To do so would, of course, have been to give up everything but the fortified towns, but still he could reasonably have expected reinforcements when once within reach of them, while, if Napoleon should be master of his communications, there was nothing for it but a desperate fight, in which, if beaten, he would be at the mercy of his conqueror. And so in fact it proved. Partly by the obstinacy of Ott in delaying to obtain the surrender of Genoa, partly by the celerity of Napoleon, very likely owing to the customary Austrian slowness of movement, Mélas found that Napoleon had seized his communications and was now advancing upon him, flushed with the success which had hitherto attended his marvellous plan, bringing with him all the prestige of superior skill, and confidently counting upon victory.

But the brave old man was not a whit daunted. He boldly came out of the fortified city of Alessandria, crossed the Bormida, and advanced resolutely upon the French. The chances were not in Bonaparte's favor. His available force was not large, for he had been obliged to leave many of his troops at Milan, and also on the Ticino and the Po, to protect his communications. Then he had just sent Desaix off to find where the enemy were. What happened at the famous battle of Marengo we probably shall never exactly know. Certain it is that during nearly the entire day the French were driven back, and in some cases with disorder. It is pretty clear that the troops fought badly. The army, as I have before said, was not a well organized army. Nevertheless it had good officers. Lannes and Victor strove to arrest the disorder. Bonaparte himself did everything that could be done, and hoped against hope. Finally, towards the end of the day, Desaix came up. Bonaparte's spirits rose. With new vigor he reanimated the drooping energy of the soldiers. Desaix's division made a formidable charge, in which that gallant officer fell. Kellerman's regiment of horse was equal to the emergency, and broke to pieces an Austrian column. Poor old Mélas, thinking the victory won, and fatigued with this long and arduous struggle, had gone back to Alessandria. The tide of battle turned. The French with the elasticity of their national temperament assumed the offensive, and drove their antagonists everywhere before them, capturing twenty cannon and six thousand prisoners. By a convention executed a few days later, the Austrian army was allowed to retire behind the Mincio, but Lombardy was evacuated, and all the fortified places were surrendered.

The moral effect of the battle of Marengo was immense. It completely dazzled the world. The dramatic character of the whole campaign, so well calculated to bewilder and astonish; the marvellous crossing of the Alps; the unopposed march to Milan and the welcome which that city gave to the liberating army, — for such was the light in which the French army was viewed; the closing of the avenues of escape; finally, the deadly struggle, with its varying chances, and the crushing victory, — all these features make the campaign of Marengo one of the most characteristic of Napoleon's campaigns. As such, we will now pause a moment and consider its leading features.

I think the thing that most impresses us in this campaign is its completeness of design. Napoleon aimed at compassing all the objects of the campaign in a consecutive series of movements which must terminate in a single battle. To gain the plains of Lombardy without a struggle; to reëstablish his former ascendency at the capital, Milan; then to possess himself of the crossings of the great rivers, so as to shut off every avenue of escape; lastly, to turn and seek his enemy, and to engage him in the decisive conflict, — this was the task he proposed to himself. It assuredly was the ideal thing to do, if it could be done. It would, if successful, accomplish more, and with less loss of life, too, than any other plan that could be devised. As an intellectual feat it awakens our admiration.

But it was equally remarkable for its audacity. The French army was inferior in numbers to its opponent. Yet the needs of this plan required large detachments, to occupy Milan, guard the crossings of the Po, and so forth. When the day of battle came, Bonaparte was outnumbered, and it was by great good fortune, as well as by hard fighting, that he gained the victory. It would not be difficult to point out certain not improbable combinations and movements on the part of the Austrians which would not only have rendered his plan abortive, but have forced him to retreat over the pass of St. Gothard, where the roads were by no means so favorable for artillery. Yet of all this he took his risk. Partly, no doubt, because the scientific completeness of the plan approved it to his intellect and fascinated his imagination, partly because he estimated correctly the want of activity of his enemies, but largely because he was a born gambler in war, because he enjoyed taking a great risk, fighting a battle in which everything was at stake, he adopted this novel, hazardous, but conclusive plan.

And here we touch upon one of the chief defects in Napoleon's character. It is evident that he had other ends in view in war than the practical result to be reached. He wanted to carry it on so as to satisfy his sense of the fitness of things, so to speak, to establish and maintain his reputation as a master of the art, or, at any rate, to make his campaigns illustrate the grand principles of strategy. For these ends, which are perfectly legitimate when subordinated to the great objects for which war is waged, he undoubtedly, in this campaign of Marengo, as afterwards in other campaigns, sacrificed a certain amount of safety, or, if you please, incurred a certain and otherwise unnecessary amount of hazard. For this he should, without question, be blamed; no ideal completeness, no possibility of overwhelming success, however desirable, should ever be allowed to obscure the clear perception of the ultimate practical ends to be obtained in war, or to render a jot more difficult or hazardous the already hazardous and difficult task of a campaign. They are not worth the sacrifices which they may cost. Moreau, as we have seen, rejected the plan which Napoleon proposed to him, of throwing his entire army across the Rhine at Schaffhausen, thereby cutting Kray's communications, and necessitating a great battle, in which success, if he gained it, would be decisive. Moreau preferred, on the other hand, the safer course of manœuvring in such a way as to render it extremely unlikely that such a decisive action could be had at the outset of the campaign, but also so as to give to him an excellent chance of driving his adversary from point to point, and thereby in time attaining the object of the war. Moreau's method was doubtless the more costly in life and in time, but it was also unquestionably safer. Manœuvring as Moreau did, he was at no time exposed to extreme peril; and although the same observation holds true of his adversary, yet it may fairly be said that, unless in the presence of a most pressing emergency, no general ought ever to expose his command to extreme peril.

Still, while we may justly criticise the tactics of Napoleon in this respect, while we may, I think, fairly enough regard him as too intent on the game of war, considered simply as a game, and not mindful enough of the practical ends for which alone it is ever justifiable to go to war, we shall not do wisely or justly if we adopt the extremely harsh tone of such a critic as Lanfrey. After all, there is something fine in this desire of Napoleon's to do this work of war with ideal completeness; to let the consideration of the ultimate results stand aside for the moment, and to play the game as it ought to be played. And it must be remembered that war is a game of hazard, at its best, and that no man can be a really good general who does not understand the enjoyment of risking a battle. All men of affairs understand this species of enjoyment; whether it be the surgeon, who trusts to the success of his newly invented operation; or the merchant, who risks his fortune on his calculations; or the master mariner, who trusts to the correctness of his dead reckoning when he is nearing dangerous ground. All men accustomed to the management of affairs on any large scale will comprehend the trait of character of which I have been speaking. In Napoleon, who was preëminently a man of affairs, it was undoubtedly exaggerated; and, holding the position he did, the undue prominence of this feature caused many and widespread evils. But when you come to sift it down, so to speak, you will find you are not dealing with a vicious propensity, calling for moral indignation. You may, if you like, have that sort of indignation which every one feels when a business man risks his fortune in speculation, when an inventor gives up his regular business and embarks his property in doubtful experiments. But even here, you will observe, you may consistently admit these rash people to be very worthy men in themselves. And you will notice another thing, if you think of it, that your indignation increases with the amount of egregious folly you perceive in the unhappy speculator or inventor, while it diminishes or even disappears if the foresight of the one or the originality of the other is evident beyond a cavil. Therefore I submit that we shall not be doing well if we join in the reproaches which Lanfrey so forcibly hurls at the First Consul for the hazards to which he subjected France and her army in this campaign of Marengo. Lanfrey was nothing but a critic, and probably never experienced the joy of the practical man in attempting something difficult and hazardous, and succeeding in it. Most men with vigorous minds and masculine temperaments will feel, I think, that they can, in a measure at least, understand Napoleon's mind about this his famous campaign of Marengo.

Let us now return from this digression.

I shall not follow the details of the war further. Suffice it to say that peace with Austria was concluded at Lunéville in February, 1801, and with England in March, 1802. Our attention must now be given to the policy of the First Consul at home.

While the great mass of the nation felt an unmistakable sense of relief from the doubts and alarms from which they had so constantly suffered during the preceding ten years, there were two factions who were bitterly opposed to the assumption of the supreme power by Napoleon. These were, first, the jacobins, and secondly, the royalists.

The jacobins clung to the form and the name of the republic. They thought they saw the beginnings of the Empire in the Consulate, and they were right. Precisely what they expected from France, they very likely could not have told themselves. It was evident enough that the republicans were in a clear minority; and where was the republic if the majority of the people were not republicans? But however illogical may have been the position of the jacobins, they still clung desperately to it. They shut their eyes to the facts. They refused to admit that the French peasantry cared for the republic only because it guaranteed to them their newly won liberty and equality, not because it gave them the power of casting ballots. For this last the people cared very little, and, if they reflected on the subject at all, they must have observed that the most distinguished apostles of the natural right of all men to share equally in the government of the state had been the fiercest and most tyrannical of rulers, when it looked as if the people desired a different kind of government from that which had been designed for them by their liberal leaders. But in truth, the masses cared very little for all this sort of thing. It had never amounted to much in their experience; what rights they had ever possessed had been possessed in theory only; some Danton, or Robespierre, or deputy of the convention, or republican general, had from time to time arranged and settled matters for them with a high hand; what had been gained in the shape of exemption from peculiar and oppressive burdens, and in the extension of equal rights, and in the levelling of all distinctions before the law, they recognized as the fruits of the Revolution, and for these, and only for these they really cared. The attitude of the irreconcilable jacobins, therefore, awakened no popular response.

The royalists had the advantage, such as it was, of knowing precisely what they wanted. They had, moreover, in the district known as La Vendée, an inexhaustible reservoir of devoted adherents of the king. Chouans, Vendeans, Bretons, were generally, and often fanatically, favorable to the exiled family. Then the sympathy of all foreign governments was with them. Louis the Eighteenth resided at Warsaw. His brother, the Comte d'Artois, afterwards Charles the Tenth, lived in or near London. The English government subsidized these unfortunate princes, and treated them as handsomely as if there had never been a quarrel between the House of Brunswick and the House of Bourbon touching the expulsion of the Stuarts, or the loss of the thirteen colonies. In the mind of the English government of that day the House of Bourbon stood for law and order, for legitimate authority against usurpation, for paternal government by the natural and God-given ruler, as against the tyranny of a soldier risen from the masses.

The royalist party in France greatly exaggerated the disaffection existing against the Directory. They took it to mean a willingness to restore the Bourbons. But in putting this interpretation upon it they were going a great deal too far. The irritation against the Directory had its causes, which every one could see. But those who murmured against the Triumvirs were not necessarily favorers of the old *régime*. Any really strong and respectable government would suit them. And such a government it was evident they had in the Consulate.

Filled, however, by the notion that nothing but the strong arm of Bonaparte prevented the nation from returning *en masse* to the ancient dynasty, some unscrupulous wretches of the royalist faction hatched the plot which, in December, 1800, nearly destroyed the life of the First Consul by the explosion of what was termed an infernal machine. At the time, it was supposed, especially by Bonaparte himself, that the authors of this outrage were jacobins, and he caused a number of the most pronounced of them, some of whom had been connected with the excesses of the Terror, to be banished. But it was afterwards ascertained that the plot was a royalist plot.

From time to time during the succeeding three years there were rumors of conspiracies, but as nothing of importance occurred, it was not unnaturally thought that these rumors might have their source in the superserviceable brains of an over-zealous police. In fact, it was not until the peace of Amiens was broken in March, 1803, that the formidable conspiracy of Georges Cadoudal was hatched in England.

Georges Cadoudal, or Georges, as he is generally called, was a Chouan of respectable origin, a staunch royalist, of unquestionable fidelity to the exiled house, and of inextinguishable hostility to the present government of France. He was a fanatic of the first rank; not a Guiteau, yet not unlike John Brown; a man for whom personally you could not but feel a certain measure of admiration, inasmuch as without any discernible admixture of selfish motives, and obviously impelled by religious and loyal enthusiasm, he undertook the perilous task of restoring the monarchy by killing the First Consul. Moreover, Georges had his own method of committing his intended murder. While he confessed having been privy to the plot of three years before, though not, as he maintained, to its details, this time, at any rate, he would have nothing to do with infernal machines. What he hoped to accomplish was, at the head of some of his own men, Chouans and fanatics like himself, to set upon the First Consul in the streets of Paris, and kill him in broad daylight, overcoming by main force the resistance of any guard that might be attending him.

While, however, this precious scheme might, and very possibly did, impose on the rude mind of this ruffian as being in its nature essentially different from any ordinary mode of assassination, it is plain enough to common-sense people that no such difference existed. What Georges undertook to accomplish was nothing else than the murder of the First Consul. His mode of doing it was his own choice; it may possibly have been confounded in his mind with lawful warfare; but no one not a fanatic in the cause of the Bourbons, and no one who did not desire to be deceived, could possibly be taken in by such a monstrous pretence.

Georges' scheme could not avail itself of the excuses which are so often made for political assassinations and atrocities. He was no enthusiast in the cause of antislavery, like John Brown; he was no opponent of despotism, like the Russian Nihilist. He was a fanatical devotee of the divine right of kings, and he meant to kill this upstart, whose existence, as he doubtless believed, was the principal obstacle to the return of the Bourbons.

It needs hardly to be said that such an enterprise as this was one with which no honorable man ought to have had anything whatever to do. Nor could any foreign government, which respected itself, and paid any regard to the most ordinary obligations of civilized nations, touch such a project without sharing in the infamy of murder. Yet nothing is more certain than that the Comte d'Artois, afterwards Charles the Tenth, was privy to the plot and personally conferred with the conspirators. And what is stranger yet, and far worse, is that the British government supplied these assassins with money, and sent them over to France in an English vessel of war, commanded by Captain Wright of the Royal Navy. A more flagrant and outrageous violation of the law of nations, it is safe to say, never took place. The discovery, that the Bourbon princes were arranging in London the details of a conspiracy to effect their own restoration by the murder of the First Consul, and that the assassins were sent over to France in English vessels of war, furnished with money by the English government, showed Napoleon that he was, by the Bourbons and the British government at least, regarded as an outlaw, that no steps were considered too atrocious to get rid of him, that the usages and customs which obtain among civilized nations, even in time of war, were not regarded as applicable to him.

These facts were ascertained when Georges, Rivière, Polignac, Lajolais, and others were arrested in the winter of 1803 and 1804. And so far as I know there is no dispute about them. One of the most curious things about this conspiracy is the evidently unconscious indifference of English historians to the infamy of the part which their government played in this affair. It is explicable only when we recollect, or rather endeavor to imagine, the enormous force of the legitimist prejudice of that day, —

a prejudice into which we Americans can hardly, even by a violent effort of imagination, bring ourselves to enter; a prejudice which makes even such a good man as Sir Walter Scott quite insensible to the enormity of the conduct of the Bourbon princes and the British government in furthering the assassination of Bonaparte, while his sense of justice and humanity is stirred to its depths by the prompt and terrible counterstroke of Napoleon in the seizure and execution of the Duc d'Enghien. But so it is. Scott is utterly indifferent to the first of these acts, for which no plea can be offered; he exhausts the vials of his indignation in dealing with the other, which had confessedly, apart from anything else, the excuse of just provocation at an infamous conspiracy, and of reasonable grounds for suspicion of the guilt of the duke.

That you may not think I am exaggerating, I am going to let Scott speak for himself. I quote from chapter xlvi. : —

"Meantime, the peace of Amiens being broken, the British government, with natural policy, resolved once more to avail themselves of the state of public feeling in France, and engage the partisans of royalty in a fresh attack upon the consular government. . . . A scheme was in agitation for raising the royalists in the west, where the Duke de Berri was to make a descent on the coast of Picardy, to favour the insurrection. The Duke d'Enghien, grandson of the Prince of Condé, fixed his residence, under the protection of the Margrave of Baden, at the chateau of Ettenheim, with the purpose, doubtless, of being ready to put himself at the head of the royalists in the east of France, or, if occasion should offer, in Paris itself. . . . Whilst the French princes expected on the frontier the effect of commotions in the interior of France, Pichegru, Georges Cadoudal, and about thirty other royalists of the most determined character, were secretly landed in France, made their way to the metropolis, and contrived to find lurking-places invisible to the all-seeing police. There can be no reason to doubt that a part of those agents, and Georges in particular, saw the greatest obstacle of their enterprise in the existence of Bonaparte, and were resolved to commence by his assassination. Pichegru, who was constantly in company with Georges, cannot well be supposed ignorant of this purpose, though better befitting the fierce chief of a band of Chouans than the conqueror of Holland."

Thus Scott. He was, you know, a contemporary of these events. I think you will agree with me that this utter insensibility of his to the enormity of the conduct both of the Bourbon princes and the British government is one of the most significant marks of the times. It shows the strength of the aristocratic feeling. Not thus would Scott have spoken if Bonaparte had landed English rebels bent upon the assassination of King George.

The discovery of this plot plunged France, and Paris especially, in a state of excitement that had not been known since the days of the Terror. The people, who had welcomed Bonaparte as their saviour from revolution and reaction, who had recognized in him the wise legislator, the restorer of the church, the healer of the revolutionary animosities, were equally amazed and enraged at this wanton, this outrageous attack upon him, hatched abroad in the interest of the Bourbon princes, and supported by the British government. Meantime the administration looked in every direction for the ramifications of the plot. The intrigues of Mr. Drake, the British resident at Munich in Bavaria, and of Mr. Spencer Smith, the British envoy at Stuttgard in Würtemberg, with the royalists in France, had lately come to light and were making a great deal of noise. French officers were sent to these countries to examine the state of affairs. They reported among other things that the Duc d'Enghien, the grandson of the Prince of Condé, was living at Ettenheim in Baden, a few miles only from the Rhine, surrounded with a little court of French *émigrés*, that he was in correspondence with the disaffected in France, and that his frequent and protracted absences from home gave good grounds for the suspicion that he occasionally crossed the border on political errands. No sooner did these reports reach the First Consul than he sent two officers, each heading a small detachment, into Baden, one to seize the duke and his retinue, the other to carry to the Margrave the apology of the French government for taking such a step. The Duc d'Enghien with all his suite, was seized on the night of Thursday the 15th of March, 1804, and carried immediately to Strasburg. Here he was kept a couple of days; on Sunday morning he was brought alone to Paris, and carried to the castle of Vincennes, near Paris, where he arrived on the afternoon of Tuesday, March 20, 1804. The same night he was brought before a court-martial, accused first, of having borne arms against France, secondly, of having been and now being in the pay of England, and thirdly, of being a party to the conspiracy against the republic; was convicted on the first two charges on his own admissions, and on the third also, though on what evidence does not clearly appear; was sentenced to death; was shot at six o'clock on the morning of the 21st, in the ditch surrounding the castle; and was buried where he fell.

This summary proceeding has always excited the severest criticism. Much of this is evidently based on the respect felt for the high rank of the unfortunate nobleman. We see plenty of this feeling in the pages of Scott, and in the memoirs of Madame de Rémusat, whose sympathies were all with the old *régime*. But the First Consul has been severely blamed by other historians, with whom this sentimental consideration has little or no weight. Bonaparte is accused of having executed an innocent man merely in order to strike terror into the ranks of his enemies. He is practically accused of having committed a counter-assassination. Let us see.

If the Prince really was, as Sir Walter Scott thinks he was, staying on the border " with the purpose," as Scott declares, " of being ready to put himself at the head of the royalists in the east of France, or, if occasion should offer, in Paris itself," it was, in my judgment, no crime to take him and shoot him. If that was the fact, the duke was virtually *particeps criminis*. He may have been, and no doubt was, ignorant of the mode employed to upset the consular government; but it is not to be suffered for an instant that a man should be allowed to escape merely because he chooses not to know the details of the plans of the villains, of whose success he has arranged to take instant advantage. The man who is waiting in the street, ready to enter a house as soon as he shall hear from the bolder ruffians who have committed the burglary that the coast is clear, can hardly be considered legally or morally free from the guilt of the murder which he finds, on entering, they have committed. It will not do for him to plead ignorance of their methods or precise intentions. He cannot place himself in the situation of one who accidentally profits by the murder, as would, for instance, the devisees in the will of the murdered man. He has distinctly participated, for he has placed himself in the street in order to take advantage of the doings in the house.

Now, if you will imagine an outrage of this character perpetrated in a country where there are no tribunals before whom the man in the street can be brought, and by whom the householder can be protected, you have the case of Bonaparte and the Duc d'Enghien in a nutshell, — that is, if the Duc was actually at Ettenheim for the purpose of crossing the border as soon as he should get word from Paris that the time had come. It is amazing to me how Sir Walter Scott can say, as he does, that the duke's residing " at Ettenheim in the expectation of having soon a part of importance to play in France" was " perfectly vindicated by his situation and connections." To my thinking, if Bonaparte believed he was there with any such expectation, he was justified in arresting him, and if, on the trial, or outside of it, it was found that this was the fact, he was justified in executing him.

Bonaparte unquestionably believed, when he arrested the Duc d'Enghien, that he was residing at Ettenheim in full communication with the disaffected royalists, and in daily expectation of being able to cross the Rhine as soon as he should hear that he, Bonaparte, had been disposed of. No one, I suppose, doubts that this was Bonaparte's belief when he ordered the arrest. To this effect had been the reports of the officers sent to inquire concerning the duke's surroundings and doings.

I think, therefore, that the First Consul was

fully warranted in seizing him. True, to do this it was necessary to violate the territory of Baden. But this was the affair of the Margrave, and was easily arranged. Besides, in a crisis of this sort, no man, not a fool, would have been deterred by any consideration of this nature.

The main question does not concern the arrest; it is whether the execution was justifiable.

As regards the proceedings of the court-martial, it is to be said that this body was constituted in the ordinary way. It was not a packed court. Brigadier-General Hulin was the president, by virtue of seniority. There were five colonels of regiments in Paris, and one captain, on the court. Another captain assisted as recorder. They were convened in a great hurry, had no previous conferences with each other, and did not know in the least whom they were to try.

Our knowledge of what took place is singularly small. The official records, with the exception of the sentence, have been stolen from the archives of the War Department. We have, it is true, a draft of the record, made by the president of the court-martial for his own use, and no doubt it is substantially correct as far as it goes, but it does not contain copies of the letters and other papers which Hulin says were annexed to the record. Savary, afterwards Duc de Rovigo, who commanded the temporary garrison of the castle of Vincennes, tells us that all the documentary evidence against Marie

Antoinette was stolen in the first days of the Restoration, in 1814, from the archives of the Bureau of Justice, and it may be, as Savary believes was the case, that for some similar reason the archives of the War Department were rifled by the friends of the Duc d'Enghien. Be this as it may, however, we are not certain by any means that we have a complete record of the proceedings.

This matter becomes important for this reason. Savary, who was present at the trial, tells us that, at the close of the interrogatories, one of the members of the court remarked to the prisoner, that it was scarcely probable that he was as completely ignorant as he had said that he was of what was passing in France; that he would hardly succeed in making them believe that he was entirely indifferent to events of which the consequences were so important for him; and that he had better reflect on the matter before replying. The duke, says Savary, after a moment's silence, replied gravely that he understood perfectly well what was meant; that it had not been his intention to remain indifferent to what was going on; that he had asked to be permitted to serve in the English army; that he had been told that this could not be, but that he was to remain on the Rhine where he would soon have a part to play; and for this he was waiting. Savary says that this was the Prince's precise reply; and that he wrote it down at the time.

It is on this reply that Scott bases his statement about the duke's purpose in staying at Ettenheim. Its authenticity rests on the single word of Savary. Neither General Hulin's copies of the minutes, nor his pamphlet published in 1824, contain any mention of it. Still, it seems clear, from Savary's account, that the remark of the officer was not in the nature of a formal interrogatory to the accused, but that it was made after the evidence, which, by the way, seems to have consisted entirely of the defendant's admissions, was in; that it was put informally, and by way of giving the prisoner an opportunity to say a word in mitigation of the sentence, and was not a part of the trial, properly so called. If this was so, and it certainly looks like it, the absence of the statement and reply from the report of the trial are accounted for.

The members of the court-martial had no choice but to find the prisoner guilty on the first two charges. The law was clear; and as regards the prisoner's having fought and still desiring to fight against France, and his being in the pay of England, his own avowals were explicit. As regards his connection with the existing conspiracies, he certainly did not admit as much as this, but he frankly stated, if we are to believe Savary, and I think there is no reason why we should not, that he was on the Rhine waiting for his part to begin.

But, — and this is by far the more interesting

and important question, — why did Bonaparte send the duke before a court which could not but find him guilty and sentence him to death?

Certainly not because Bonaparte wished to punish him for having fought against the republic; no one has ever pretended this.

Was it, then, as so many have supposed, an act done solely to strike terror into the hearts of the Bourbon princes, and without any evidence showing the complicity of the duke with the plots of the royalists? '

I think not; I think that Bonaparte had evidence before him which convinced him that the duke was cognizant of the existence of a royalist conspiracy, and was residing near the border in the hope of being soon called upon to take an active part in affairs. I am not now referring to the duke's avowal at the trial, of which Savary informs us. Bonaparte, of course, never heard of this till after the execution. I refer to the duke's papers, which were seized at Ettenheim when he was arrested. The mistake most historians have made is to look solely to the trial for the evidence on which the duke was put to death: the real question is, Why was he tried? To get light on this we must look in a wholly different direction.

That there were some papers seized at Ettenheim, we know, for we have the duke's own journal containing a narrative of his arrest, and of his being carried to Strasburg. On the 15th of March, the day of his arrest at Ettenheim, he says: "My papers were carried off and sealed up." On the 16th he says: "At half past four, they come to examine my papers, which Colonel Charlot, accompanied by a commissary of safety, opens in my presence. They read them superficially. They do them up in separate bundles, and leave me to understand that they are to be sent to Paris." On the 17th he says: "They come to get me to sign the *procès-verbal* of the opening of my papers. I demand and obtain to add to it an explanatory note, to prove that I have never had other intentions than to serve in and make war."

Now, if the duke's papers contained nothing of a suspicious or compromising nature, why did he accompany them with this note? If they did not contain something that indicated pretty clearly his being implicated in some doings that could by no means fall under the head of open warfare, why did the duke append this explanatory note, that he never had any other intentions than to serve in and make war? Or, may we not at any rate fairly infer that these papers contained evidence of somebody else's intentions to embark in enterprises that were very different from honorable warfare, and that the duke was anxious to clear his skirts of the connection? Something of this kind, depend upon it, induced the duke to ask permission to add this explanatory note to the *procès-verbal* of his papers.

But this is not all. On the 18th of March, Napoleon had the papers. On that day we find him writing to Talleyrand about the behavior at Vienna of a certain man mentioned in them, and on the 19th, the day before the court-martial was ordered, we find Napoleon sending the papers to Réal, one of the Council of State, who was afterwards charged with the examination of the prisoner. (I need hardly remind my readers that in the whole matter of criminal procedure, the French method is a wholly different one from that prescribed by the common law.)

On the next day, the 20th, the First Consul decrees that the duke should be brought before a court-martial, and he also writes a long letter to Réal, which the latter receives that evening, ordering him to go to Vincennes at once, and giving him eleven points on which he wishes him to have the duke examined. I will give one or two of these questions: "5. Have you not proposed to raise a legion, and to cause the troops of the republic to desert, in saying that your sojourn for two years near the frontier had put you in the way of having an understanding with the troops stationed on the Rhine? . . . 8. What correspondence is this that you have with people in Alsace? And what is this that you have with people in Paris? What is this that you have with people in Bréda and in the army of Holland?"

These are questions contained in a letter which

Napoleon sent to the councillor of state, whom he had charged with the examination of the duke. They are not statements made in an apology for the execution of the duke. They are not contained in a manifesto of any kind. The letter in which they are to be found was never intended to reach the public eye, and was published, I believe, for the first time, in 1865. These are points in regard to which Napoleon, after he had read the duke's correspondence, desired the duke to be questioned. These questions are manifestly framed after reading that correspondence. There can, I submit, be no reasonable doubt that some of the letters found at Ettenheim came from Alsace, Paris, Bréda, from officers in the army in Holland; that in some of these letters reference is made to letters received from the duke, in which he had said something about his sojourn near the Rhine for two years having enabled him to have an understanding with some of the French officers stationed in that neighborhood, that he thought he could induce the troops to desert, and so forth. No one can believe that Napoleon, writing to Réal, after having read the duke's papers, invented out of his own head the subject-matter of these questions. It was with reference to the contents of those letters that the duke appended that explanatory note to the *procès-verbal* of his papers, for the duke says so himself; and from the questions framed by Bonaparte after he had examined the papers, we can get a pretty good notion of the duke's motive in so doing.

But we are not left in this matter to mere inference. The Count Miot de Melito, who was also one of the Council of State, and was especially charged with investigating the charges against Moreau, states in his memoirs that among the papers seized at Ettenheim was "a list of persons in France on whom the duke might have relied. This list," he says, "was said to contain the names of certain councillors of state, such as Barbé-Marbois, Siméon, Portalis, and others. It has been proved by subsequent events that these imputations were not unfounded; it is therefore all the more remarkable that no injury resulted from them to the persons involved. They continued to enjoy Bonaparte's favor, and to serve him as long as his power lasted." Melito also gives us Bonaparte's explanation, made a few days after the affair, to the Council of State, in which he says: "It will be seen by the papers we have seized that he (the duke) had established himself at Ettenheim so as to carry on a correspondence with the interior of France."

One other thing may be mentioned in this connection. When the duke signed the *procès-verbal* of his evidence at the trial, for by French law his own evidence is read to the accused, and he signifies his admission that it is correctly reported by signing the document, he wrote an urgent demand that he might be permitted to have a private audience with the First Consul. There was, therefore, unquestionably something to be explained; not that any of the facts which he had so frankly admitted at the trial about his participation in the wars against the republic, or his having been in the receipt of an allowance from England, needed or were capable of an explanation; still less can we suppose that he wished to humiliate himself before the man whom he considered a usurper, and implore his pardon. No; there was evidently something which weighed on his mind, something in the papers which had been seized that looked as if he had entertained projects which were not those of honorable warfare; and he wanted to see Bonaparte and explain this. Probably, what the duke wanted to say was that his own personal share in the enterprises disclosed by the papers was to be a purely military one, and no doubt this was true. Nevertheless, if he resided at Ettenheim rather than in London, for instance, in order, as his correspondence seems to indicate, that he might act with certain advantages, when the time should come for him to act, he had, in fact, made his arrangements to profit by the conspiracy of Georges, ignorant as he preferred to remain of its methods.

Accordingly, I cannot doubt that Bonaparte, who examined the papers found at Ettenheim before the duke's arrival in Paris, found quite enough in them to satisfy him that the duke had been cognizant of all sorts of political intrigues in France; that he was in correspondence with disaffected persons, and was preparing to play his part when his way should be made clear. He therefore had him brought before a court-martial, and ordered one of the members of the Council of State to charge himself with the examination of the prisoner on the points raised by an inspection of his papers.

We come now to the only really obscure thing in this whole matter. How did it happen that the trial and execution were hurried through with such precipitation that the First Consul's intentions as to the examination of the duke were not carried out? Why did not Réal arrive in season to propound to the duke the interrogatories which the First Consul had so carefully drawn up? or rather, as the First Consul points out in his letter to Réal, to instruct the officer who would act as judge-advocate to put the questions, Réal being unable, as being a civilian, to take part in the proceedings? Why was not this done? It seems perfectly clear that Bonaparte expected the questions, which he had prepared, to be put, and he no doubt expected to get something out of them. But at eight o'clock in the morning, Colonel Savary, on his way to Paris, meets Councillor Réal, — who had the evening before, received the First Consul's letter, — with the list of questions in his pocket, and, probably, the duke's papers also, ready to hold a consultation with the judge-advocate, and see that the information which the First Consul expected to extract from the prisoner was obtained, if possible.

The amazement of Réal on hearing of the duke's execution was so great that Savary, as he tells us, determined to go straight to Malmaison without going home first, and tell Bonaparte at once what had occurred. The First Consul was equally astounded, and told Savary that there was something in the matter that he could not understand; not that the court should have condemned the duke upon his own admissions, but that the trial should have taken place before Réal had had the duke interrogated.

That Murat, then military governor of Paris, was to a certain extent responsible for the precipitate action of the court-martial, seems very probable. His order appointing the court-martial contains every justification for haste. "Cette commission se réunira sur-le-champ au château de Vincennes, pour y juger, sans désemparer, le prévenu."

But this is not enough of itself. After the trial, the proceedings ought to have been sent to Murat for approval. This was not done. Hulin, the president of the court, says that the court had no purpose of carrying out the sentence immediately; that he supposed the proceedings were to be sent, as was customary, to the proper authorities. He evidently thought Savary was responsible for the promptitude with which the sentence was carried out. But in this opinion he was mistaken. All that Savary did was to furnish the detail of men to carry out the sentence, when requested to do so by the judge-advocate. The real truth seems to have been that the members of the court were, as General Hulin says. entirely ignorant of law, and the judge-advocate and recorder had had hardly more experience than the rest. The first draft of proceedings, which was signed by the seven officers who constituted the court, contained the following sentence : "Ordonne que le présent jugement sera executé de suite, à la diligence du capitaine-rapporteur." The judge-advocate (capitaine-rapporteur) conceived himself bound to carry out the sentence at once, and he asked and obtained from Savary, as has been said, a detail for the purpose. It seems to me more likely that this extreme haste was due to the fact that the words "de suite" slipped unobserved into the sentence, than that it was the result of any more occult cause. In fact, this first draft of the record is full of imperfections of various kinds. But I do not find any evidence whatever tending to show that Bonaparte was in any way responsible either for the trial having taken place on the night of the 20th and 21st, or for the execution of the sentence before it had been sent to the proper authorities for revision and approval. On the contrary, there is every reason to believe that the First Consul expected that the trial would not take place till the morning of the 21st. And there is no evidence, one way or the other, as to his intentions in regard to following up any such sentence by the execution of the duke. The truth seems to be, the Duc d'Enghien was tried and executed with a promptitude that was entirely unexpected to the First Consul; and, although he preferred to assume the responsibility for the act, no one has a right to say what would have been the duke's fate had not Bonaparte's decision been thus anticipated.

LECTURE III.

NAPOLEON IN GERMANY.

The conspiracy of Georges Cadoudal and the execution of the Duc d'Enghien occupied a large portion of the last lecture; nevertheless, I cannot dismiss the subject without a few words more. Georges and a few of the chief leaders were executed; but the First Consul pardoned several whose guilt was confessed. There was not only no indiscriminate severity, but there was a great deal of leniency shown in dealing with the authors and abettors of this plot. Moreau, who was proved to have had interviews with Pichegru, whose association with Georges was admitted, was brought to trial, and sentenced to two years' imprisonment. It was a light sentence, certainly, but the First Consul gladly commuted it to exile, and, by purchasing Moreau's house for a round sum, placed it within his power to live as became a man who had rendered such distinguished service to his country. The execution of the Duc d'Enghien stopped further royalist plots. The Bourbons perceived that the new chief of the French nation was not a man against whom it was safe to conspire.

We must return for a while to the domestic policy of the new government. This was a course confessedly energetic, wise, liberal, and conciliatory. Bonaparte found the finances in extreme disorder; it was difficult to raise the money needed for the army. But if there was one subject which Bonaparte understood better than another, it was finance; his vigorous intellect enjoyed mastering those problems of economy which have always been so attractive to great statesmen. Assisted by the best talent he could procure, he initiated a series of changes which at once stopped the leaks, and laid all the resources of the country under fair and equal contribution. The funds rose in value; the world of business recognized very clearly that affairs were now in the hands of a business man, and a man, too, of first-rate business capacity.

Yet it is hard to satisfy some men. Lanfrey, whose perverse ingenuity is rather severely taxed on this occasion, in speaking of Bonaparte's "decided preference for upright administration," asks, "what can be more skilful than the employment of honest agents in a crooked policy?" This is, by the way, not an unfair specimen of Lanfrey's method in dealing with facts; he is an adept at throwing out an insinuation so skilfully that the careless reader will swallow it as if it were propounded to him as a fact. Here, for instance, Lanfrey is dealing with Bonaparte's admitted preference in his administration for honest men. But the suggestion of the crooked policy positively has the effect of making us think there is almost something culpable in preferring honest to dishonest men. But what is the justification of this suggestion? Absolutely none. The work which Bonaparte's cabinet were to perform was straightforward hard work in all the departments of government; there was nothing crooked about it at all; and Lanfrey knew it. France was in a state of administrative disorder; the finances, especially, needed attention; the law regulating assessment of land, which formed the basis of one of the principal taxes, was very defective; the schools and universities needed supervision; there was a great deal of hard and faithful work to be done, and it was done by these honest and capable and laborious men whom the First Consul called about him; and Lanfrey gives them credit for it too. Yet he throws out the slur about "a crooked policy" to prevent his victim from having even the merit accorded to him of having selected these worthy men for their several tasks. Why does he thus go out of his way to asperse the motives of Napoleon? In other words, why this virulent hatred of Napoleon? Because Lanfrey and all his school confuse political rights with political and legal liberties; they do not see that it was the latter only that had been conferred by the Revolution, and that the granting of political rights by the decrees of the National Assembly did not result in the possession and exercise of political power by the French people, who were as despotically governed from 1792 to 1799 as either before or after that date. Lanfrey and his school accordingly detest Napoleon because of his assumption of the supreme authority, forgetting that, in assuming it, he deprived the people of no political power that they then were exercising, or ever had exercised; that to them the Eighteenth of Brumaire meant merely a change of masters, a change from men who were cordially detested and distrusted, to a man whom every one admired, and in whom everybody placed confidence. Excuse this digression upon Lanfrey: but I am very anxious to make this part of my subject perfectly clear, and for this purpose I cannot do better than to show where this historian, writing from the extreme republican standpoint, has fallen into grave error.

The most important measure of the Consulate was undoubtedly the Code Napoleon. No other work of Napoleon's will live as long as this. It is to day the framework of law in France, Holland, Belgium, western Germany, Switzerland, and Italy. In France it replaced a chaos of laws and decrees, and welded the old legislation which was worth retaining with the new improvements of the revolutionary epoch.

The importance of the share taken by Napoleon in this matter of the Code is not to be measured by the legal learning, or even by the practical common sense, which he contributed to its provisions. Without a doubt, the credit of combining into a consistent whole the immense mass of law and custom which had to be considered and sifted, belongs to the eminent jurists whom the First Consul employed in the work. Napoleon very likely made many valuable suggestions; it is certain that when it was necessary to come to a decision, his clear mind, instructed by the discussions of his counsellors, found little difficulty in arriving at the right conclusion, and it is equally certain that he permitted no unnecessary loss of time in announcing the decision at which he had arrived. But however valuable his contributions may have been to the composition and structure of the Code, it is not in this direction chiefly that we are to look, if we would find the great service which he rendered to his country in this matter. It is rather to the fact that he saw at once on his accession to power that such a measure was absolutely necessary to consolidate the newly acquired benefits which the Revolution had conferred on the French people; and that, military man though he was, he carried through with promptitude, wisdom, and energy this gigantic task to a speedy termination. It was not that he was the first man who had thought that a codification of the laws would be desirable; the subject had been broached for fifty years, and in fact the work had been planned by the decrees of the convention. It was not that he was the first among rulers actually to set about a codification of the laws; this may be true, but it is also true that a measure of this sort was more obviously desirable, in the condition in which he found France, than any similar undertaking could have appeared to the rulers of countries which had escaped the disorganization incident to a revolution, and into which the new system had not yet gained an entrance. But what he is to be credited with is this: with having taken at once the true view of the needs of France in this regard, — the true view, the view which a real statesman would take; and, furthermore, with having, promptly and persistently, and at a very considerable expense to himself of time taken from other and perhaps more congenial duties, and of labor for which neither his education nor his habitual occupation had fitted him, pushed the work through to an eminently satisfactory conclusion.

This task was undertaken by Napoleon in the spirit and with the energy which belonged to him as a first-rate man of affairs. His appreciation of its importance showed him to be far more than a mere soldier, in fact, to be a great statesman; and it is not unlikely that his name will be more widely known through the Code Napoleon than by the lustre of his victories. It was a work of which he was always very proud; he always spoke of it as one of the principal labors of his life. And it is morally certain that, had it not been for the systematic arrangement and codification of the legal results of the great liberal movement through which France had just passed, and for the ten years, from 1804 to 1814, during which the Code was the law of the land, entering into and determining the public and private relations of the French people, becoming to them a rule of justice and a priceless possession, the restoration of the Bourbons would have swept away most of the reforms of the revolutionary period. It is equally certain, as we shall ere long have occasion to observe, that the Code became in the hands of Napoleon a sure and a most convenient means of introducing the new system into the German and Italian possessions which afterwards came under the dominion of the Empire.

Another measure of the Consulate was the Concordat, which reëstablished the Roman Catholic Church in France under the protection of government, much as the Church of England is established in that country. This important step was not taken without meeting with violent and sincere opposition on the part of most of the prominent men who had supported the Revolution. It seemed to them a step backwards. It was true that all religions were to be freely tolerated, as much as they ever had been, or are to-day. But the political character of the Roman Church, the danger that the allegiance due from its members to a potentate independent of France might in some way conflict with the obligations of its powerful officers to obey the laws of the land, the opinion held by very many in the France of that day as it was then and is now held by nearly everybody in the United States, that civil government has no concern whatever with church establishments, all these considerations were urged against the First Consul's project. And there was undoubtedly force in these arguments. Yet I am inclined to think that Bonaparte did wisely in giving to what he termed "the church of the majority of the French people" the inestimable advantage of public recognition and support. France was not far enough advanced in her education, that is, the masses of her people were not, to make it safe to rely solely on the voluntary system. The alternative was either the restoration of the Roman Catholic Church, or leaving France without the regular institutions of Christianity. He chose wisely, I think, in taking the former of these courses.

In his negotiation with the Pope, he held out for state nominations to important posts in the church, and for a strict regulation by the government of ecclesiastical institutions. But his system was too artificial; he did not thoroughly understand the subject; he gave more power to the bishops over the clergy than they had been hitherto possessed of; but his new bishops were not the important functionaries of state that the bishops of the old *régime* had been; they not only had no political power, but their doings and sayings were closely watched by a not very friendly government-superior; they fell back upon their purely spiritual powers, and hence upon the Bishop of Rome, becoming with each decade less Gallican and more Ultramontane. But, for all this, the restoration of the Catholic Church was, as it seems to me, an almost indispensable step in the then demoralized condition of France.

One more step remained to be taken, — one more change in the form of government to be made, — that from the Republic to the Empire. But how much did this change amount to? It certainly did not carry with it any alteration in the laws which affected life, liberty, and the pursuit of happiness, to use the words of the immortal Declaration. The great fundamental changes for the better which the Revolution had wrought in the condition of the people of France were not in the remotest degree affected. In truth, the nation demanded the change, because it believed that the great benefits which the Revolution had conferred would in the then existing state of public feeling in France, in the stage of political development at which the French people had then arrived, and in the face of the unmistakable and unscrupulous hostility which the success of the new order of things in France had evoked throughout aristocratic and legitimist Europe, be more secure under a liberal monarch like Napoleon than under the forms of a republic. And it is certainly not for the republican theorist to quarrel with the wish of the people. Sad and deplorable as it may seem to such a man that his country, at a certain stage of its history, should care less about further experiments in self-government than about protection by a strong arm from foreign attacks and domestic conspiracies, yet, if the fact be so, he, as a professed republican, ought to bow to the will of the people. But, without troubling ourselves further, as we easily might, to imprison our republican philosopher in the web of his own construction, we cannot repress a smile at the unhappy Lanfrey, who finds his people so far below the level of what he considers manly pride in their beloved republic. It is necessary for Lanfrey to ride two horses in his discussion of this subject; when on one horse he assumes that the people desire the Republic, that the Empire is forced upon them. When upon the other, he bewails the actual fact: "France," he says, "was passive and subdued; she had no longer either will or opinion, she was credulous and ignorant." It never seems to occur to him, that if the people of a country are passive and subdued, ignorant and credulous, have neither opinion nor will of their own, they certainly are not fit to run a republic. Such a people are sure to have somebody to govern them, and whether it be four or five Directors, or two or three Consuls, or an Emperor, it matters little. But there is no need to make the foolish lamentations in which Lanfrey and his school indulge when they speak of the Empire. The people of France had advanced in the Revolution one stage, and that a very important one, in their political development; they were not at that time ready to advance the remaining steps; what they had done was, they felt, and very rightly too, quite enough for one generation; and they had grave reason to be alarmed at the foreign and domestic hostility which seemed to be awakened everywhere and to threaten seriously their ability to retain what they had gained. They knew perfectly well what they were about; in fact, it was the Empire which not only consolidated and preserved for France the great reforms of the Revolution, but by extending them into the neighboring countries, prevented France from being left alone in her experiment with the new system, gained for her hearty and intelligent allies, and, in spite of the terrible mistakes which the new Emperor made in the later years of his rule, shattered the power of the old system throughout a great part of Europe, and rendered the triumph of the reaction when it came, in 1814, a far less serious and important matter than it would have been had it occurred fifteen years before.

In dealing with the subject which these words naturally introduce, — the foreign relations of the Empire of Napoleon, — it is not my purpose to weary you with an attempt at a connected and full narrative. We have not time for anything of that sort. All we can do is to get some general notion of Napoleon's policy, its purposes, and its results.

The peace of Lunéville, which followed the campaign of Marengo, not only secured the withdrawal of the Austrian influence in Northern Italy, but left Piedmont and the republics which had recently been organized out of Lombardy and some of the lesser states, under the influence and protection of France. As a natural consequence, Piedmont was annexed to France, and the new republics were united in one, under the presidency of Bonaparte himself. As regards Germany, the territory on the left bank of the Rhine was given up to France. Her acquisitions in Belgium and her protectorate over Holland were also sanctioned. More than this, France was by the same treaty admitted to share in the negotiations which the recent changes had rendered necessary in the Holy Roman or German Empire, of which the Emperor of Austria was the head, which at that time, it will be remembered, still existed; and it needs hardly to be said that France exercised her full share in the decisions which were arrived at by the Diet. In his general policy, Napoleon took the natural course of furthering the interests of the south German states, which had for centuries, as a rule, had France for a friend and ally in their interminable quarrels with the House of Hapsburg. The influence of France was also exerted in favor of the extinguishment of the petty principalities, of the suppression of the (so called) free cities, of the secularization of the enormous possessions of the Roman Catholic Church. In these changes, every one of which was a beneficial change for the people, Bavaria, Würtemberg, and Baden received great accessions of territory, and, what was very important for Napoleon, were brought under the influence of France, both as regarded their internal and external relations. On the one hand, they were attracted to follow in the steps of France, to abolish the antiquated abuses and inequalities which survived to such a deplorable extent throughout Germany, and to introduce the administrative efficiency and simplicity which they saw prevailing in their neighbor's territories; and on the other, by taking these very steps in the direction of reform, they were separating themselves still further from the reactionary policy of which their nominal superior, the Emperor of Germany, was the chief representative.

For thus exerting his influence in these schemes for the reorganization of Germany, Napoleon has been severely blamed by those who bow down to the newly invented deity of German nationality. Take an illustration. Among the antiquated nuisances that were abated by Bavaria and the other states of western Germany, when, under the impulse of France, they entered upon the path of reform, was the Order of the Knights of the Empire. These gentlemen lived upon certain vexatious imposts, and enjoyed a sort of irregular and anomalous jurisdiction over their neighbors. To abolish their privileges was a manifest gain for the cause of good administration. One of these chevaliers was the celebrated Stein, afterwards, as minister of Prussia, the great organizer of the German uprising of 1813 against the Empire of Napoleon. Stein told the Duke of Nassau that he was protected by the same laws of the Empire that the duke was, and that he and the other petty princes had much better attach themselves to the two great monarchies of Austria and Prussia than be following foreign counsels in abolishing vested rights like his. With such a position I have no sympathy. As I stated in my first lecture, the vital question for continental Europe at that time was not a question of political rights, but of personal liberty, of equality before the law, of religious toleration, of the continuance or the abolition of a host of anomalous and oppressive privileges that lay like a burden upon the trade of the bourgeois and the labor of the peasant. But there is another way of looking at these questions. I have before me a valuable contribution to the history of these times, Fyffe's "Modern Europe." Mr. Fyffe says, "that the consolidation of Germany should be worked out in the interest of French hirelings, instead of in the interest of the German people, was justly treated by Stein as a subject for patriotic anger." Let us examine this assertion a little.

Mr. Fyffe tells us, in regard to the sovereignties of the ecclesiastics and the free cities, which were both suppressed in this reorganization, that "the internal condition of the priest-ruled districts was generally wretched; heavy ignorance, beggary, and intolerance kept life down to an inert monotony;" that "the free cities, as a rule, were sunk in debt; the management of their affairs had become the perquisite of a few lawyers and privileged families;" and that "for Germany as a nation the destruction of these petty sovereignties was not only an advantage, but an absolute necessity." If this be a true picture of the state of the case, it is certainly matter for sincere thankfulness that Bonaparte put a little practical common sense and a little wholesome pressure into the reorganization of western Germany, and that the poor people there were not obliged to wait until the cause of equal rights should be taken up by the King of Prussia and the Emperor of Austria. Moreover, that in exerting his influence in the matter of these reforms Napoleon was not outraging any national or patriotic feeling is admitted by Fyffe himself. "The peoples of Germany," says he, "cared as little about a Fatherland as their kings. To the Hessian and the Bavarian at the centre of the Empire, Germany was scarcely more than it was to the Swiss or the Dutch, who had left the Empire centuries before. The inhabitants of the Rhenish provinces had murmured for a while at the extortionate rule of the Directory; but their severance from Germany and their incorporation with a foreign race touched no fibre of patriotic regret; and, after the establishment of a better order of things under the Consulate, the annexation to France appears to have become highly popular. Among a race whose members could thus be actually conquered and annexed without violence to their feelings, Bonaparte had no difficulty in finding willing allies." So far Mr. Fyffe.

Very well, then, if his allies were willing, if the annexation to France was satisfactory to the people, as you say was the case, why, I should like to ask the learned author, why and of whom do you complain? Of Bonaparte? How can you, when his annexations were popular and his allies willing? *Volenti non fit injuria.* Of these German communities? Why should you undertake to put your opinion against theirs? What business is it of yours to revise their judgment? And have you considered at all, have you not entirely forgotten to consider, what was the alternative presented to them? Is it not possible that the obstinate aristocratic and ecclesiastical despotism of Austria might appear more terrible than participation in the political career of the freest nation on the Continent, even if that nation was France? Or that the peasantry of the west bank of the Rhine might well prefer the position of French soldiers, drawn as they were from all classes in life, each man certain to be promoted in due time if he was brave and competent, to that of serving in the Prussian army, where no one but a nobleman could by any possibility become an officer, and where the free use of the cane took the place of emulation and ambition?

I am tired of these theorists. Men like Lanfrey, instead of looking coolly and fairly at the actual state of the French people in 1799, at what they had gained in the way of legal and political reforms, at what they actually needed, and what they were fit for, pour out no end of reproaches upon their own nation for having decided to remain content for the time being with their acquisitions, and to consolidate the state in order to defend them. Men like Fyffe, instead of comparing the relative advantages and disadvantages of the alternative presented to the peoples of western Germany of allying themselves either with Austria and Prussia or with France, and then telling us in so many words which they consider the wisest course, omit one branch of the alternative altogether from the discussion, and by the way they speak of the other clearly convey the impression that the right thing for these western Germans to do would have been to stand by Austria and Prussia, and postpone to an indefinite future, at the bidding of those powers, the much needed practical reforms which they either received when incorporated into France, or which were introduced into their respective countries by French influence during their alliance with France. If they really think this, then I have the honor to differ from them, *toto cœlo*. To my mind, neither Austria nor Prussia had any claim on the loyalty of the citizen of Cologne or the peasant of the Palatinate. The policy of both powers had always been grasping and unscrupulous. At this very time they had just finished the third partition of Poland. And not a single movement in the direction of practical relief to the middle and lower classes could reasonably be expected to come from either power.

To my thinking, too, the inhabitants of western Germany acted like sensible people in disregarding this vague talk about the Fatherland, and in taking the shortest and most efficacious course to secure the sweeping reforms which they so urgently needed. It is a great thing, no doubt, for the people of a country to be patriotic. But in order that any people should be patriotic they must first have a country. And by a country, I mean not a vision in the indefinite future, but a fact of to-day, and of a hundred years ago. That several communities speak the same language does not constitute them one country, however distinctly it may point to their common origin. One's country is not an inference from the fact of a common language; still less is it a dream of the future. The country which has claims upon its citizens must in the nature of things be an organized community, with a history of which all its citizens can be proud, a present tangible existence in which they all participate, and a future to which they can all look forward. I am not reproaching those who have in recent times brought about the political unity of Germany under the hegemony of Prussia, whether they went to work by songs, or books, or secret societies, or by the more efficacious method of the Bismarckian blood and iron. We have at any rate no concern with their conduct here. But I do mean to say that to reproach the Germans of the Rhine with a lack of patriotism because in their several states they stood by and fought for Napoleon against Austria and Prussia backed by Russia, is absurd on its face.

More than that, — it was to France that western Germany had always looked for support from the time of the Thirty Years War; it was France that had all along prevented the absorption of these communities in the Austrian Empire. The Germans of the Rhine had much more in common with the French than they had with the inhabitants of Hungary or Pomerania, with Paris than with Berlin or Vienna. They shrank back with merited dislike and dread from the crushing conservatism of the three eastern military monarchies, Russia, Austria, and Prussia; they gladly and thankfully, and, let us add, wisely, took the hand which France stretched out to them, and entered cheerfully and hopefully on the path of reform, in which she had led the way. What was it to them that the military aristocrats of Prussia spoke German, that the Kaiser of Austria was the nominal head of Germany? Ought considerations like these to influence intelligent public opinion in western Germany to receive the word of command from the successor of the Great Frederic, or its institutes of civil and religious liberty from the hand of a Metternich? Let me speak my mind on this matter. I have no patience with people who, led away by a notion of a patriotism which at that time could have had no real existence, refuse to see that the side of France was, throughout the wars of the Revolution and the Empire, the side of civil and religious liberty.

The important changes in western Germany, of which we have been speaking, greatly increased the predominance of France. The Italian republic had recently followed the example of its elder sister, and had become a kingdom. Napoleon was crowned at Milan with the iron crown of Lombardy, amid great enthusiasm; and his title thenceforward was that of Emperor of the French and King of Italy. He delegated his authority in the latter country to his stepson Eugene Beauharnais, a man of high character and good abilities, who assumed the title of Viceroy of Italy.

These peaceful victories aroused anew the jealousy and perhaps even the alarm of Austria. England had broken the Peace of Amiens in the spring of 1803, and Russia had entered into alliance with her in 1804. In 1805 Austria joined the coalition. The ostensible cause of this combined attack on Napoleon was the disturbance of the balance of power in Europe, caused by the aggrandizement of France; and this was unquestionably a real cause. But there was something behind and below this: there was the feeling that Napoleon represented the Revolution. Not certainly that he represented the excesses of jacobinism; but rather that he was the champion of the liberal cause, and the foe of those unequal and oppressive privileges and vested rights, which constituted the very framework of society in Austria, Prussia, Russia, and, I might almost add, in England also. There was, in short, the conviction entertained by the ruling classes everywhere that he and his system must be broken down, or the old order of things in Europe would fall. Hence these repeated coalitions.

Napoleon had been for more than a year assembling and organizing a large force at Boulogne for his projected invasion of England. He undoubtedly meant, if circumstances should favor him, to undertake it. He gave such directions to his admirals as he judged would enable them to elude the vigilance of the British fleet, and to sweep the English Channel for the brief period during which his crossing could, as he calculated, be made. He had drilled his men in embarking and disembarking, and I am afraid to say in how few hours he expected to be able to land 160,000 men in England. Had his plans succeeded, he could no doubt in a few days after landing have destroyed the arsenals and dockyards at Woolwich and Portsmouth, and taken London. But that seems to me to be all he could reasonably have expected to do. After all, 160,000 men of all arms were certainly not too many for his needs. The English government could doubtless have collected 60,000 or 70,000 regular troops, and volunteers would have been at once forthcoming in crowds. The best drilled militia would be used to fill up the regular regiments and batteries to the maximum strength. It would not have taken long to put into the field a formidable force of at least 100,000 men, nearly all of whom would be regular troops; and, making all necessary deductions for garrisons, guards of communications, and so forth, Napoleon could not have taken the field with a much larger force than this. Under these circumstances any great success in battle would have been improbable. The English regular troops were at least quite as good as the best that he carried with him; and, though the English army would in the case I have imagined have been more or less diluted with recruits, still it would have been a force exceedingly hard to beat in any event; and, had it played a waiting game, and its commander been wise enough to remain on the defensive and receive the assault of the French, there would have been an extremely good chance for a victory of the class of Busaco, Talavera, or Gettysburg. And it must be remembered that Napoleon could have got no reinforcements, while the English army would have been augmented daily. If he was to succeed at all in the invasion of England, it would have been necessary for him to conquer the country, and actually possess himself of its resources; and, without reinforcements, this would not have been possible. But, to return from these speculations on what might have been, the French navy utterly failed the Emperor. It has always been hard to beat the English on their favorite element, and the French admirals of that day were certainly no match for Nelson and Collingwood. These great captains and their able subordinates headed off the French squadrons, prevented their junction, collected their own forces, secured an unimpeded control of the English Channel, and finally, in the famous battle of Trafalgar, fought on the

21st of October, 1805, annihilated the French and Spanish navies.

Long before this, however, Napoleon saw that his plan had miscarried; and, as Austria had declared war, and was invading Bavaria, he abruptly put his army in marching order, turned the heads of his columns to the southeast, and commenced the masterly series of movements that opened the brilliant campaign of 1805 by the capture of Ulm and ended it with the battle of Austerlitz.

Already had his political combinations begun to yield fruit. Bavaria had refused to join with Austria and Russia in this new attack on France. She was invaded, to be sure, but her territory was soon freed from the enemy. Würtemberg was passive at first, but in the first days of the campaign joined the French. Baden and Hesse Darmstadt had already taken sides with France. Hanover, which at that time belonged to England, had since the rupture of the peace of Amiens been occupied by a French army. Possessed of these advantages, it was possible for Napoleon to pour his columns through Hanover, Hesse Darmstadt, Bavaria, and Würtemberg upon the communications of the Austrian general Mack, who had advanced to Ulm, on the western frontier of Bavaria, without his suspecting any movement of the sort. Mack had expected that Napoleon would operate from Strasburg as his base, and he was quietly waiting till he

should hear that his adversary had got through
or got round the Black Forest, when he found
to his amazement that the French, in overwhelming numbers, were in his rear, and in fact all
round him. Only a resolute dash could possibly
have saved him; even that might have failed;
there was, however, still a chance. But Mack
was not the man to take the risk, and after a few
days of vacillation he surrendered, on the 19th
of October, with 30,000 men.

Following up this striking success without an
instant's hesitation, and driving before him the
fragments of the Austrian army and the van of
the Russian contingent, which had just begun to
enter Bavaria, Napoleon entered Vienna without serious opposition on the 13th of November.
Here he offered peace, stipulating only for the
cession of the Tyrol to his ally Bavaria and of
Venice to his new Kingdom of Italy; but the
Emperor Francis refused. Large reinforcements
of Russian troops had arrived. The allied armies retired into Moravia, in the neighborhood
of Brunn, some seventy or eighty miles north of
Vienna. Thither Napoleon followed them. He
was in a situation of considerable peril. The
detachments which must always be made in an
invasion to cover and protect the communications are necessarily very large. He had opened
the campaign with six corps and the Guard; he
had with him here but four corps and the Guard.
The army had been marched without mercy;

the ranks were much thinned; the French were doubtless outnumbered. Defeat would have been most disastrous, for Napoleon was in the heart of a hostile country. Moreover, Prussia, alarmed at the success of his invasion of Germany, was preparing to take up arms; her ambassador had arrived in the French camp bearing the *ultimatum* of his government; the cabinet of Berlin fully expected war. They were counting confidently upon sending a strong Prussian army upon the exposed communications of the French, and compelling an instant and disastrous retreat. But Napoleon was not a man easily frightened. He had no notion of leaving his prey, now that it was practically within his grasp. He preserved perfect presence of mind. He refused even to talk with the Prussian envoy, and packed him off summarily to Vienna. He then coolly waited to see what the military genius of the two Emperors in front of him would devise in the way of an offensive movement against him, for at that comparatively early period in the wars of the Empire it was generally possible for Napoleon to calculate upon some stupendous blunder in the conduct of his adversaries. The allied armies were occupying loosely a long line of heights lying to the west of the village of Austerlitz. Their line faced the west. Napoleon confronted them. His base of operations in his movement into Moravia had necessarily been Vienna, but he had now with great judgment shifted it to the west, and had made his arrangements, in case of retreat, to fall back into Bohemia. Of this the enemy were ignorant. Their plan was to seize the Vienna road, turning the French right, and thus to force them into a region where they could procure neither supplies nor reinforcements. This scheme Napoleon, who was always indefatigable in personally watching the movements of the enemy, and spent the best part of the day of the 1st of December on the picket line, to see for himself what was going on, penetrated without difficulty. It was precisely what he would have had them do. In his exposed situation he was naturally desirous to avoid such a perilous and doubtful enterprise as that of attempting to drive his antagonists by main force from the strong positions they held on the heights of Pratzen. But it was quite another thing if they should voluntarily abandon the heights. Therefore, when on the morning of the famous 2d of December the sun of Austerlitz arose, Napoleon quietly waited until he saw the strong Russian columns leaving the heights in his immediate front and marching off to turn his right; he prepared his counterstroke by strongly reinforcing his own centre; when he judged that the key-point of the enemy's position, the heights, had been sufficiently denuded of troops, he gave the word to Soult to advance; and in a few hours the Austrian and Russian army was completely broken to pieces. The

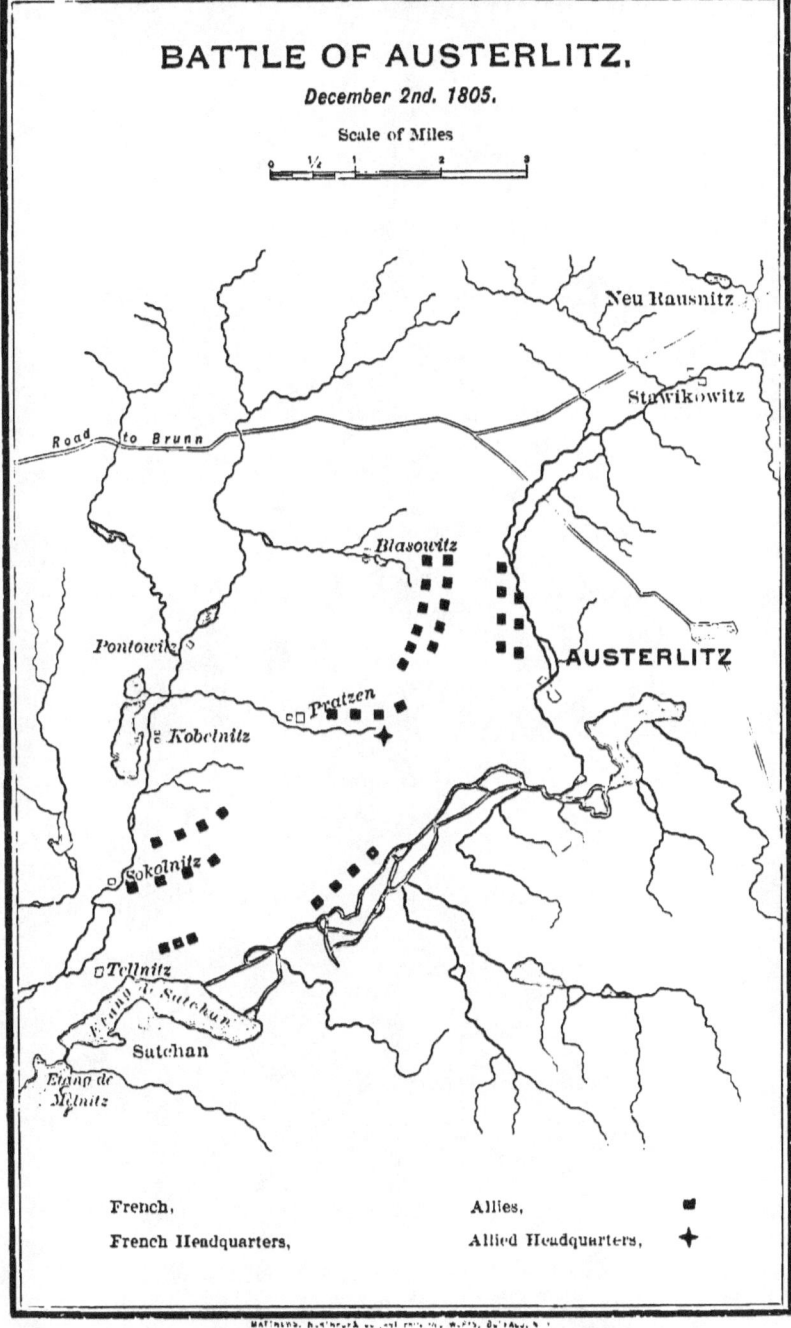

allied right and reserve fought hard, but the French had always a superiority of force at the point of contact. In vain the Russian Guards displayed heroic courage; in vain did the young Czar animate his men by fearlessly exposing himself: the French made good and maintained their advantage; until finally, the allied right and centre being routed, Napoleon was able to surround and almost to destroy their separated left-wing, and complete the success of the day.

Napoleon, it is said, was more proud of this battle than of any he ever fought. It certainly was a most decisive victory. Never was an army better handled than was the French army on this memorable field. Not only was Napoleon then in the zenith of his physical and mental strength, but his lieutenants were men of first-rate capacity. Soult, Davout, Lannes, Murat, were among his ablest officers. Bernadotte, to be sure, was not their equal, but he was a good soldier. Then the army was probably the best that in all his long career he ever handled. It was an army that had at Boulogne received special instruction, and had imbibed a strong *esprit de corps*. It was nearly all composed of French troops; and there are certainly great advantages in a homogeneous force. The army which he had at Jéna was perhaps as formidable, but that which fought at Wagram was by no means as good an army as that which he had at Auster-litz; it was made up from detachments from other armies, got together in haste to repel the unexpected invasion which Austria undertook in 1809. At Borodino his troops, especially his cavalry, were a good deal worn with long marching. At Waterloo he did not have with him corps commanders of the exceptional capacity of Lannes and Davout. But though at Austerlitz he was fortunate in the ability of his lieutenants and in the discipline and *morale* of his troops, it was the enormous blunder of his antagonists that enabled him to win such a crushing victory over them. Had a cool, sagacious, military head like the Duke of Wellington's directed the Austrian and Russian movements, such a defeat could not have been inflicted upon the allies. Their true policy was to play a waiting game. The necessity which obliged Napoleon to strike a blow quickly, if he would prevent the armed intervention of Prussia, would have forced him probably either to attack his enemy in position, or else to undertake a difficult campaign of manœuvres, having for its object to compel them to attack him. In either case a good general ought to have been able to make a respectable stand, even against Napoleon, hampered as he was by his situation in the midst of a hostile country. And nothing but a decisive victory, it must be recollected, would have answered Napoleon's needs. A drawn battle like Eylau, or a doubtful success like Borodino, accompanied, as such a struggle must always be, with great loss of life and great expenditure of ammunition, would certainly have necessitated his retreat. In such an event Prussia, who was waiting her opportunity, would without doubt have declared war on the instant; and to say the least of it, it would have required all the unrivalled genius of the French Emperor to withdraw his army and garrisons from the Austrian dominions without suffering very serious loss. Of all this Napoleon was perfectly cognizant; but, in pursuance of his usual hazardous policy, he chose to take these risks in the hope of winning a decisive success by the mistakes of his foes. And he certainly succeeded this time. But, as we shall see before finishing our study, he was not always so fortunate.

Austria was now obliged to accept the terms which a few weeks before she had rejected. The Tyrol was ceded to Bavaria, and Venice to the Kingdom of Italy. No serious complaint can be made of these conditions. Venice had been in Austrian hands for only eight years, and all the interests and political fortunes of its population attracted it to the new Kingdom of Italy. Here, then, was, as every one will admit, an unquestionable benefit conferred on the Italians. As for the Tyrol, it was annexed to Bavaria mainly on account of its strategical importance in the event of another war. It is true that the population were attached to the House of Hapsburg, and that the annexation to Bavaria was unpopular with them. Still, such cessions of territory as the result of an unsuccessful war were common enough then, and have been tolerably common since. There seems to have been nothing specially remarkable about this one. Austria had begun the war by the unprovoked invasion of Bavaria; it was not on the whole very harsh that she should be compelled to end the war by ceding her frontier province to her injured neighbor. The principal question for us in considering these changes and annexations is not whether they are in our eyes justifiable or not: to arrive at any decision on that question, we shall have first to determine from what standpoint we ought to view them, whether from the standpoint of the Austrian and Russian and Prussian and French statesmen of that day, — for they all viewed such matters pretty much in the same way; they all of them, Alexander, Napoleon, Thugut, Haugwitz, held stoutly to the old course of adding whatever, according to the customs of civilized warfare, they could add to their respective countries, — or from the standpoint of abstract political morality; we shall never make much headway in determining that question, and shall, if we undertake the task, very likely end in condemning all the continental politicians of the period and their doings. The only question that it is worth while for us to consider is this: What was the result, in each particular case, of the annexation? Was it a change in the direction of progress and good government, or in the direction of the preservation of ancient systems of oppression, inequality, and intolerance? In determining this question, we can have facts to aid us in almost every case. If, on the contrary, we take up the other, we become mere casuists, undertaking to decide questions of conscience for other people, long since dead and buried, and who had different standards of right and wrong on such matters from any that commend themselves to our minds to-day. This is an unprofitable and a hopeless task. What we want to do is to understand, if we can, the real nature of the great political changes which took place in the Napoleonic period.

Looking now from this point of view at the result of the war, the events of which I have just sketched, we can all, I think, agree that it was a gain for European progress that it ended in the triumph of Napoleon and not in the triumph of the allies; that it added the Italian territory of Venice to the new Kingdom of Italy; that by increasing the strength of the western states of Germany, it added to the stability of the liberal institutions they had, under the lead of France, recently adopted; that it did not end in subjecting Italy and western Germany to the domination of Austria and Russia, and in the reintroduction of the abuses which Napoleon had swept away. For, let me add (and I assure you it is not an unnecessary reminder), as nearly all wars end in the triumph of one party or the other, we must.

in considering these continual conflicts of the Napoleonic era, always keep in mind what would have been the consequences if his antagonists had beaten him. On which side in these wars, on the whole, do we find the interests of human progress, of liberal, modern, equal, and just government? That is the question throughout our whole examination of the history of these times.

On his return from Austria, Napoleon, in the spring and summer of 1806, carried out his favorite project for the consolidation of the French predominance, as opposed to the Austrian predominance, in southwestern Germany. He established the Confederation of the Rhine, of which Bavaria, Würtemberg, and Baden were the principal members, and to which nearly all the lesser states of southern Germany gave in their adhesion. In all these communities the new system of things was introduced to a greater or less extent; the general principles of the Code, if not the Code itself, became the fundamental law; equal rights, universal toleration, no exemptions or privileges, a free career for every man, took the place of oppressive restrictions, of antiquated institutions, of unjust and unequal privileges. Napoleon was styled the Protector of the Confederation; and it was definitely agreed what should be the contingent furnished by each state in time of war. By this masterly scheme the new order of things in western Germany received a definite political constitution.

The Peace of Presburg had not included Russia, between which power and France war still existed. England, also, secure in her insular position, jealous, with her old national jealousy, of the aggrandizement of her ancient rival, wholly out of sympathy with the new liberal movement on the continent, equally ignorant and careless of the real needs of the masses of the people in France, Italy, and Germany, viewing the whole conflict as the work of an aggressive democracy led by a successful military usurper,[1] clinging with aristocratic and invincible prejudice to her determination to restore the old social order of things, and reëstablish at any cost the former balance of power, continued the war. If we would understand the course taken by England during these wars of the French Revolution and the Empire, we have only to recall her attitude during the late civil war in this country. Notwithstanding her professed abhorrence of slavery, her sympathies were plainly with the States that were fighting for slavery. Why was this? Because by its characteristic features Southern society was allied to the aristocratic element in English society. Because the South was fighting a pure democracy, and the victory of that democracy in America would give a great impulse to the democratic cause everywhere. Lastly, England preferred that there should be two nations in North America in place of one.

[1] See Appendix III.

Hence she assumed the rightfulness of secession; she pretended to believe that the North was fighting for mere lust of dominion; she chose to ignore the question of slavery, and prated about the tariff; and her philanthropic lamentations about the devastations and bloodshed of a war that she wanted to see terminated by the recognition of the Southern Confederacy could be heard across the Atlantic. Sixty years before, had such a struggle broken out in the United States, no one can doubt that she would have openly taken part against the great Northern democracy. It is, therefore, I submit, not so very difficult for us Americans to discern the real causes which actuated England in her fierce and persistent struggle against the French Republic and the Empire. We can tell how likely it is that she should have taken any sympathetic and intelligent interest in the welfare and fortunes of the populations of the continent, since we know how incapable she was of comprehending the great political crisis in the history of her own child. We can put the proper value on English denunciations of the ambition of Napoleon, and on English diatribes on the miseries caused by his wars, because we know how in recent times England has chosen to mistake the real nature of our great conflict, and to ignore the necessity which we were under of carrying it through at any cost, however tremendous.

Returning now to our narrative. Mr. Pitt,

then Prime Minister, had got up the coalition of
1805. England had furnished Russia and Austria with a great part of the money which had been so uselessly expended in the recent disastrous campaign. She had also tried her best to induce Prussia to join the allies, and throw her sword into the scale against Napoleon.

But in this she had not succeeded. It was not that Prussia was not at bottom as hostile to Napoleon and his doings as were Russia and Austria. Her sympathies could not but be with the conservative side, so far as the lines of the European conflict were drawn on general principles of social and political policy. The intensely aristocratic constitution of her army was sufficient of itself to determine her preferences. Still, she was probably not displeased at witnessing the repeated humiliations of her ancient rival, Austria. And she was not without hopes that her abstention from the coalition might be rewarded with a considerable accession of territory.

The net result of these opposing forces was a timid, unstatesmanlike, and dishonorable course of action. While the king and some of his advisers were favorable to the maintenance of friendship with France, the military and aristocratic party were bitterly hostile to it. The crossing by some of Bernadotte's troops of two of the outlying territories of Prussia, in the movement upon Ulm, though a mere temporary matter, gave, as indeed it well might, serious cause of offence at Berlin. It was, of course, promptly apologized for, but it nevertheless gave a great impulse to the war party. The Czar Alexander besought the king to join the coalition, and finally a treaty of alliance, offensive and defensive, was signed between the two powers. Hence the despatch to the French camp before Austerlitz of the Prussian envoy, Haugwitz, with an *ultimatum* which it was supposed Napoleon would at once reject. But if Napoleon ever saw it, it was not until after the battle of Austerlitz. In fact, it is questionable whether it ever was presented in due form; certainly it never was insisted on, Haugwitz, doubtless, feeling very clear in his mind that it was no time now for *ultimatums* of any sort. The two powers patched up a new arrangement, and seemed to be better friends than ever. Hanover was to go to Prussia; the territories which Bernadotte had crossed were to go to Bavaria.

But the breach had gone too far to be healed; or, to speak more definitely, the continued inaction of Prussia greatly irritated the war party, which was equally opposed to Napoleon's system and to his growing predominance in Germany, and which was also eager to try the result of an encounter between the army of the Great Frederic and the veterans of Austerlitz and Marengo. There was no real *casus belli;* but there was an irrepressible feeling of irritation and alarm felt at the growth of French influence in Germany. The formation of the Confederation of the Rhine, the introduction into these German states of the democratic ideas of the French Revolution, the abolition of the powers and privileges and exemptions of the nobility, awakened in the minds of the military aristocracy of Prussia and her immediate neighbors and dependants, Brunswick and Hesse particularly, sentiments of the bitterest hostility. Then, there was no state in Europe more martial than Prussia. She had won her position among the nations by her eminence in war. She had been, as it were, born and bred in camps. She had recently had in the Great Frederic a king who was confessedly the best general of his day. The veteran officers of the Seven Years War still reviewed her battalions. She had counted France as her foe in the time of her direst extremity, but she was able to point to Rossbach as one of her proudest days. Her army had always been sedulously cared for. Its manœuvres were as perfect and its drill as exact as in the days of the exercises at Potsdam before the great king; but they were also the same manœuvres and the same drill. Prussia had forgotten that the world moves; that even in war something is gained by experience under new and enterprising leaders. And she forgot also that it was not a man of the stamp of Marshal Soubise with whom she would now have to deal.

These feelings of jealousy and hostility overcame in the end every prudential consideration. On the 1st of October, 1806, Prussia declared war. The Duke of Brunswick commanded the army. He had been a general of some mark in the Seven Years War, but now he was upwards of seventy years of age. The other leading officers, Prince Hohenlohe and General Mollendorf, were also too old and infirm for the labors and duties of an active campaign. The army was in fact full of superannuated officers, although containing, of course, many of the younger nobility. The troops were of excellent material, but their tactics were antiquated.

The Duke of Brunswick favored taking the offensive. Occupying Saxony, and obtaining a reinforcement of Saxon troops, his plan was to move westwardly through Jéna, Erfurth, and Eisenach until he had passed the westerly extremity of the Thuringian Forest, and then, turning to the south, to strike the communications of the French army, which was massing in the northern part of Bavaria, near Bamberg. Apart from the temerity of adopting such a project when opposed to such an adversary as Napoleon, which should have been a sufficient objection to it, there was no time to carry it into effect. Before they were well on their way, Napoleon was upon them. Pushing his troops over the Saale, he planted himself upon their communications with Saxony. The forward movement of the Prussian army was at once arrested; at first it was resolved to concentrate on Weimar, and fight; finally it was decided to retreat upon Magdeburg. But these hesitations took time, while Napoleon did not lose an hour. Sending Davout and Bernadotte still farther to the north to seize the enemy's dépots of supplies, and block their retreat into Saxony, he, with the main body, consisting of the corps of Ney, Soult, and Lannes, a portion of the cavalry of Murat, and the Imperial Guard, came up with the Prussians in force on the 13th of October. The Emperor supposed that he had before him the whole Prussian army; but in fact it was not more than half of it, under Prince Hohenlohe. This force was acting as a rear guard, the main body having retired some miles to the north. To divide their army when about to fight Napoleon was a blunder indeed, and dearly did they pay for it. In the battle of Jéna, fought on the 14th, the Prussians had no chance whatever. Outnumbered through their own folly, outmanœuvred by the superior skill of their antagonists, opposed to troops inured to war and led by the best generals of the day, there was nothing to do but to stand up and fight like soldiers, and accept their fate. And fight they did, with great resolution and obstinacy, though to no purpose. The same day, a few miles further to the north, at Auerstädt, Davout, who had been sent to threaten the Prussian communications, encountered their main body, led by the Duke of Brunswick, accompanied by the king in person. He was, of course, at once attacked. But Davout was one of the ablest of Napoleon's marshals, and was moreover a man of great firmness. He took up a strong position, and held it with unyielding obstinacy all day long. In vain did the magnificent Prussian cavalry throw themselves upon the French squares; their efforts were as useless as those of the French cavalry against the English squares at Waterloo. The king, sword in hand, again and again led the troops in person; the Duke of Brunswick was mortally wounded; Mollendorf, Schmettau, Wartensleben, and other officers of rank were wounded at the head of their men. But Davout held his own, and finally, at the close of the afternoon, the arrival of his last division enabled him to take the offensive, and put his enemy to rout. For his services on this memorable day, Davout was made Duke of Auerstädt, and to him was accorded the honor of entering Berlin before the Emperor himself.

On this fatal 14th of October, 1806, the military power of Prussia was destroyed. The French went from city to city and from fortress to fortress, only to receive surrenders. On the 25th Davout entered Berlin. In three weeks nearly all the fortresses in Prussia proper had surrendered; and the French had advanced to the Oder. Before winter set in, the King of

Prussia had retired to Königsberg, at the easterly extremity of his kingdom, and Napoleon was at Warsaw, near which city he established his army in winter quarters.

Of the operations in Poland and East Prussia during the winter and early summer, I have no time to speak. In the Russians, Napoleon found an obstinate and enterprising foe. At Eylau on the 7th of February, 1807, he came very near suffering defeat. But his presence of mind, clear head, and unshaken firmness carried him through, and he gained the day. Finally, after several bloody and useless encounters, the Russian general, Benningsen, made one of those egregious tactical blunders, on which, as I have before remarked, Napoleon could generally calculate in the first half of his career, and at Friedland, on the 14th of June, 1807, the Russian army was practically destroyed. Hopeless now of accomplishing anything more for his ally, the King of Prussia, to whom out of all his kingdom a mere remnant now remained, — Königsberg having fallen as the result of the battle of Friedland, — the Czar came to terms. The famous interview on the raft in the Niemen took place at Tilsit on the 25th of June, 1807, between the two Emperors, and a general peace was concluded on the 7th of July.

LECTURE IV.

TILSIT TO MOSCOW.

The Peace of Tilsit restored to Prussia most of her own proper territories. She even retained Silesia, which, sixty years before, the Great Frederic had wrested by main force from the Empress Maria Theresa. But she was compelled to relinquish her last ill-gotten acquisitions. Warsaw, Posen, and the surrounding territories were formed into a new state called the Grand Duchy of Warsaw, of which the King of Saxony was made the head. Into this country, lying between the three great military and reactionary monarchies, the French Emperor introduced his new *régime* of equal laws and equal *status*. The Grand Duchy of Warsaw was thus an outpost of the new system.

The most important result of the war was the creation, out of Brunswick, Hanover, Hesse, and some other of the lesser states of northern Germany, of a new kingdom, to which Napoleon gave the name of Westphalia, and over which he placed his youngest brother, Jerome.

Into these communities, full as they could be

of all the vexatious and oppressive features of feudal right and military officialism, Napoleon introduced the humane, enlightened, just, and equal laws embodied in the Code. Never was there a country more in need of them. They brought comfort and hope to the hovel of the peasant. They enlisted the untitled middle classes in support of the first government they had ever known that had condescended to recognize their existence. True, there was in the constitution of Westphalia but small provision for popular representation. To our eyes, — in fact to any eyes, — the frame of government looks very autocratic. But it was not the monarchical feature that gave this constitution its distinctive character. It was no innovation in that part of the world to concentrate all power in the hands of the head of the state. To this, and to the most arbitrary exercise of that power, the Hessians and the Brunswickers, at least, were well accustomed. It was barely thirty years since the predecessors of some of these very princes whose states were merged in the new kingdom had actually sold the military services of their subjects, and had defrayed the expenses of their petty courts with the money which England gladly paid for the assistance which their soldiers rendered in fighting her battles on the Hudson and in the Carolinas. There was nothing in the monarchical provisions of the new **constitution** calculated to give offence to anybody. But the abolition of all the pecuniary and other exemptions of the privileged classes, the extinction of all their vested rights to labor, service, tolls and charges on land, and the introduction of a system of equal legal rights for all persons, were certain to awaken indignation and opposition. It was to these features in the constitution, therefore, that Napoleon gave the most attention, because they would make the difference between Westphalia and her Prussian and Austrian neighbors, and would, when thoroughly accepted by the people, attach Westphalia to the cause of the new order of things.

Hence we find him writing to his brother to follow the constitution faithfully, and calling his attention to its characteristic provisions. "What the German peoples desire with impatience," says the Emperor, "is that individuals who are not noble and who have talents shall have an equal right to your consideration and to public employment" with those who are of noble birth; "that every sort of servitude and of intermediate obligations between the sovereign and the lowest class in the people should be entirely abolished. The benefits of the Code Napoleon," he goes on to say, "the publicity of legal procedure, the establishment of the jury system, will be the distinctive characteristics of your monarchy. And to tell you my whole mind on this matter, I count more on the effect of these benefits, for the extension and strengthening of your kingdom, than upon the result of the greatest victories. Your people ought to enjoy a liberty, an equality, a well-being, unknown to the German peoples. . . . This kind of government will be a barrier separating you from Prussia more powerful than the Elbe, than fortresses, than the protection of France. What people would wish to return to the arbitrary government of Prussia, when it has tasted the benefits of a wise and liberal administration? The peoples of Germany, France, Italy, Spain, desire equality, and demand that liberal ideas should prevail. . . . Be a constitutional king."

In this remarkable letter, Napoleon gives us not only his ideas of the political needs of the continental nations, but also his general view of the state of Europe. He recognizes that what the people of the continent needed at that time was not *self*-government, of which they were then wholly incapable, but *better* government, — equal rights and an enlightened policy on the part of their rulers: and his language leads us to infer that he considered the whole west of Europe as united in a desire to obtain these advantages. It is plain, also, that he anticipates that these newly emancipated nations will have to defend their rights against their reactionary neighbors, and will need all the help that natural barriers, strong fortresses, the protection of France, and, above all, a union of opinion among their own people, can give them. What he evidently was aiming at, was the union of the western states of Europe, so soon as they should all have received the new system, in a common league to defend their liberties against the hostile coalitions which would certainly be formed against them. You observe, that he does not say that the populations of Prussia and Austria demand equality and liberal ideas in government. By Germany he means the German states, which, outside of these two powers, then comprised much the larger part of the German people. Here he had determined to draw the line. Attaching these populations to the new system, welding them together in a confederation under the protection of France, he hoped that in time this part of Europe at any rate would be able to maintain itself, and to retain the great social, legal, and political reforms introduced by the French Revolution.

It has probably not escaped your observation that the Emperor included Italy and Spain in his enumeration of the countries that demanded the new system. Of Italy he had the right to speak thus, although it certainly was more true of the northern than of the southern portion of the peninsula. Still, at this time his brother Joseph was King of Naples, was introducing the Code, and was governing in a wise, humane, and liberal spirit, to the great satisfaction of the better classes of the population. But Spain was still under the rule of the Bourbons, and a most corrupt, inefficient, bigoted rule it was. How came he, then, to include Spain?

There is no need that I should take up your time with any account of the highhanded and entirely indefensible course pursued by Napoleon towards the king and royal family of Spain. No justification for his acts in seizing from their weak grasp the country which they governed, or rather misgoverned, can be made. Let us frankly admit this. There was an excuse, and a good one, for his banishment of the Neapolitan Bourbons. Ferdinand of Naples had deliberately made a treaty by which he had agreed to preserve neutrality in the war which England, Russia, and Austria had in 1805 undertaken against Napoleon. Yet when the French cause seemed to be compromised by the perilous advance of the Emperor beyond Vienna, the court of Naples put its army on a war footing, and received with open arms an English and Russian force. There was not a shadow of cause for this hostile course; it was wholly unprovoked. It was taken six months after a solemn promise to keep the peace. The breach of faith was the more heinous in that the time selected was when Napoleon was supposed to be in great straits. Lastly, there was the additional aggravation, that it was not an ordinary war between the two countries that Naples undertook to wage, but it was a combination, a coalition, against France, into which she so eagerly and so dishonorably entered. Naturally,

Napoleon felt that this was practically joining a conspiracy, and that with a monarch capable of this no terms could be made. Hence he determined once for all to bring Naples permanently into the French alliance. He made his brother Joseph king; liberal institutions were introduced; the new *régime* met with the countenance and support of the middle classes and of many of the educated and influential nobility.

No excuses of this kind can be made for Napoleon's course towards Spain. True, the Spanish ministry had taken a hasty step which looked like a rupture with France, at a moment when Napoleon was fighting in the marshes of East Prussia and Poland in 1807. This step was, however, soon retracted, and the two countries were apparently on terms of amity again. There was, I repeat, no justification for Napoleon's dethronement of the Spanish Bourbons.

Yet it will hardly be pretended that Napoleon had any hostile intentions towards the Spanish people. He undoubtedly supposed that, like the populations of Italy and of most parts of western Germany, the population of the Spanish peninsula were ready for the great reforms in government in which France had led the way, and in which Holland, western Germany, and Italy were then cheerfully and hopefully marching, and that the better and more enlightened part of the Spanish people would be thankful to see a liberal, intelligent, and conscientious man like Joseph take the place of the bigoted and profligate Charles IV. In Napoleon's view, all the states of western Europe were ripe for political and legal and social progress; and he thought that what had proved so successful in Italy and Germany would be cordially welcomed by Spain.

In this he was mistaken. There was, it is true, a certain amount of liberal sentiment in Spain; but there was also a deep feeling of patriotism, which the course pursued by the French Emperor towards the Spanish king and his son aroused into fierce action. Not only were the masses of the people averse to any changes, not only were the clergy zealous beyond measure in inciting the population against France and her revolutionary policy, but even the liberal party in Spain, though some men of influence in it declared for King Joseph, as a rule preferred the continuance of the existing wretched and despotic form of government to any improvements which could be introduced under the rule of a foreigner. On this Napoleon had not calculated. His arrangements had been made on the supposition that the experiences of Lombardy and Naples would be repeated in Spain. Accordingly, the new king made a royal progress in great state to Madrid, but he soon had to abandon it; and although he afterwards returned under the escort of his powerful brother, his reign was one of incessant war. There were periods when he ruled, with the aid of French armies, over the greater portion of the country. Had it not been for the assistance of the English there can be no reason to doubt that the resistance to him would have died out in time, and there can be equally little reason to doubt that Joseph would have made the Spaniards a good king. He brought with him the principles of a far better government than any to which they had ever been accustomed. But he found in Spain a national or patriotic feeling, pure and simple, which resisted all his efforts at conciliation. This the previous experience of the French on the Rhine and in Italy had not prepared them for. They had forgotten that while the religious wars and the wars ensuing on the disintegration of the German Empire had rendered a strictly patriotic feeling out of the question in Germany, that while Italy had been from time immemorial parcelled out between the kings of France and Spain and the Emperor of Germany, Spain had maintained her integrity, and that she had a great and glorious history.

Napoleon, in fact, made a capital error in attempting to force a liberal government upon Spain. But there can be no sort of question that it would have been a great benefit to Spain had Joseph been able to establish himself. As between him and the principles of government which he represented, and Ferdinand and the principles to which he was committed, we cannot for a moment hesitate in expressing our preference for the former. Under Joseph, in 1808, the Inquisition was abolished; under Ferdinand, in 1814, it was restored. The opposition to Joseph was not an intelligent opposition; it was a movement of an unreasoning, and, so to speak, bigoted patriotism. The Spanish people in fighting the French were not resisting tyranny; nor were they fighting against the imposition of a foreign yoke, for there was no intention of conquering Spain and annexing the country to France. They were opposing the advent of a new *régime* which brought, or would, if they had suffered it to enter, have brought to them in its train incalculable benefits, — would have made them a freer, more intelligent, more liberal people, have placed them in line with the advanced nations of Europe, and would have saved them innumerable revolutions, atrocities, executions. But they shut their eyes to all this, because the way in which their legitimate king had been treated deeply wounded their national pride. With the aid of the English they finally expelled the intruder, and succeeded in restoring Spain to nearly the same condition of degradation, poverty, misrule, and intolerance in which she was before the French invasion. The liberal element, unable to rally around the reactionary government, was soon forced into revolution, and the history of Spain since 1814 has been a bloody story of insurrection and civil war.

Undoubtedly, the true course for Napoleon to

take when he discovered the almost universal opposition in Spain to his projects was to have at once abandoned them. This, however, it needs hardly be said, was a course totally opposed to his disposition. Having undertaken to put his brother on the throne of Spain, he did not propose to desist because of the opposition of the people. He attributed this opposition entirely to the prejudices of the ignorant masses and the bigotry of the clergy. He refused to give sufficient weight to the fact that the French policy had few supporters, even among the liberals. He thought he could crush all resistance by main force.

Accordingly, he invaded Spain at the head of a large army, dispersed the wretched troops which the Spanish junta had set on foot, forced Sir John Moore, who at the head of a small English army had penetrated a long distance into the interior, to beat a precipitate retreat to the coast, and departed for Paris, leaving the conduct of further operations to Joseph and the marshals. His stay was, in truth, too short to do the work thoroughly, and, what is more, he left no one behind him who was competent to finish the task. But the attitude of Austria alarmed him.

The fact was, that Austria believed that Napoleon had got himself so entangled with the affairs of Spain that she might reasonably hope to recover some of her lost possessions, and some part, at any rate, of her former ascendancy in Germany. There was absolutely no pretence of France having given her any new ground of quarrel. To the mind of the Austrian statesman of that day there was a standing cause of war with Napoleon. No matter what had been agreed in treaties, if there was an unexpectedly good chance, it was always the thing to attack him again. You will find this view defended by Scott, Fyffe, and others, on the ground of Napoleon's aim being the conquest of Europe. But the facts at that time certainly warranted no such conclusion. Take Austria, for instance. Of the three wars in which she had been engaged since the outbreak of the French Revolution, she had begun each one of them herself. In not one of the three does any historian, to whatever political belief he may hold, seriously claim that France was the aggressor. To be sure, in every one of these three wars Austria had been badly beaten, and there is no question that Napoleon improved to the full the advantages he gained. But in this there was nothing to complain of. I see no reason whatever to doubt that Austria might have had peace just as long as she was willing to keep the peace.

Nevertheless she determined on war, and, as usual, began it by invading Bavaria. The campaign of 1809 is an interesting one. Every one has heard how for the first time in his experience Napoleon found that the Austrians had effected a concentration of their forces, when his own were as yet separated. The Emperor arrived at the front not a moment too soon. He applied himself with wonderful activity to the problem before him. For six days he did not take off his clothes. Fortunately he had in Masséna, Davout, and Lannes three first-rate lieutenants. With their cordial, intelligent, and vigorous help the army was soon got together, and in the brilliant actions of Abensberg and Eckmühl the troops of the Archduke Charles were beaten and dispersed, and the way again opened to Vienna.

The French entered Vienna without further serious opposition about the middle of May. The Austrian army, now again concentrated, lay on the northern side of the Danube, just below the city. It numbered somewhere about 80,000 men. Napoleon was naturally anxious to lose no time; he desired to preserve the moral effect of his success hitherto. Accordingly, although his army was considerably weakened by the casualties of the campaign as well as by the troops required to guard his communications, he determined to cross the Danube at once and attack the Archduke Charles. At the point selected, the channel of the river is separated by the large island of Lobau into two branches, of which the southern is much the wider. In less than a week from his arrival at Vienna this large arm of the Danube was bridged, and troops were crossing on smaller bridges thrown from the island to the north bank. But these arrangements being hastily made were imperfectly made, and, besides, the river rose, and the increased velocity of its current imperilled the bridges, particularly that crossing the larger or southern branch. Nevertheless, Masséna crossed with his corps, occupied the villages of Aspern and Essling, and was immediately attacked. He however maintained himself during the day (May 21st). The corps of Lannes and some other troops crossed during the night, raising the total of the French force on the north side of the Danube to about 55,000 men. With these troops Napoleon managed to hold his own during the greater part of the 22d against the repeated and desperate assaults which the Archduke directed against him. Such was the precarious state of the bridges that he was unable to get Davout's corps and the other troops across the river; all he could do was to maintain his position against largely superior numbers, and wait till he could be reinforced. But in the afternoon came the terrible news that the great bridge across the main channel had given way entirely, leaving Davout with his corps and some other troops on the south side of the river. It required all Napoleon's firmness and coolness, and all the splendid fighting capacity of Masséna and Lannes, to bring the force they had in hand in good order back to the island of Lobau. But they did it. The Emperor's nerve never failed him for an instant; nothing could exceed the skill and bravery of his corps commanders. One of them, Lannes, was mortally wounded at the close of the action; the other, Masséna, for his conspicuous services on this terrible day, was created Prince of Essling.

Once on the island of Lobau, the army was for the time being safe. But it was a very serious question whether to remain there or to recross to the south side of the river. Napoleon decided to stay where he was. He ordered new and solid bridges to be built. He surveyed the whole field, and made up his mind that the game was not half played out. He sent for reinforcements from France, Italy, Germany. Fortune favored his plans. The Viceroy Eugene beat the Austrians in the Tyrol, and made his way to the Danube at the head of a powerful corps. Marmont and Bernadotte joined him, each with strong reinforcements. His army numbered on the 1st of July no less than 150,000 men.

On the 4th of July pontoon bridges were laid from the island to the north bank, and on the 5th the whole army was over in excellent condition for an army made up of such heterogeneous elements, the main body fully rested by the enforced stay on the island, encouraged by heavy reinforcements, and expecting a striking and decisive victory.

It is always within the power of a good general who commands an army equal or nearly equal to that of his opponent, to prevent anything like a catastrophe. Rosbach, Leüthen, Austerlitz, Jéna, Friedland, Waterloo, Sedan, are all instances of great mistakes made by the defeated commanders or their subordinates. Even Napoleon himself could not score a decisive victory where no serious errors were made by the opposite side. And it always ought to be possible for a thoroughly trained and educated officer to avoid serious errors. Such an officer may of course lose battles; but he never loses a battle without inflicting heavy loss on his antagonist, and without retiring his own troops in respectable order.

The Archduke Charles at Wagram, while he certainly failed to manœuvre his army as skilfully as did Napoleon, counted, and had apparently a right to count, on the reinforcement of his left wing by a corps commanded by his brother, the Archduke John, which did not come up in time. Doubtless some allowance should be made for this. Still, as it was, the Archduke fought a very good fight, and pushed the French hard. The main battle was on the 6th of July.

The immense plain of the Marchfeld, on which the great battle of Wagram was fought, is as flat a tract of country as can be found anywhere, and is as well suited for the manœuvring of 300,000 men as can be imagined. It is not surprising, therefore, to find that marching and manœuvring are the characteristic features of this battle. Of course, there was a great deal of hard fighting too; the Austrians were animated by the recollection of Aspern, two months before; the French felt that with a fair field and no bridges that could be broken, and with Napoleon commanding, they must win. Still, their army, though large, was not a homogeneous army, and contained troops of various degrees of merit.

Napoleon, as usual with him, took the offensive. He found the Archduke occupying generally a semicircular position, extending from Neusiedel on the east to a point not very far from the Danube on the west. Pushing his corps forward, he attacked their left and centre simultaneously. But neither operation was at first successful. The Austrian left defended Neusiedel against Davout, and their centre held Wagram and Aderklaa against the repeated efforts of Bernadotte and Masséna. Then the Archduke took the offensive himself. Bringing up his right wing, he pushed it straight towards the island of Lobau and the bridges across the Danube. Masséna's efforts against the Austrian centre ceased at once, and he hurried off his corps as fast as it could go towards the threatened point. This attack had apparently not been foreseen by Napoleon. With his customary skill, Masséna disposed his troops, holding the most essential point in the line, stubbornly defending himself, on the whole losing ground, but still preserving the communications of the army.

His departure had left a gap in the French line of battle, which it took time to fill, and time was precious, for it was evident that the French left was outnumbered and that the bridges were in serious danger. But Napoleon had watched the operation with his accustomed clearness of vision. He saw that his best, if not his only chance of a victory lay in piercing the Austrian centre, in which case their right wing, which was fighting Masséna, would be forced to retire at once. He saw the risk he ran of the contest at Essling ending in Masséna's defeat, but he knew Masséna, and he decided to take that risk. He again pushed forward Davout, supported by Oudinot, against the Austrian left at Neusiedel. He himself organized the attack on the centre, between Aderklaa and Süssenbrunn. It was to consist of two divisions of infantry under the command of Macdonald, the cavalry of the Guard and the cuirassiers of Nansouty, and an enormous artillery force of a hundred pieces of cannon, of which sixty belonged to the Guard. It was on the fire of this tremendous battery that Napoleon chiefly counted to do the work. He had himself been an artillery officer, and in all his battles he placed great reliance on that arm of the service. In this case, the guns, supported by the infantry, were advanced to within a short distance of the hostile lines, under a very heavy fire. When they opened, the effect was terrible. The Austrians were evidently much shaken.

But Macdonald's divisions had suffered so much in the advance that it was impossible for them to complete the work of defeat. Seeing this, the Emperor at once orders in the cavalry, together with two fresh divisions of infantry. By this attack the enemy's lines are soon broken. The Archduke Charles has no available reserves at this point. His right wing is engaged a long way off near Essling; he perceives by the receding smoke that his left wing has been compelled to retreat; in fact, part of the troops of Davout and Oudinot are rapidly coming up from Neusiedel to aid in the attack on the Austrian centre; there is nothing left but to retire. This is effected in good order, the French being too much exhausted to pursue their antagonists vigorously.

The Austrians in this battle fought with great courage and obstinacy. And they were well handled by the Archduke Charles, although he probably erred in strengthening his right at the expense of his centre. But if Masséna could be routed, it was certain that the French must retire; and the Archduke thought that his centre could hold its own until the superior force which he had directed against Masséna should have gained the bridges. In this he was mistaken, to be sure; but it was a very close thing. Had the Archduke John come up as it was expected he would, and had the Austrian left wing, thus strengthened, been able not only to repel the

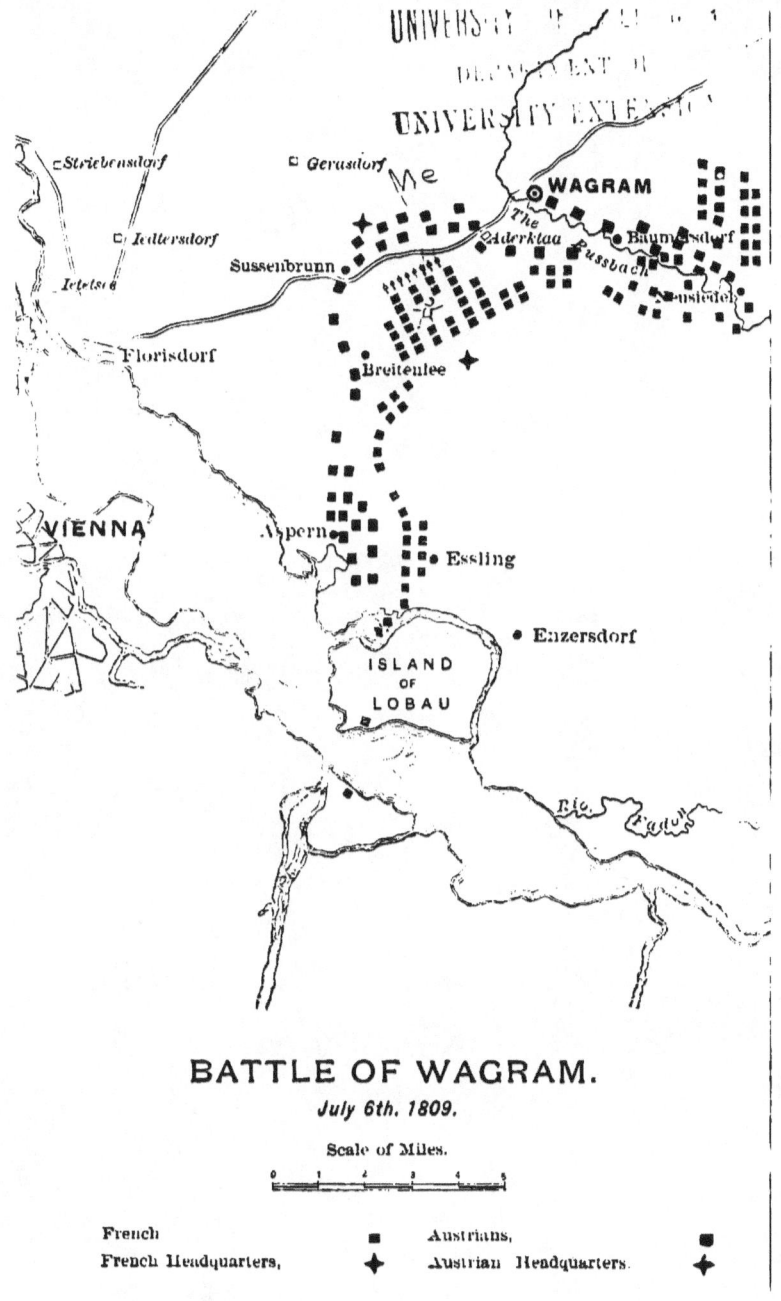

BATTLE OF WAGRAM.
July 6th, 1809.

attacks of Davout and Oudinot against Neusiedel, but to take the offensive, Napoleon's attack on the Austrian centre must have failed utterly. And if, with or without the aid of the Archduke, the left could have maintained itself, Napoleon's attack on the centre would have failed of half its effect. It may be remarked, also, that the Austrian right in its movement against Masséna ran no such risk of being cut off as did the Russian left wing at Austerlitz; its line of retreat was always open. On the other hand, there is no reason to suppose that Napoleon's skill was not what it had been at Friedland or Austerlitz; the whole cause of the difference between the victory of Wagram and those just mentioned lay in the fact that the Austrian commander here made no blunders. Napoleon was here pitted against a master in the art military. He won, it is true, but that was all. He did not destroy or entirely cripple his antagonist.

Nevertheless, the battle of Wagram was a terrible blow to Austria, although she still had powerful armies in the field. It discouraged her. Negotiations began, and peace was at last concluded at Vienna. Its terms were perhaps not unreasonable, taking into account that Austria had begun the war without any provocation. To the Grand Duchy of Warsaw, which in the beginning of the war had been invaded by an Austrian army, was added a large part of Austrian Poland. Bavaria likewise received a large accession of territory. The Illyrian provinces of Austria on the Adriatic were ceded to France, thus shutting out Austria from the sea. The Empire of Napoleon reached at this moment its largest extension of territory.

Let us pause a moment here in our narrative. The continent, with the exception of Spain, was at peace. In that unhappy country, war, and war of the worst kind, was still raging. The Spanish liberals had, as a rule, preferred to stand by their old monarchy, intolerant, oppressive, and inefficient as it was, rather than accept the only mode by which Spain could receive the benefits of the new system. But in Italy, Holland, western Germany, and Poland a great improvement in the condition of the middle and lower classes, and also a marked change in the notions of government entertained by the ruling classes, had been effected, and was bringing self-respect, happiness, prosperity, and a laudable ambition to those who, under the old order of things, had not only always been oppressed by a sense of legal and political inferiority, but had also grievously suffered in their persons and property from unjust and unequal legislation. This change had certainly not been effected without war; it had not been effected without a radical alteration in the European "balance of power;" it had come about chiefly, as you have seen, as the result of wars which were undertaken against France to restore the balance of power, and to bring

back the old order of things in government and
legislation. But it had not come about as the
result of any purpose of Napoleon's to extend
his Empire, or to propagate the new system at
the point of the bayonet. Napoleon's course in
Spain is undoubtedly open to these criticisms;
but I submit that they cannot fairly be made in
respect to his course with regard to Italy, western Germany, or Poland. These countries came
under his disposition as the result of wars in
which he was, though the party ultimately victorious, the party originally attacked.

England still continued the war. To force
her to make peace Napoleon established what
was known as the Continental System, which was
simply the exclusion of English trade from the
continent, a measure which, while it undoubtedly brought the English merchants and manufacturers to the brink of ruin, caused among the
peoples of the continent also great and widespread distress. This was not so manifest in
France, where the various industries of the people enabled them to dispense to a great extent
with English products; it was most severely felt
in Russia, which depended largely on English
commerce for the sale of her staples.

So long as England kept up the war, standing ready, as she always did, to assist with her
subsidies any continental nation that might desire to join her in a new attempt to break down
Napoleon, — so long as Russia, her military re-

sources undiminished, was chafing and suffering under the system which destroyed her commerce, — no one could feel that the international conflict which had begun in 1792 was over. Still, for the present, at any rate, the continental horizon was clear; the Empire of Napoleon seemed to be firmly established and to be working well. The Emperor himself was untiring in his labors for the improvement of the condition of the people and the development of the resources of the country. Every year added to the hold which the new system was acquiring over the modes of thought of the peoples of Italy, Germany, France. Let but this state of things continue twenty years longer, and the west of Europe at any rate would safely pass through its epoch of transition, and might defy the worst efforts of the oligarchical and legitimist nations to bring back the old *régime*.

But how much this possibility of continuing the present state of things depended on the life of one man! That was the thought which was continually arising to interfere with the prospect of stability. Nobody could succeed Napoleon. Whether one turned towards France, or looked across the border, it was plain that on his death, unless that event was to be deferred to the dim future, there was certain to be trouble. Nor was this forecast of danger much mended by the establishment of the Empire. True, the succession to the throne was defined strictly in the constitution. The Emperor had, to be sure, no children, but for this contingency the constitution had made provision. His brothers and their issue would in this event become in turn entitled. There was no difficulty about the law, and the law, if not satisfactory, could have been easily changed. The trouble lay in this, that neither the Emperor's brothers, nor his stepson Eugene, nor any of his marshals, nor any one else whom he might make the heir to his crown, could hope to command the obedience of France, still less to maintain the Empire. Jealousy, insubordination, open hostility were certain to arise, should either one who was merely the brother or stepson of the great Emperor assume to wield his sceptre, or should any one of those generals who had simultaneously received the marshal's baton undertake to command his peers. The difficulty lay in the very nature of man. It seemed as if there was no way out of it.

Yet some of those about Napoleon thought they could see a chance of escape. If, said they, Napoleon could leave his heritage to a son of his own, he might die without anxiety. Hundreds of thousands of bayonets would protect that boy's claim to his father's throne. His advent to power would clash with no one's pretensions, would awaken no jealousies, arouse no animosities. Child though he might be when some chance bullet found its way to his father's heart, he would possess power, to him would be transferred the allegiance of the soldiers, the ready obedience of the people, for he would be Napoleon's son.

There was, to my thinking, a good deal in this reasoning. It was sound enough as far as it went. It would have been an exceedingly desirable thing for France if Napoleon could have had a son. It would have been far preferable to devolving the crown upon the brothers or the marshals. No doubt whatever about that. But Napoleon had no son by the Empress Josephine, and was not likely to have one. Then, it was argued, let him divorce the Empress Josephine and marry another wife. The good of the country demands this sacrifice. Done as an act of public duty, the divorce would be justifiable.

It is hardly necessary to point out the fallacy of this reasoning. To those who have any regard for the sacredness of the marriage tie, the suggestion that it may be justifiably broken, provided the motive be to benefit the public, is as inadmissible as would be the suggestion that an innocent man may be justifiably killed, provided only the motive be to benefit the public. Among those, however, who surrounded Napoleon were many who took a very low view of the obligation of the marriage relation, and a very practical view of the political desirability of Napoleon's having a son and heir. For years they had been urging the divorce of Josephine upon him, and for years he had resisted. In an evil hour he yielded to the arguments which were so constantly thrust upon his notice. Josephine, at his desire, reluctantly gave her consent. The whole affair was managed without any attempt at concealment; the Emperor and Empress carried themselves throughout with great dignity and propriety of demeanor; and, to the honor of the French people be it said, no voice was raised in slanderous accusation or insinuation. All this is, I think, true, and it ought to be remembered. Still, to divorce man and wife on grounds of state policy is at complete variance with our ethical notions respecting marriage. We ought, however, to remember that this divorce proceeded from no unworthy or scandalous grounds. Both Napoleon and Josephine are entitled to be treated with respect in this matter. But it is impossible to approve his course.

By his marriage to the Austrian Archduchess Maria Louisa and the subsequent birth of a son, Napoleon seemed to have indeed consolidated his power, and to have assured for France and for the continent a long period of peace and prosperity. It was taken for granted that by this union the alliance of Austria was rendered certain, and that the two powers together could settle the policy of Europe.

These happy prognostications were, however, to be disappointed. The principal cause of the wars between France and Austria was not a dynastic rivalry between the Hapsburgs and the Bonapartes, capable of being terminated by a marriage between representatives of the two families. Nothing of the sort. There were in reality two causes for the wars which had been devastating the continent for the last eighteen years. The first in order of time was the great social and political Revolution begun by France in 1789, and carried by her into the territories of her neighbors. At the epoch of which we are now speaking, however, 1810, this cause had apparently lost much of its force, or, perhaps, it would be more correct to say that the second of the two causes, alarm at the extension and growing power of the Empire of Napoleon, had to a great extent supplanted the first in men's minds; yet the fundamental differences in legal and political *status* which existed between the French Empire and the other states of Europe continued to the end of the Napoleonic conflict to be a most efficient barrier in the way of a permanent peace, and a constant incitement to war. In the French Empire there were equal rights, no exemptions, no privileges, no monopoly by the nobility of the honors and employments of the public service. Between such a country and such nations as Russia, Austria, and Prussia, where the general system of things was the entire opposite of this, both in theory and practice, it was not possible for any cordial understanding to exist so soon after the French Revolution. Such essential differences in the ideas of nations in regard to the fundamentals of civilization and government have again and again in the world's history been the cause of war. Witness, in ancient history, the Peloponnesian war, — a contest, by the way, very like in some respects to this of the Napoleonic era, where Athens stands for France and Sparta for England, and where, underlying all the particular causes of quarrel, is the great difference between Athens and Sparta in their views of government. In modern times, there is our own civil war, in which culminated "the irrepressible conflict" between the civilizations of the slave-holding and the free States.

At the time of which we are now speaking, however, the second of the two causes, alarm at the enormous aggrandizement of the Empire of Napoleon, was certainly more prominent in men's minds. So far, every coalition against him had not only been defeated, but the result of each defeat had been to strengthen and increase his power. Austria and Prussia had been crippled. They had lost terribly in men and money, and they had been obliged to cede a large part of their territories. Nor was this all. These conquered districts, which were incorporated into the French Empire, by the very act of adopting the new system of equal rights, could not but array themselves in opposition to their former political affiliations; could not but adopt views of government diametrically opposed to those held at St. Petersburg, Vienna, Berlin; could not but maintain a close alliance with France. The French Empire, in fact, seemed capable of overpowering all its neighbors. It was no longer a question of driving French influence out of Germany, or of restoring Lombardy and Venice to the House of Austria. The question was larger than this: it was whether or not France and French ideas should dominate the continent from the Vistula to the Tagus.

Here, then, were the two causes of war, each of them adequate of itself: first, the underlying hostility with which the states which adhered to the old order of things regarded the French Empire, with its radically opposite constitution, so destructive of those institutions which to the privileged classes in Russia, Austria, Prussia, and England seemed to be essential to the welfare of civilized society; and, secondly, the natural alarm at the enormous preponderance which France had so recently acquired. It is plain to every student of history that here was an "irrepressible conflict" in regard to the fundamental notions of civilized government, which, having originally been the cause of the coalitions against France, had since occasioned such sudden, great, and violent disturbances in the balance of power in Europe that further shocks were sure to come.

Accordingly, you will find, I think, nowhere a clear statement of the causes of the great war between Russia and the rest of the continent in

1812. There was no doubt a mistrust on the part of the Czar of the Emperor's intentions in regard to Poland, dating from the augmentation of the Grand Duchy of Warsaw by a part of Austrian Galicia, which was provided for in the Treaty of Vienna. There was a grievance of Russia regarding the continental system. There was a grievance of France regarding a Russian tariff. There was the incorporation of the little Duchy of Oldenburg into the French Empire, for which for a while the Czar refused to accept either apology or equivalent. But these, with perhaps the exception of the Polish question, were probably all pretexts. The fact was, that all the three great monarchies of the continent only waited for a chance to recover their power and prestige, and to roll back the tide of modern ideas in government and legislation. Austria in 1809 had no *casus belli;* she had no grievance, hardly a pretext, but she attacked Napoleon because she thought he was embarrassed and entangled in Spain. In like manner Russia determined on war in 1810. With all convenient speed she completed her conquest of Finland. She sounded public opinion in the Grand Duchy of Warsaw, which she greatly coveted. She endeavored to bring her war with Turkey to a conclusion. She began the preparation of formidable armaments. She communicated her intentions to the courts of Vienna and Berlin. For various reasons, however, she could not get ready as soon as she had at first intended, but she placed a large part of her army on the frontier. Napoleon likewise strengthened his force in the Grand Duchy of Warsaw and increased the garrison of Dantzic. During the next two years negotiations went on constantly between St. Petersburg and Paris. Russia's peculiar complaint was this, that Napoleon refused to pledge himself never under any circumstances to restore Poland. At the same time, he said that to restore Poland was no part of his plans. Whether Russia really feared the reëstablishment of Poland, or merely pretended to do so, it is not easy to say. It was certainly of vital importance to her to retain her Polish provinces. But it was not so much the question of retaining what she had, as of adding to it, that was at the bottom of her military activity. There is conclusive evidence of Alexander's schemes, concocted when a nominal ally and friend of Napoleon, for conquering and incorporating into his empire the Grand Duchy of Warsaw.[1] That Napoleon might have avoided the war is perhaps probable; but it is certain that Alexander might have done so. The latter seems to have been the first to take up the idea of war; he seems to have regarded a contest between himself and Napoleon as inevitable. The truth was, that in the enormous aggrandizement of the French Empire which resulted from the

[1] See Appendix IV.

defeat of the Prussian and Russian coalition in
1807, and of Austria's isolated attack in 1809,
people lost sight of the fact that in neither of
these wars was the French Emperor the aggressor. Up to this time, certainly, with the exception of Spain, Napoleon cannot be charged with
having entered on a career of conquest. His
conquests had been made in wars begun by his
enemies. It may be, as most people believe,
that in 1812 Napoleon wantonly invaded Russia.
The enormous extent of his preparations and
the time occupied in organizing the army of invasion, certainly support this theory. Nevertheless, I think it on the whole far more probable
that the Russian war was in its causes and objects essentially like the Prussian war of 1806 and
the Austrian war of 1809; that is, that it was undertaken by Russia in the hope of changing the
existing state of things in Europe, and breaking
down the increasing influence of France. She
expected to remain on the defensive, and to be
invaded. But she believed that the task of conquering her immense and barren country would
be an impossible one even for the genius of Napoleon; and, if she did not actually entertain the
hope of some such catastrophe happening as
that which subsequently occurred, yet she did
expect that she would be able in the end to
parry the blows and to break the prestige of the
great conqueror, and then to place herself at
the head of a new coalition into which, as she

well knew, Austria and Prussia would eagerly enter.

On the other hand Napoleon, in accepting the challenge, hoped to be able, as the result of the war, to reëstablish Poland. It was only sixteen years since the last partition. The country was ripe for insurrection. Already had the hopes of the patriots been excited by the establishment of the Grand Duchy of Warsaw. For some years Polish regiments had served in the French armies. The invasion of Russia was not like other invasions. In his march to Moscow, Napoleon would not set foot on hostile ground until he should reach the city of Smolensk. Kowno, Wilna, Polotsk, Witepsk, Minsk, the whole population for nearly two thirds of the distance from the Prussian frontier to Moscow, were certain to receive the French with open arms. Napoleon had a right to consider that if the result of the war should be to rescue this unhappy country from the grasp of the Russian Czar, to reorganize it on sound and liberal principles of government, so that it might again resume its place among the nations of the earth, mankind would not be likely to accuse him of having committed a very heinous offence. Such a result of the war would be, in fact, a great benefit conferred upon the world. I do not think he went to war for this purpose. But I have no question that he intended that this should be the outcome of the struggle. And I am free to say that I think it was a great misfortune for Europe and especially for Russia, that Napoleon's enterprise failed, and that the cause of Poland perished in the snows of that terrible winter.

I have not time to give the details of the immense preparations made by Napoleon for this gigantic expedition. He recognized fully the peculiar military difficulties of the task, arising from the nature of the soil and the great extent of country to be traversed. His arrangements for forage and provisions were on an enormous scale. Everything was done that human foresight could suggest to provide for the subsistence of 450,000 men in a country which could not be expected to furnish anything like the entire support needed for the troops and their horses.

All the nations of the continent except Turkey had their contingents in the grand army. That of Prussia was to operate on the extreme left; that of Austria on the extreme right. Between these outlying corps, the Emperor organized three armies. The left or northernmost one, comprising three corps of infantry and the Guard, with three cavalry corps under Murat, numbering in all about 225,000 men, under the Emperor himself, crossed the Niemen at Kowno on the 23d of June, 1812, and marched straight upon Wilna, where it arrived on the 28th. Here the city authorities welcomed Napoleon and presented him the keys of the city in due form.

The Viceroy Eugene, with two corps, comprising about 75,000 men, crossed the river at Pilany, to the south of Kowno, about the first of July, and marched also on Wilna. The Emperor's brother Jerome, with three corps of infantry and one of cavalry, making altogether a force of about 80,000 men, crossed the Niemen on the 30th of June at Grodno, still further to the south.

The Russians had formed two principal armies: the first or main army under Barclay de Tolly, with its headquarters at Wilna; the second under Prince Bagration, with its headquarters at Wolkowysk, a place a considerable distance to the south. The Russian generals made the mistake of underestimating the force which the French Emperor could collect at such an immense distance from his own country; they supposed that he would be able only to form one considerable army. This, they rightly judged, would be directed upon Wilna. Alexander had calculated also on the neutrality of Prussia and Austria. Barclay also expected to have plenty of time to concentrate his main army, and, in falling back to the interior, to be able to obstruct and delay his adversary. The part which Bagration's army was to play was to operate on the flank of Napoleon's army, and harass its operations. But the army under Jerome directed against Bagration's force was something he had not counted upon; and the army under the Viceroy, manœuvring, as it did, between the two Russian armies, not only preserved the flanks of the two main French columns from annoyance, but threatened the movements of both the Russian armies, and specially of the southern one under Bagration. Furthermore, the Emperor marched so quickly upon Wilna that Barclay had all he could possibly do to assemble his own army, and some of its detachments were even cut off and obliged to attach themselves to the second army.

Both Barclay and Bagration, therefore, found themselves obliged to fall back in haste. But in Bagration's rear were the marshes of the Beresina, over which there were but two or three practicable roads. To occupy these and so cut the second Russian army off from all possibility of uniting with the first army under Barclay de Tolly, was now Napoleon's aim. Eugene's force was, as we have seen, unable to cross the Niemen simultaneously with the army commanded by the Emperor. Napoleon therefore detached from his own army Davout, with a large force, who moved in a southeasterly direction endeavoring to reach the important points in this region before Bagration. He was to coöperate with Jerome, but his superiority to the Emperor's brother was so manifest that Napoleon soon gave him the command of Jerome's force in addition to his own. Davout acted with his usual activity and military capacity; but he could not cut off the Russian general, who, moving very rapidly by a large circle to the southward, finally brought up at Smolensk about the 3d of August.

Meantime the first Russian army, under Barclay de Tolly, on evacuating Wilna, gave Napoleon a great opportunity, which he unaccountably failed to improve. Previous to the declaration of war the Russian military authorities had thought it wise to fortify in advance an entrenched camp to which both their armies could retire, where, it was to be hoped, they would be able to hold their own behind regularly constructed works. They had selected for this purpose the position of Drissa, a town lying more than a hundred miles northeast of Wilna. A glance at the map will show the mistake of making such a choice as this. It is to the north of the main road to Smolensk, and its occupation thus not only left that road open to the French, but enabled them completely to interpose between the two Russian armies. Nevertheless there Barclay went. He got there on the 11th of July. But when once there the absurdity of the situation dawned upon the Russians. In three days they left their carefully prepared redoubts and were off on the road to Smolensk. Their movements were quickened by hearing that Napoleon was trying to gain this road so as to be between them and Smolensk. Why he did not succeed in doing this, it is impossible to say. No doubt he was detained at Wilna by the cares of the enormous army under his charge. But it

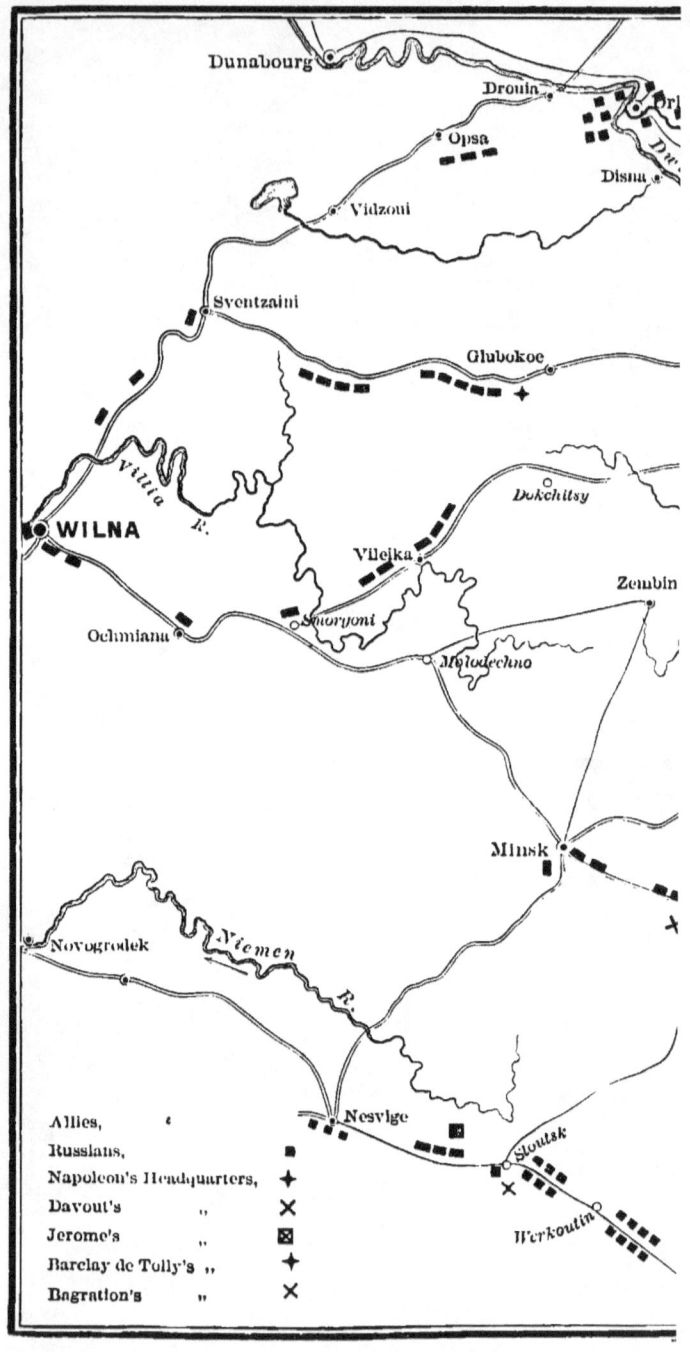

does seem that if Napoleon had manœuvred on his arrival at Wilna with anything like the activity and energy which he displayed three years before in the opening of the last Austrian campaign at Abensberg and Eckmühl, he would have thrown Barclay back upon St. Petersburg, if not upon the Baltic sea.

As it was, however, Barclay gained Smolensk before him, and united his army to that of Prince Bagration. The Russian forces now numbered some 117,000 men. It was the 12th of August. The French columns which composed the main army were much exhausted and in great need of repose. On approaching Smolensk, Napoleon halted on the north side of the Dneiper to give his soldiers needed rest. Of the eight corps which had crossed the Niemen, three were detached and posted on the lines of communication. The remaining five had suffered greatly on the march; the Guard had, however, suffered less than the other troops. The four cavalry corps had lost severely in horses from fatigue. Probably, Napoleon's force at Smolensk, deduction being made for these losses, and for garrisons and detachments at various points on the line of march, did not exceed 150,000 men.

For convenience' sake the French corps were somewhat separated from each other. The Russian generals conceived the idea of attacking them while in this condition. Moving from Smolensk in a northwesterly direction with great circumspection, they simply gave warning of their purpose. In a moment Napoleon united his forces, crossed the Dneiper, which here runs from east to west, a little to the west of Smolensk, and marched upon the city, the principal part of which is situated on the southern bank of the river. But the Russian troops who were encountered defended themselves obstinately and showed an admirable countenance; the alarm was sent to the Russian headquarters; and before the attack could be made Smolensk was held by a force of a hundred thousand men.

Why Napoleon attacked this city it is not perhaps quite easy to see. Superior as the French were in numbers, an occupation in force of the great road between Smolensk and Moscow might certainly have been made, and the Russian army must have evacuated the town. Probably he thought his own army needed the encouragement of a successful battle, and that, if he compelled the retirement of the enemy by manœuvring, his own soldiers would lose courage, and feel that they were being drawn farther and farther into an unknown country without even having a chance to show in a fair fight that they could bring the war to a sudden and glorious termination. If this was his object, he certainly miscalculated, for the action at Smolensk, — it can scarcely be called a battle, — was indecisive, though very bloody.

The night after the battle the Russians evacuated the town. But from some incomprehensible motive, Barclay's army did not retire at once on the Moscow road, but made a détour to the north, leaving the troops of Bagration to take the straight road. Ney at once attacked them, but was severely handled. Napoleon then ordered Junot to move to Ney's assistance, and if he had done so, a decisive advantage must have been gained, as Barclay's army could not possibly have joined the force that was attacked in season to prevent a disaster. But Junot would not stir. The disease which finally incapacitated him for active service, insanity, had begun to show itself. Thus the opportunity offered at Valoutina was also lost, and the united Russian armies stood between Napoleon and Moscow.

I have no doubt that it was no part of the original plan of Napoleon to advance beyond Smolensk. The evidence for this is very strong, and there is every reason to believe it. He probably expected to repeat on a grand scale the experience of 1806 and 1807 in Poland and East Prussia. He had then wintered, and even manœuvred and fought during the winter, in a country situated on nearly the same parallels of latitude as the region in which he was now operating. He saw, therefore, no insurmountable difficulty in passing the winter of 1812 and 1813 in Lithuania, a friendly country, which, during his stay at its capital, Wilna, he had organized as a military department, and where he had every reason to expect that the immense stores which he had accumulated in Germany and which could not be carried in the wake of his rapidly marching armies, had now been safely transported. He also, without doubt, had counted on winning a decisive victory before arriving at Smolensk. This he had not succeeded in doing; and he could not but recognize among the generals and in the army generally a restlessness and an uneasiness hitherto unknown, and also a feeling of profound disappointment, which he himself could not help sharing, that this great expedition had so far accomplished so little. One great victory would change this atmosphere to one of confidence and elation. True, if he went beyond Smolensk it must be to go to Moscow, and Moscow is 280 miles from Smolensk. And if he should go to Moscow, he might have to retreat from Moscow. There was certainly that chance. On the other hand, there was the Russian army between him and the capital, and he was sure that they would never give up the Holy City without a great battle. This battle he felt confident of winning. He would be able to bring to the task a good army, worn and tired, to be sure, but still certain to be alert and vigorous on the day of trial, lieutenants of great ability and experience, and his own unrivalled energy and skill. To oppose this the Russians had simply their obstinate courage to rely upon. He knew they would fight hard, but he saw no reason why he could not be reasonably sure of beating them, and thus winning the prize of Moscow. Once there, he expected that the Czar would treat for peace.

Accordingly he again set his army in motion. The Russians fell back before him. But this continual retreating before the invader had begun to try even Russian patience and obedience. People thought that Barclay de Tolly and Bagration had fallen back far enough. The original intention was that both the Russian armies should unite at the camp at Drissa, and there fight for the defence of the Empire. But Napoleon, as we have seen, had prevented this. Lithuania was now entirely under French control. Still, the separated Russian forces had now at last effected a junction. The army was anxious to measure swords with the foreigner, who was now no longer treading the soil of the recently acquired Polish province of Lithuania, but that of old Russia. A change was called for, and Prince Koutousof, an old and distinguished officer, took command of the forces of Barclay and Bagration. This meant that Moscow should not be given up without a battle.

On the 4th of September the French came up with the Russians in position near the little village of Borodino, on the banks of the Moskwa. The men of both armies prepared for a desperate conflict: the French to fight as men will fight in an unknown and hostile region, thousands of miles from home, where victory is their only salvation; the Russians to fight for their homes and their country.

The whole of the 6th was spent by Napoleon in a personal, close, and careful examination of the enemy's lines. They were strongly entrenched. Several redoubts, besides other works, increased the defensive capacity of a position naturally good, and gave every chance that could be desired to an infantry of well-known steadiness and endurance. It was clear that this was to be no Austerlitz, no Jéna, no Friedland. If the Russians were to be driven from the field here, it must be by main force.[1]

It would be in vain for me to attempt to give you in this lecture the terrible details of the bloody battle of Borodino. The main French movement was directed against the Russian left; but partly from hindrances occasioned by the nature of the country, and partly from the obstinate resistance everywhere encountered, it did not succeed in accomplishing what was expected of it. Ney attacked the Russian centre, and was the hero of the day. The Viceroy commanded on the left. The grand redoubt in the centre of the Russian position was captured and recaptured more than once. The Russians had a strong position and excellent infantry; the French were superior in cavalry and artillery. The battle was fought at close quarters, and the

[1] See Appendix V.

carnage was terrible. The Russians admitted a loss of 50,000 men. Bagration was mortally wounded. The French probably lost at least 30,000. The Russian commander fought a strictly defensive battle, and he fought it skilfully. Whenever the assailants seemed to have gained a point, Koutousof brought up fresh troops from other parts of the field, and for hours he maintained his position substantially intact. At last, however, the superior fighting of the French began to tell. One by one the Russians were forced out of their works. Davout, Ney, and Prince Eugene united their commands, and beat back the Russian left and centre. It was evident to these experienced officers that a severe blow struck now would do the business for the army of Koutousof. They sent to the Emperor, and begged him to put in the Guard. Napoleon hesitated; he had not been able to see for himself what was happening as clearly as he generally could in a battle, owing to the nature of the Russian position, and he was by no means sure that they had not other reserves. Bessières, who commanded the cavalry of the Guard, reminded him that he was more than 1,500 miles from Paris. Napoleon would not give the order. The exhausted troops at the front went on fighting and did their best; but the Russian army, though dreadfully cut up, still maintained its order and discipline, and, falling back a short distance, gave up to the French only the field of battle.

This refusal of Napoleon's to put in the Guard at Borodino has been severely criticised, and I think with reason. He himself defended it on the ground that it was absolutely necessary for him to have a *corps d'élite* to rely upon in case of disaster, such as happened in the retreat from Russia. But such considerations are out of place, in a death struggle like Borodino. In fact, if Napoleon did not mean to fight the Guard, it was a mistake to advance beyond Smolensk; for advancing beyond Smolensk meant a great battle, and it is not common sense to engage in a great battle and not do your uttermost to win it. In other words, if the Guard was to be reserved in the day of battle, the question for the Emperor in advancing beyond Smolensk was whether, with the rest of the army without the Guard, he could reasonably count on a decisive victory; if he could not answer this question in the affirmative, and he certainly could not have done so, it was clearly unwise to advance beyond Smolensk. But, in point of fact, Napoleon did count the Guard in when he made his calculations for the advance to Moscow; he undoubtedly intended to put it in whenever the critical moment should arrive; yet when, from the best information he could get, that moment had arrived, he yielded, in a way very unlike himself, to the suggestions of an unwise caution. It was a terrible mistake: the Russian Colonel Bourtourlin, in his admirable history, states that, had

Napoleon put in the Guard at three in the afternoon, he would have succeeded in overwhelming the Russian army, and that he could have completed its rout during the four hours of daylight yet remaining. Had the Russian army been destroyed as an organization, Alexander would probably have made peace; but as his army fell back in perfect order, it was simply necessary to recruit and reinforce it to make it as formidable as ever. Hence Napoleon gained nothing by the battle except the undisturbed road to Moscow, where he arrived on the 14th of September.

LECTURE V.

MOSCOW TO ELBA.

NAPOLEON had arrived at Moscow. He had with him somewhat over 100,000 men, a good deal tired out, to be sure, and a large park of artillery. His cavalry, though numerous, was not in good condition, having suffered much from lack of forage. But he now expected to be able to repair all these defects. He had, moreover, arranged for reinforcements being sent to him from the various dépots. The army was ably commanded. It is unnecessary to speak of the military capacity of Davout and Ney. The Viceroy Eugene had throughout this campaign showed that he possessed the highest qualities as a corps commander. Murat was unrivalled as a leader of cavalry. Besides these men of the first distinction were many other officers whose capacity and courage had made them men of mark. The weather was excellent. The Russian autumn is a good deal like our own, and no months in the year are finer than September and October. The army had arrived at its objective point, and was looking forward to rest, recruitment, a speedy peace, and a safe return.

You all know how these expectations were disappointed; how Count Rostopchin, the governor of Moscow, after vainly trying to get old Koutousof to fight another battle for the defence of the city, proposed its abandonment as a patriotic duty; how the inhabitants, animated with a desperate hate of the invaders, only to be found among a people imperfectly civilized, fell in with the Count's suggestion, and, before the arrival of the French, left the doomed city; how Rostopchin then set fire to it, and how during the three days of the conflagration nine tenths of the city were laid in ashes.

No more appalling catastrophe ever befell an invading army. It could not but have a profound effect even upon the veteran soldiery of Napoleon, — nay, upon Napoleon himself. It should have convinced him of the implacable hostility of his enemy; that to negotiate for peace was useless, and worse than useless, for it consumed valuable time, and a Russian winter was approaching.

A reasonable time certainly it was worth while to stay in Moscow, sufficient to refresh the troops and rest the worn-out horses. Let it even be granted that it was worth while to send an envoy to St. Petersburg, and to wait until he should have had time enough to deliver his message and to return. But to wait longer than this was simply to tempt fortune. It is true that there was still plenty of accommodation for the troops. There were also provisions enough in Moscow to last the men for many weeks. But after these should be exhausted, there was no means of procuring more. For an army to occupy a large and populous city is one thing; to occupy the houses in which the population formerly lived is a very different thing. In the one case the army merely increases the population of the city; and it avails itself of the usual channels by which the population is supplied with food. In the other case there is no such machinery to be availed of; the army must supply itself.

But, even if with the strictest economy the troops themselves could have been fed during the long Russian winter from the stores found in the cellars and magazines of Moscow, there was no hope of finding anywhere sufficient forage for the horses; and an army without horses is helpless. There was therefore nothing to do, but to prepare to go, and the sooner the preparations could be made, the better on all accounts.

Yet Napoleon lingered. A retreat through a desolate and hostile country was likely to be accompanied with considerable losses of men and material. Moreover to retreat was to confess himself foiled, that the object of the war had not been attained. To avoid this painful necessity it was, he thought, justifiable to risk something. He thought it possible that Alexander might still recede from his high ground, and negotiate for peace. He waited, in the hope that fortune might have some good thing in store for him. But luck never helps a man who relies on it. The only sound and rational course in any emergency is to be governed by the ascertained facts and to act on them, without regard to a possible turn of the tide. If Alexander intended to treat with Napoleon at Moscow, Napoleon would have heard of it in a week or ten days at furthest. When that time had elapsed without any negotiation being begun, the only thing to do was to get the army into safe winter-quarters.

This, though doubtless a difficult task, was by no manner of means an impracticable one, had Napoleon set about it seriously and in good season. There was an abundance of horses, such as they were, and an abundance of wagons of all sorts. There were certainly provisions for two or three weeks, besides plenty of superfluous horses, which would furnish an excellent substitute for beef. There was also no difficulty in supplying the troops with winter clothing. The officers generally did provide themselves with furs. And it would have been easy to obtain sheepskin coats, such as are worn by the Russian peasantry, for every private in the ranks. The army might have left Moscow provided for every emergency so far as the men were concerned, certainly until Smolensk should have been reached. As for the horses, forage could have been found for them by taking roads not hitherto traversed. But in order to carry all this out successfully it was necessary for Napoleon to bend his mind to it; to realize fully the difficulties of his position, and to feel that in the emergency in which he now found himself, it would be a great feat for him, a task, moreover, to which he was called by every consideration of honor and duty, to bring the army back in good order and condition. This, however, seems really not to have seriously entered his mind. He appears to have shut his eyes to the perils which were manifest to every one else, to have culpably delayed his departure, and, when he did undertake to retreat, to have neglected the most ordinary precautions. If he had waited in Moscow a fortnight only, and had left on the 1st of October, Smolensk might have been reached by the 15th or 16th. Here were large supplies. In four or five days more, that is on the 20th or 21st of October, Orcha could have been reached, where was another dépôt of supplies. To reach the Beresina, if he had marched that way, was only a matter of three or four days, and as early as October 24th or 25th no Russian army was anywhere near it. From the Beresina to Wilna is a march of only ten or eleven days; that is, Wilna might have been reached before the 6th of November, which was the first very cold day, and at Smorgoni, on the road to Wilna, there was another dépôt of supplies. Or, if it had been thought best, the army, or a part of it, might have gone to Minsk, where were large stores. In fact, had Napoleon with his army been at Smolensk on the 14th of October instead of on the 14th of November, as was the case, he could have disposed of his army in Lithuania without difficulty and without serious loss, and he would thereby have added greatly to his military reputation.

Napoleon remained in Moscow till the 19th of October. He had been there more than a month. He had utterly failed to engage the Czar in any negotiation. He had undertaken nothing against the Russian army, which had increased in numbers and improved in organization and condition. True, his own army, though somewhat reinforced, was not equal to any very difficult task. But, unless he was determined to destroy Koutousof's army, Napoleon should have commenced his retreat while that army was still suffering from the effects of the battle of Borodino. He had now to encounter all the difficulties of the march and run the gauntlet of the Russian army into the bargain.

Nor was this all. While Napoleon was wasting time at Moscow, the Russian forces which were operating on his long line of communications were strengthened, and were now dangerously near cutting that line in two. Wittgenstein on the north was fighting St. Cyr at Polotsk, and on the very day when Napoleon left Moscow, Polotsk was evacuated. Tchitchagoff on the south was eluding Schwartzenberg, was fighting Dombrowski, and was drawing near to Minsk. Oudinot, with the second corps, and Victor with a fresh corps of 30,000 men, were vainly endeavoring to make head against these powerful Russian armies.

Whichever way one looked, the situation was a gloomy one.

Various causes, moreover, contributed to lower the morale and impair the discipline of the grand army. Among these may be mentioned the fact that it was composed of such mixed materials. The same corps would contain Germans, French, and Italians. Anything that renders the men of the same military unit strangers to one another, impairs their confidence in each other, and weakens the bonds of discipline. Then the difficulty in finding food and forage on the march to Moscow had induced pillaging, than which nothing is more antagonistic to military order. The ransacking of the deserted houses and cellars of Moscow, and the appropriation of the good things found there, of food, drink, and clothing, had only made matters worse. Moreover, when the army did march, it was accompanied by an innumerable crowd of wagons of all sorts, carrying sick and wounded officers and soldiers, French residents of Moscow, women, booty, provisions, encumbering the roads, delaying the march, and distracting the attention of the generals.

To have checked these disorders, to have enforced rigid discipline, to have seen to it that the army was fully equipped for cold weather, and that, while its transportation was sufficient, it should be encumbered with no additional *impedimenta*, would certainly not have been an easy task, yet it was a task imperatively demanded by the exigency in which Napoleon found himself.[1] It is true that the Guard maintained their usual strict discipline and admirable countenance. But the rest of the army was in no condition to resist an unusual strain.

Napoleon's plan was to return by way of Kalouga through the southern provinces of Russia. Koutousof's army, however, barred the way, and after a sanguinary and indecisive action at Malo-Jaroslawetz on October 24th, the Emperor determined to return the way he had come. This affair caused a delay of some days, and even before the army could reach Smolensk, the cold and snow had come. On November 4th and 5th there was snow; on the 6th it was very cold; on the 9th it was only 5° above zero, on the 13th it was 5° below zero. The losses were frightful both in men and horses; and in the bodily suffering caused by the severe cold, discipline became fatally relaxed. Different portions of the army also suffered considerably at Viazma and other points from the attacks of the enemy before reaching Smolensk.

[1] The Emperor, however, did all that man could do to send the sick and wounded to the rear.

Napoleon seems now to have become aroused to a sense of his danger and his responsibilities. He remained at Smolensk five days, attending to the reorganization of the army, to the distribution of provisions to the troops, and sending off the sick and wounded. But things had become very much worse since he had left Moscow. Out of the 115,000 men which marched out of the Russian capital, not 50,000 were with their regiments. Nearly 400 cannon had been abandoned. There were no frost-nails to insert into the horses' shoes, such as the Russians habitually use on slippery roads, and it was sometimes almost impossible for the artillery and wagons to proceed. The sick, wounded, and stragglers accompanying the army numbered some 30,000.

On the 14th, Napoleon with the Guard left Smolensk. The other corps were to follow, first, that of the Viceroy, then that of Davout, finally that of Ney. Why the Emperor chose to march his army in detachments, it is hard to say. No good reason that I know of can be given for it. In the state in which the troops then were, the isolation of a corps was, of itself, a cause of demoralization. Besides, the Russians were pursuing by parallel roads, and were certain to intervene between the columns.

The succeeding fortnight is the critical part of the retreat from Russia. As might have been expected, the detached corps were attacked separately. The Emperor arrived at Krasnoi on the

15th, and found himself confronted by a considerable Russian force. He put a bold face on it, however, and maintained his position. In the night of the 15th and 16th the Viceroy arrived. He had been intercepted, and nothing but perfect presence of mind and great military skill extricated him from his toils. But Eugene brought no word of either Davout or Ney. There was great cause to fear that they with their weak commands were cut off. The Emperor however was determined to wait a while longer, and see. He disposed his troops with excellent judgment, and actually from time to time took the offensive. All day of the 16th Napoleon and his step-son stoutly held their own against a largely superior and steadily increasing force. On the 17th Davout arrived. He had waited for Ney, but having heard of Eugene's misfortunes, judged it more important to go forward and join the Emperor. He brought no word of Ney. It had now become impracticable to wait longer at Krasnoi, as the enemy had begun a movement which would cut the line of retreat, and on the afternoon of the 17th Napoleon with his corps, such they were, united, set off for Orcha, where he arrived the next day.

Napoleon's conduct at Krasnoi deserved and has received the highest eulogiums. Had he selfishly pursued his course, Eugene and Davout could not have escaped being captured. "It was," says Sir Robert Wilson, who was serving at the time at the Russian headquarters, "a day of honor for Napoleon, who had shown "great presence of mind, dauntless intrepidity, and consummate practical skill."

At Orcha Napoleon was rejoined by Ney. That indomitable officer, having found the direct road completely occupied by a large force, which he made a gallant but unsuccessful attempt to dislodge, recrossed on the ice to the north side of the Dneiper, and, keeping in the woods, suffering terrible privations, and losing the greater part of his command, succeeded in bringing the remnant of his corps safely into the lines on the 20th, to the great joy of the Emperor and the army.

It would seem as if the larger part of the losses sustained in these terrible days from the 14th to the 20th was attributable to the separation of the corps in marching. The weather had from the time of leaving Smolensk begun to moderate. On the 19th a thaw had commenced. The march from Smolensk to Orcha could certainly have been made in three or four days; and, supplied as the army had been from the stores at Smolensk, and in weather which ought not to have been insupportable to men well fed and properly clad, it might have reached Orcha in good order and condition, had it only been kept together.

Napoleon remained at Orcha two days, organizing the army and especially the artillery.

There were still twenty-four batteries, of six pieces each, besides those belonging to the Guard. Arms, ammunition, and provisions were served out to the men, and the army prepared for a fresh wrestle with adverse fortune. Some reinforcements also were received. It was expected that at the Beresina, towards which the march was directed, the army would be augmented by the comparatively fresh troops of Victor and Oudinot, and by the division of Dombrowski.

Napoleon wrote to Oudinot to prepare for the crossing, and sent him the able and experienced engineers Eblé and Chasseloup, and also the famous General Jomini. These officers preceded the march of the army.

Fortunately for the French, Koutousof had conceived the idea that Napoleon was intending to cross the Beresina at a point some fifty miles south of that which he had in reality selected, and the march of the French army towards Borisow was therefore uninterrupted. But Admiral Tchitchagoff was holding the right or western bank of the river, and Wittgenstein, who was on the eastern side, had it in his power to impede any attempt at crossing.

On arriving at Borisow the wearied and discouraged troops under Napoleon met the two fine corps of Oudinot and Victor. These troops having been well fed and cared for, and not having been subjected to the unintermitted marching and fighting which, together with the severe weather, had so disorganized and demoralized the principal column, were in good order and condition. Oudinot and Victor were men of well-known energy and courage. There were now about 40,000 fighting men in the army, under the colors. There were actually some 260 guns, "tolerably well horsed," as Sir Robert Wilson tells us. The great difficulty came from the enormous mass of stragglers, and from the wagons and carts containing the sick and wounded. Probably these followers of the army were as numerous as the army itself.

Napoleon on his arrival approved at once of the position at Studianka which Oudinot and the engineer officers had selected for the crossing. Through gross recklessness the pontoon trains had been destroyed at Orcha, and it was necessary to build bridges. Had the pontoons been on hand the army could have crossed in one day without the least trouble. As it was, all day of the 26th was occupied in building the bridges. Napoleon was there on the spot, from which he never moved till the work was done. During this time a feint of crossing was made at Borisow, and the Admiral was deluded into remaining in that neighborhood. The troops of Oudinot crossed in the afternoon over the first bridge. The second bridge, which was built specially for the transit of the artillery and wagons, was finished at dark. The artillery of Oudinot's corps and of the Guard then passed over. In the afternoon of the 27th, Napoleon with the Guard crossed, as did also a multitude of the stragglers. Up to this time there had been no serious fighting. Late the same afternoon, however, one of Victor's divisions, that of Partonneaux, in marching from Borisow to Studianka, was surrounded and obliged to capitulate. During that night all the other troops crossed the river, save Gérard's division of Victor's corps.

From a purely military point of view the operation was now finished. To withdraw the remaining division as speedily as possible was obviously the prudent thing to do. But there yet remained the greater part of the army-followers, a great many carriages, containing sick and wounded, officers' wives and children, disbanded troops, stragglers of all sorts. Most of these had become so torpid from the effect of continued privation and suffering that they made no effort to avail themselves of the facilities which the bridges had hitherto offered them. Napoleon was willing to delay one day more to give them another chance. This decision, unquestionably dictated by motives of humanity, cannot, however, be defended. Napoleon hated the thought of abandoning these poor people; yet the safety of the army imperatively demanded that he should march at once. The care of the army, with whose existence was bound up so much that was of vital importance to the Empire, was the paramount duty.

Nevertheless, as I have said, he gave these poor wretches another day. But to do this, it was necessary for him to fight the Admiral, now awake to the fact that he had been outwitted, on the western bank, and to recross another of Victor's divisions to the eastern bank to assist Gérard in fighting Wittgenstein. On both sides of the Beresina, all through this terrible day of the 28th of November, the French held their own, though with severe loss. It was not until nine in the evening that Victor crossed to the western side with his two divisions. From time to time during the day, the apparently inert mass of humanity concealed in a multitude of wagons, or standing round fires made of *débris* of all sorts, had been fired into by the Russian guns, and then and only then was there a rush for the bridges. Such was the confusion among those that made the attempt, that the bridges were often blocked, and the next morning, the 29th, a vast crowd still remained on the eastern shore.

The Emperor could wait no longer. His losses in the battle of the preceding day had been very severe. Several generals had been wounded, and among them Oudinot; Victor's corps, which had covered itself with glory, had suffered severely. The necessity for continuing the retreat was imperative. Eblé was ordered to burn the bridges at eight o'clock of the 29th. When the smoke began to ascend, the miserable creatures on the eastern side realized that they had lost their last chance. Of course, they all fell into the hands of the enemy.

Such was the terrible passage of the Beresina, in which one cannot fail to mark the great ability and courage displayed throughout the whole affair by Napoleon. His energy, coolness, presence of mind, the skill with which he deceived his foes, ensured for the operation an almost complete success. The distressing circumstances, the sanguinary affairs of the 28th, the sufferings of the multitude who were left, are not to be attributed to any military fault, but to the unwise, almost culpable, compassion which led him to risk the lives of his brave soldiers and to imperil gravely the fortunes of the army, to afford another day of opportunity to the miserable people whom, as he should have known, nothing could rouse from the torpor and apathy produced partly by suffering and partly by having cast off the bonds of discipline. Had the bridges been burnt on the morning of the 28th, many valuable lives would have been saved, and the disorganization always consequent on a battle, and which is especially productive of harm when a bloody battle is followed by a hasty retreat, as in this case, would have been entirely avoided.

From the banks of the Beresina the army made its way as rapidly as possible to Wilna. Even if there had been food enough for the men and forage enough for the horses, it would have been a very severe experience, for the weather now became and continued extremely cold, the thermometer ranging from 29° to 35° below zero. But there was not anything like sufficient forage and food, and the losses were frightful. In addition to other sufferings, the Russians from time to time caught up with the rear guard, and often inflicted severe loss. Still, there was nothing to prevent the *débris* of the army from reaching Wilna, where were abundant stores of all sorts, a friendly population, and a French garrison.

This being so, Napoleon deemed it unnecessary to remain longer with the army. He had made up his mind that unless he appeared on the Vistula the next spring, a new and formidable coalition against him was certain to be formed, and that to maintain the Empire as it was, it would be necessary to take the field in great force. In this belief he was doubtless correct. He saw, too, that there was no time to be lost. The sooner he was in Paris the better.

Accordingly he set out on the 5th of December, accompanied by Caulaincourt, Duroc, and Lobau, and one or two other officers. He ran great risk of being captured by Cossacks, but arrived safely at Wilna, and thence proceeded to Paris. Of this decision, which some writers have harshly criticised, it is sufficient to say, in the words of Sir Robert Wilson, that " the motives " of it " were too apparently reasonable and prospectively beneficial not to satisfy every one, after a short time, that it was not a flight for personal safety, but a measure of paramount necessity for the common welfare."

On the 9th of December, the wreck of the grand army arrived at Wilna. Such, however, was the disorganization that prevailed, that it was deemed best by Murat, to whom Napoleon had confided the command of the army, to evacuate it at once. The weary soldiers were soon on the march again for Kowno, where, less than six months before, hundreds of thousands of brave troops had crossed the Niemen. But even Kowno could not be held, and the few troops that survived retired without delay into Prussia.

Thus ended the Russian campaign, the most terrible of which we have any knowledge. From all the accounts, I gather that somewhere about 530,000 men took part in the campaign under Napoleon.[1] Of these, the Russians estimate that 125,000 were either killed in battle or died of wounds; that 132,000 died of privation and disease; that 193,000 were taken prisoners; that only 80,000 returned.

I think this estimate erroneous in more than one point. The 80,000 who are put down as returned, returned in December. Yet, without question, a great many of the sick and wounded must have been sent back long before that time. These would serve to diminish the number of

---

[1] See Appendix VI.

those who are set down as having perished by privation and disease.

Besides, there were more than 80,000 that returned in December. The greater number of those that returned consisted of the Austrian contingent under Schwartzenberg, the seventh corps under Reynier, which accompanied it, and the Prussian contingent under Macdonald; these troops numbered nearly 70,000 men. And 35,000 to 40,000 men of the main army re-crossed the Niemen. Of these, it is true, a large part had not shared in the campaign; they were portions of the garrisons of towns on the line of march. Many of them in fact had recently entered Russia from Germany. The total of those that returned, however, cannot be far from 110,000 men.

That a very large part of the loss arose from preventable causes is certain. The Duc de Fezensac, who commanded the 4th regiment of the line, tells us in his most interesting narrative what became of the officers and men of his regiment. Of 3,000 enlisted men, only 200 returned with him in December. But of some 96 officers who set out from Moscow, 49 returned in December. This shows a loss which, though certainly severe, is by no means unparalleled in war. Many regiments suffered much more in officers in Grant's campaign from the Rapidan to Petersburg. Had the men been as provident as their officers, they would no doubt have fared as well.

This was one of those cases where superior intelligence goes for something. We may also be certain that had it been possible to preserve strict discipline, the men could not have suffered in the proportion they did. But this seems to have been found impracticable.

Sir Robert Wilson tells us that, after passing the Beresina, the Russians suffered nearly as much as the French from want of food, fuel, and clothing, and of course quite as much from cold, and that the various Russian commands lost about 90,000 men from these causes. Nevertheless the Russian army perfectly preserved its organization and discipline; it only needed reinforcements. Whereas the allied army, with the exception of the Prussian and Austrian contingents, and such French troops as served with them, — which had not really made the campaign, — was practically dissolved.

Murat, ably seconded by Eugène, Ney, Davout and a host of gallant officers, made every effort to collect the men under the colors and to present a bold front to the enemy. And had the Prussian contingent stood by their allies in this emergency, their efforts would have measurably succeeded. But the disasters of the French aroused in the Prussians a fierce hope that they might now shake off the burden alike of French alliance and of French superiority. General Yorck, who commanded a Prussian division in Macdonald's army, arranged with the opposing

Russian commanders to allow them to get upon his line of retreat, so as to give him a technical reason for entering into a capitulation. On the 30th of December, this officer signed a convention, in which he included the other Prussian division, that of Massenbach, which was at the time actually serving with Macdonald's column, by the terms of which the Prussian forces were to remain in a sort of neutral territory. This desertion of his military comrades in a moment of supreme danger, cannot be viewed by honorable men as other than an act of duplicity and perfidy. Many writers have excused it, some have even praised it. To their minds the grievances of Prussia against Napoleon were so intolerable, that any course of conduct, no matter how opposed to the ordinary rules of good faith and honest dealing, is justified on the score of patriotism. I do not so regard the matter. It may sometimes be the duty of a nation, as it certainly is sometimes the duty of an individual, to put up with evils from which there is no honorable and righteous way of escape. It might well have been repugnant to General Yorck's feelings to serve in Marshal Macdonald's army. If so, then he should have resigned. In a certain crisis in this country, many officers of the United States army found themselves unable, on account of their political views, to continue in service, and, as soon as they had an honorable opportunity, they resigned. But with a single exception, that of the infamous General Twiggs, they did not surrender the forts or the troops in their charge, even to their own States. In several cases, notably in the case of an officer who was at Fort Sumter, such officers fought against the cause to which they were personally attached, because they could not honorably desert the flag under which they were serving in presence of the enemy. They in fact subordinated politics to the inflexible requirements of duty. When they had turned over the property in their hands and the troops in their charge to the United States authorities, they resigned, but not until then. With the exception above mentioned, there were no deceptions or disgraceful contrivances of any kind. But Yorck's surrender was a deliberate compact with the enemy. When he wrote to Macdonald that he "had no alternative but either to sacrifice the greater part of his troops or to save the whole by making a convention," he told Macdonald a deliberate falsehood. When he wrote to the King of Prussia that his position was desperate, that he should have sacrificed the whole corps had he tried to escape from the Russians, etc., he was lying to his own sovereign. Had the facts been as he stated them to the king, his defence was an easy one, and one which depended entirely on military reasons. But he discloses the real truth when in the same letter he harps upon his having acted as "a true Prussian," as "a patriot who only sought the welfare of his country." This conclusively shows the falseness of his pretence about his extreme danger being the justification of his conduct. It is well to call a spade, a spade; there can be no question that General Yorck in these letters lied to Marshal Macdonald and to the king. Love of country is doubtless a great virtue, but it cannot excuse such flagrant disregard of military honor and of common veracity as Yorck displayed on this occasion.

The conduct of the Austrian contingent under Prince Schwartzenberg, though not open to the charge of doubledealing, was characterized by an anxiety to avoid above all things an engagement with the advancing Russians. It was perhaps to be expected that the Austrians should be unwilling to see the stress of a doubtful struggle fall upon their own troops, especially when they were simply serving as allies to the French. Schwartzenberg retired into Galicia, leaving Warsaw to its fate.

Thus the wreck of the grand army, abandoned by its allies, was unable to withstand the invaders; Warsaw was evacuated early in February, and the much coveted Grand Duchy was occupied by Russian troops.

But the Czar was not satisfied with this triumphant ending to the invasion of Russia. He aspired to accomplish, as he termed it, "the deliverance of Europe." By his orders Koutousof issued a proclamation promising the aid of Russia to all peoples who desired her help. He counted specially on the patriotic party in Prussia compelling the king, who still faithfully adhered to the French alliance, to shake it off, and to join heart and soul with Russia in an attack on the Empire of Napoleon. The action of Yorck had given a tremendous impulse to this party throughout Prussia, and it was easy to see that that proud-spirited people would ere long embrace the opportunity offered them to avenge Jéna and Auerstädt, and to restore to Berlin its former dominating influence in northern Germany. Prussia had indeed suffered grievously since her overthrow. She had been obliged to maintain an army of occupation. She had paid a heavy war indemnity. Her territory had been from time to time, and especially during the late war with Russia, marched over by the troops of the grand army. Then her army had been restricted to 40,000 men, a restriction especially galling to her martial spirit. She craved revenge.

With Austria the case was different. She had lost territory, to be sure, and some of it was territory she could ill spare, such as her provinces on the Adriatic. But she had never been subjected to that most irritating of all the consequences of an unsuccessful war, the presence of the conquering troops after peace has been declared. Besides, she was now, since the marriage of Maria Louisa, the ally of France. Nevertheless, there was quite reason enough to hope that Austria would make use of this new chance to recover her lost provinces, or some of them, and to resume, if she could, her predominance in the states of southern Germany.

Besides these considerations, which were plainly acting on Prussia and Austria, were others to which I have often alluded before. There was the cause of the dispossessed princes and potentates of western Germany, who hoped to see their vassals restored to them in the destruction of the recent Kingdom of Westphalia and the reduction of Bavaria and Würtemberg to their ancient limits. There were even men who cherished a fanatical belief that they would yet live to see all the work of the French Revolution destroyed, all its sins against legitimacy and political order expiated and avenged; who looked confidently to God to prosper what they fully believed was the cause of religion and order; whose devout aspiration it was that they might live to behold the Bourbons again on the thrones of France, Spain, and Naples, the Austrians again ruling in Italy, while the emigrant nobility of France and western Germany, now returned to their own country, should again be holding their petty courts and living on their ancestral acres on the tolls and taxes which they had an immemorial right to exact of their less privileged neighbors.

To this bundle of aims and hopes and beliefs the ancient courts and aristocracies gave the general name of the cause of the deliverance of Europe from the yoke of Napoleon. Never has there been exhibited to more advantage the power that resides in a name. Let it be granted that it would be in some respects for the advantage of Europe if Prussia and Austria should recover a part, at any rate, of what they had lost by the fortune of war. But that the cause of good government or the welfare of the populations would be advanced by bringing back the old order of things in France, western Germany, or Italy, no intelligent man ought to have believed for a moment.

It is true that the continent was suffering from the evils of war. For the evils of war, however, the remedy is peace; and peace could have been had at any time if only the ancient monarchies and aristocracies of Europe had been willing to accept the reorganization of western Europe under the new system of equal rights and government for the people which had taken place in consequence of the French Revolution. But the change was so sudden and so violent, and involved such a loss to them of power and prestige, that they could not and would not accept it. Perhaps it would be asking too much of poor human nature to expect that they should have resigned themselves both to the predominance of France and to the triumph over so large a part of Europe of the fundamental social and political changes embodied in the Code Napoleon. It could hardly be hoped that they would recognize the real truth which underlay and explained the unwelcome facts which made the Europe of 1813 such a different country from the Europe of 1783, namely, that western Europe, with the exception of the Spanish peninsula, had during these thirty years passed through a great and most wholesome transition as well in the ends and aims of government as in the social and political status of the people. Still less could the reactionary party be expected to recognize the fact that the preponderance of France was by no means a permanent concomitant of the great transformation which western Europe had undergone, although it was during the epoch of transition a necessary element of that transformation. In the minds of the leaders of the allied cause in 1813, the war was a sort of holy crusade for legitimacy and privilege against the all-devouring ambition of an aggressive usurper.

On the other side, Napoleon, undismayed by his reverses in Russia, was raising a new army with which he expected in the spring to overawe Prussia, and to drive the Russians back over the Niemen. He felt, and no doubt rightly, that unless a vigorous stand was taken, the tide of reaction might sweep over the Empire. France, though grievously suffering from the frightful losses of the Russian campaign, came bravely forward to meet the emergency. Hardly less energetic were the efforts put forth by the states of the Confederation of the Rhine, and by Italy. The Emperor himself worked day and night.

Meantime Prussia was putting her army on a war footing, her ministers all the while assuring the French ambassador at Berlin, with a duplicity well nigh unparalleled, that their preparations were made only in order that she might make a suitable appearance in the coming campaign on the side of France. For a month after a treaty of alliance with Russia, offensive and defensive, had been signed, Prussia continued warmly to protest her adhesion to the cause of Napoleon. But her warlike preparations, as well as a thousand other indications of popular feeling, showed clearly enough that she had made up her mind to fight a desperate struggle with France. The army and the nobility hated France and Napoleon with an implacable enmity, born not less of wounded pride than of actual and tangible grievances.

Great efforts were made to give to the reactionary movement a liberal and popular character. Proclamations were issued by Russian and Prussian generals promising liberty and equality to the people, and in the heat and excitement of the war fever, and in the midst of the patriotic fury that prevailed, few people had the sense to see the patent and absurd deception involved in raising and cherishing expectations of this nature from such sources.

Even this was not sufficient. The new crusade in favor of liberty and equality carried on by the autocrat of all the Russias must take on a pan-Germanic coloring also, to make it, if possible, attractive to those German communities which were living under the Code Napoleon, and could not be supposed to be specially anxious for the bestowal of that particular variety of liberty and equality dispensed by the Czar. Accordingly, Koutousof proclaims the dissolution of the Confederation of the Rhine. Wittgenstein refuses to recognize as a German any man who prefers to remain quiet in this emergency. Blücher urges the Saxons to raise the standard of insurrection against foreign usurpation. But appeals of this sort were evidently not much relied on. The generals in the service of Russia had a much shorter mode of convincing their opponents. Wittgenstein says: "You must choose between my fraternal affection and my sword." And Koutousof demands of the princes of the confederation "faithful and entire coöperation," and menaces with destruction those among them who are traitors to the cause of the German fatherland.

I have admitted that Prussia had serious and tangible grievances, which, taken in connection with the hatred and desire for revenge caused by her complete overthrow in 1806, may account for the state of feeling among her people. Still it is clear enough that these motives needed to be supplemented. Else why these wild appeals

to the people, these delusive promises of liberty,
this talk about the German fatherland? All this
sort of thing was done simply for effect, as the
event abundantly proved. None of the promises
were ever kept.

And what shall we say about the threats uttered so freely against the German communities
which adhered to the Empire? What was this
terrible foreign yoke which they were to throw
off, in order to join the Czar and the King in
their crusade for popular liberty? Let me read
a few words from a recent English work written
by a man who is wholly in sympathy with this
crusade, and who cannot therefore be charged
with misrepresenting facts against the cause
which he favors: —

"All Italy, the northern districts of Germany which
were incorporated with the Empire, and a great part
of the Confederate Territory of the Rhine, received in
the Code Napoleon a law which, to an extent hitherto
unknown in Europe, brought social justice into the
daily affairs of life. The privileges of the noble, the
feudal burdens of the peasant, the monopolies of the
guilds, passed away, in most instances forever. The
comfort and improvement of mankind were vindicated
as the true aim of property by the abolition of the devices which convert the soil into an instrument of family pride, and by the enforcement of a fair division
of inheritances among the children of the possessor.
Legal process, both civil and criminal, was brought
within the comprehension of ordinary citizens, and
subjected to the test of publicity." "Even the misused

peasantry of Poland had been freed from their degrading yoke within the borders of the newly founded Grand Duchy of Warsaw."

Still, while all this was true, it was unfortunately no less true that the burden of war pressed heavily upon the shoulders of the people. Napoleon's obstinate persistence in trying to accomplish the subjugation of Spain was costing every year thousands of valuable lives, sacrificed in a contest in which no one had any interest. The course he pursued in regard to Spain was in direct contravention of his true *rôle* in European politics. When the unwillingness of the people to receive Joseph and the liberal institutions which he brought with him was definitely ascertained, there should have been an end of the whole matter. Moreover, if Napoleon was to prosecute the war at all, he certainly should not have delegated such a difficult task to his lieutenants. Had he in 1810 or 1811 gone to Spain himself, he would have probably driven out the English and subdued the country. As it was, the jealousies and limited powers of the king and the marshals gave Wellington opportunities of which he never failed to make good use. He was a better general than any of the marshals sent against him, Masséna possibly excepted, and he played his cards admirably. Talavera, Busaco, Torres Vedras, Salamanca, Vittoria, illustrate his varied military talents.

Besides the annual drain of men necessitated

by the Spanish war, there had now come upon the populations of the Empire the terrible catastrophe of the Russian campaign. Such calamities do a great deal to dispose people to listen to appeals for a change of government.

Then, all the while, was the unintermitted hostility of England, showing its deplorable effects no less in the distress produced by the continental system than by the encouragement and assistance which she afforded to the allied powers of the continent, without which they could not have continued the struggle. The entire cessation of foreign trade for so long a period was getting to be felt as a grievance well-nigh intolerable. Maintaining this policy after experience had abundantly shown that the English aristocracy had the power and the determination to carry on the war, in face of the disastrous effects which the continental system had on the commercial and manufacturing interests of the English people, was another of Napoleon's mistakes. Had Napoleon in 1813 retired from the contest in Spain, he could have availed himself, for the campaign about to open in Germany, of a very large army of veteran troops, and could have spared France and her dependencies the great sacrifices which he demanded and which they so generously made. Had he, before calling upon the Empire to put forth its strength again in another war, repealed the continental blockade, frankly announcing its failure as a war measure, he would have done much to reconcile the people to the really necessary step of a new campaign in Germany. He would thus have shown to France and Holland, Italy and western Germany, with the clearness and point which the crisis demanded, the real nature of the impending contest. Stripped of the two most unfortunate accessories of the Spanish war and the continental system, the question was, whether the old *régime* should be restored throughout western Europe under the lead of the Russian autocrat and the Prussian king. Had this single issue been clearly offered, and had Napoleon, recognizing the gravity of the situation, devoted himself to the task thus presented, and only to that, the Empire would easily have maintained itself against the coalition.

The new grand army, organized to take the place of the one that had perished in Russia, numbered some 270,000 men. It was no doubt organized as well as an army can be organized in three months, but that is not saying much. The skeletons of the regiments were indeed composed of old soldiers. When, as frequently happened, the survivors of the Russian campaign did not number enough for this purpose, veterans from regiments serving in Spain or elsewhere were imported. The list of officers and non-commissioned officers being thus filled, with, in most cases, a certain number of private soldiers drawn from the regimental dépots at home, the conscription furnished the rest of the rank and file. The army was to be ready by the middle of April, and it is easy to see that the mass of the private soldiers must have had very insufficient instruction. Napoleon himself specially prescribed the tactics which were to be taught to the recruits. Besides the manual of arms, a few simple manœuvres, such as forming square to resist cavalry and the like, were to occupy all their attention in the few weeks allotted for drill. The Guard was reconstituted entirely from veteran soldiers, largely taken from regiments which had not served in Russia, but it numbered less than 20,000 men. An extraordinary amount of artillery accompanied the army, Napoleon recognizing the fact that the presence of a battery is a great moral support to raw infantry. Cavalry was lacking; but some good troops were brought from Spain.

During the winter and early spring the French forces under the Viceroy had retired before the enemy from step to step, until in April, 1813, they were on the banks of the Elbe. Saxony had been evacuated, and the allies were endeavoring to secure its adhesion in the crusade against Napoleon. The attitude of Austria was equivocal.

Suddenly, in the last days of April, the Emperor appeared at the head of the new army, and marched at once on Leipsic. With an audacity which disclosed a very different temper from that which prevailed in the Prussian army seven years before, the allies attacked Napoleon on the 2d of May, on the great plain between Lützen and Leipsic. But after a sanguinary contest they were compelled to retire, and Napoleon in a few days entered Dresden. Following up his advantage, the Emperor came up with the allied forces at Bautzen near the Austrian frontier. Here the enemy had taken a strong position. Napoleon now had his troops all in hand. On the 21st of May he attacked the allies in front, and sent Ney with a large corps to turn their right flank. The operation was on the whole successful. Owing, however, to the necessarily isolated character of the movement prescribed to Ney, and probably also to the fact that he felt that he could not count with certainty upon his inexperienced troops, that officer did not dare to avail himself fully of his opportunity, and the results of the battle were by no means what they might have been.

Thus far, however, Napoleon had accomplished quite as much as he could reasonably have expected. The allied invasion of the Empire had been checked; the Russian and Prussian armies had been defeated and driven back. Napoleon had a large superiority of force. It was plain that if Austria remained neutral, the new coalition was doomed.

But Austria recognized to the full the advantage she possessed. Napoleon was at that

time in no condition to fight all the three powers
together. His army was too small and too
poorly disciplined for any such task as that.
Hence the Austrian cabinet felt that they could
exact a price for the neutrality of Austria. It
was not an exorbitant price; it was, substantially, the restoration of what had been taken
from Austria in Poland, Illyria, and Germany as
a consequence of her disastrous campaign of
1809. But to Napoleon these demands seemed
most unwarranted. The treaty of Vienna had
not been broken. France had given Austria no
ground of offence. Metternich did not pretend
there was any *casus belli*. He simply said:
" We are strong, stronger than you suppose; we
want these provinces back; if you do not give
them up we shall join your enemies, and we shall
be too many for you." Such language was intolerable to Napoleon. He regarded it as an out
and out threat, — that it assumed that he, Napoleon, could be intimidated into resigning territory which had become his by valid treaties.
To his mind the attitude of Russia and Prussia
was far more intelligible. He recognized that
they had good grounds for hostility. He could
understand and appreciate their position. Russia had her invasion to avenge. Prussia since
Jéna had never been treated as an equal; she
naturally desired to recover her position as a
great power. But that Austria, with whom he
had so recently been connected by a marriage

alliance, should take advantage of his misfortunes, and, without any allegation even of a breach of good faith on his part, should exact a price for not joining in the crusade against him, this was to him irritating to the last degree. It was a repetition of Austria's conduct in 1809, when, without the least excuse, she attacked him simply because he was embarrassed in Spain.

Mortifying, however, as it might have been for Napoleon to yield to such demands as these, it was clearly for the interest of his Empire to make these concessions. After all, it was natural that Austrian statesmen should embrace the first opportunity of recovering the seaports on the Adriatic. Here, in all probability, lay the stress of the Austrian demands. Had Napoleon yielded the Illyrian provinces, he could without much doubt have arranged everything else. Then, Austria's neutrality secured, the defeat of the Russian and Prussian coalition was morally certain. Russia had by no means recovered so fully as France had from the losses of the preceding year. Prussia's new organization had so far yielded but a moderate army. The chances were two to one that by the 1st of September Napoleon could occupy Berlin, relieve Dantzic, and reënter Warsaw.

Instead of taking this course, so manifestly demanded by ordinary prudence as well as by a sense of public duty, he allowed his indignation at the attitude of Austria to direct his policy.

He accepted, indeed, the offer of mediation which Austria made, and agreed to the armistice which she proposed. In fact, he did not feel himself strong enough in May to withstand a coalition of the three great powers. But he continued his preparations for war, in the hope that Austria, when later in the season she came to see the magnitude of his armaments, would recede from her selfish attitude, and keep the peace without being paid for it. He also calculated that, if she should act the contrary part, he would, by the time the armistice terminated, have a force adequate to all emergencies.

Hence, instead of buying off Austria by making the moderate concessions which she demanded as the price of her neutrality, and finishing the contest as speedily as possible with the enfeebled and discouraged forces of the Czar and the King, he chose to tempt fortune by engaging in an unequal contest against the three nations combined. Of the certain losses and miseries of such a gigantic struggle, he apparently took no heed. Of defeat, and of the disastrous consequences of defeat to the populations who had, under his guidance, begun a new career in political and social life, he took his chance. To his mind, it is true, there was small probability of his being beaten; and with Austerlitz, Jéna, and Friedland to look back upon, who can wonder at his feeling? Yet it is almost incomprehensible that he should have left out of the account, as he certainly did, all the considerations which made a speedy termination of the war most desirable, — the exhaustion of France and her allies, the discontent arising from the constant conscriptions, the suffering caused by the blockade, the miseries caused by such tremendous wars, and above all the disproportionate importance to the French Empire of retaining the Illyrian provinces compared with having Austria added to the coalition. Nothing but an inordinate reliance on the use of force, a professional soldier's forgetfulness of the blessings of peace, a gambler's willingness to risk everything on the issue of a battle, and a wholly inadequate appreciation of the importance of the preservation of the Empire, and of the consequent duty of preventing any dangerous combination against its integrity, can account for Napoleon's course at this juncture.

When the armistice terminated in the middle of August, Austria had joined the coalition. Napoleon had indeed largely increased his army. He had also been able to improve somewhat the drill and discipline of his troops. But the army was a poor one. The men were too young and too green. There were a great many inexperienced officers. Nevertheless Napoleon, as usual, despised his enemies. His own mind was as fertile as ever in plans, and he looked for great results.

You all know how fatally his expectations

were disappointed. I have not time to tell how the brilliant success at Dresden which followed close on the termination of the armistice, was succeeded by the four crushing defeats of Vandamme, Oudinot, Macdonald, and Ney, and how the remainder of the army, under Napoleon himself, sadly diminished in strength and confidence, and largely outnumbered by its foes, was defeated and discomfited in the great battle of Leipsic, and driven across the Rhine.

But perhaps you do not all of you know that Napoleon was so insanely confident of success that he had at the time of the battle of Leipsic nearly 200,000 men in the various fortresses and fortified towns of Germany, the larger part of whom could, had he so ordered, have been fighting under his eye in that tremendous struggle. Had they been there, the result might very possibly have been different. It is true that if Napoleon's plans of campaign had turned out well, these garrisons would have secured for him all the strategic points in northern Germany. But to deprive himself of the services of such a mass of troops when the fate of his Empire was trembling in the balance, only that success, if he won it, might be more decisive, is such reckless and insensate conduct that it is impossible to speak of it with moderation. When he crossed the Rhine also, he left large garrisons in the important places, so that when he returned in the spring he might find them ready to his hand.

This is the conduct of a gambler. The crisis was indeed a grave one; it needed that all the available resources of the Empire should be concentrated. Yet Napoleon scattered them. In Spain and northern Germany were armies that would have amply sufficed to guard the Rhine frontier from invasion. But to Napoleon's mind such extreme measures were uncalled for. It was impossible, he felt, that he should not succeed, in the end, in beating Schwartzenberg and Blücher, and then, of what immense advantage would be the possession of Hamburg and Dresden and Magdeburg and Dantzic!

Nothing can show more clearly than this how thoroughly he regarded the whole thing as a game; a game of war, to be sure, but still a game; and how completely he lost the character of monarch, of the defender of the integrity of the states composing the Empire, in that of a mere general of an army, and a most recklessly imprudent general too. The manifest want of serious appreciation of his real position during the years 1813 and 1814 seems to indicate in Napoleon a deplorable and radical defect in mind and character. It does not seem to me to show what we call moral perversity, so much as an inability to grasp the essential conditions of the problem, which in any ordinary man of the world we should be surprised to find, combined with a total deficiency in that sobriety and seriousness with which a man of strong character deals with great emergencies. He seems to have been incapable of listening to the dictates of prudence, of common sense. Still less did he appreciate that a ruler is, in a true and real sense, a trustee for his people; and that risks, which, to an individual or to a soldier of fortune, are permissible enough, are wholly out of place when they put at hazard the destinies of states.

The rest of our story is soon told. Napoleon's part in it is characterized throughout by an obstinate and reckless reliance on military success as the only means of escape from the difficulties which environed him. Peace, and an honorable peace, he might have had when he wanted it. In fact, the Emperor Francis was far from being desirous to ruin him; he was satisfied with having regained for his country her ancient predominance in southern Germany and Italy. Alexander would have willingly retired on his laurels. It was only in the Prussian camp that the desire to push the war to the bitter end was manifested. Thus, after Leipsic, Napoleon was offered peace on terms which would have left France bounded by the Rhine, Belgium being included in the French frontier. These terms he had the incredible folly to reject. He was counting on the three or four months of winter in which to bring out a new army. But the allies did not give him the time he needed. In January of 1814 their armies crossed the Rhine.

Not much, of course, had been accomplished

at this date by Napoleon towards a reorganization of his shattered forces. What little could be done after such terrible disasters and mistakes, was certainly done, but meantime French territory was being occupied. Not only were Alsace and Lorraine invaded, but on the southern frontier also, Lord Wellington had crossed the Pyrenees.

Of the resolute, daring, brilliant fight that Napoleon made in the winter and early spring of 1814, — of Brienne, Champ Aubert, Montmirail, Montereau, — I have not the time to speak. Nor would it be possible for us to follow the complicated movements of this remarkable campaign in a lecture. Admire, however, as much as we may, the indomitable spirit of the man, his unfaltering nerve, his clear judgment, his untiring activity, his great skill, his daring courage, we cannot but recognize that during this whole period he was playing the part of a mere military man, he was totally ignoring the duties of a ruler of states. It is true that the Great Frederic was at times, during the Seven Years War, well-nigh as hard pushed as Napoleon, and that no thought of giving way ever entered his iron soul; and he finally succeeded in holding his own. Such an example may well have had an influence in shaping the line of conduct which Napoleon proposed to himself. Be that as it may, it remains true, that during this very campaign in France, offers of peace were repeatedly made which would at any rate have saved France from the terrible misfortune of having her form of government settled for her by her enemies, a misfortune which was destined to bear its bitter fruit to succeeding generations in revolution after revolution. But Napoleon had chosen his *rôle*, and he stuck to it. If fortune favored his military combinations, he would come out of the contest with flying colors; he would not have compromised the honor of the flag, nor have yielded a foot of soil which France had ever owned; if the fates were against him, it would be said of him that he had made a brave and skilful defence, and that France, having been overpowered by numbers, had not lost her proud name. Suffice it to say, that all that a military man could do to defend his country against invasion with the utterly inadequate force, which, owing to his reckless and insane folly in failing to withdraw his garrisons from Germany and his armies from Spain, was all that remained to him to use against the allies, was done. The question, however, being in Napoleon's hands a purely military one, and all his skill not sufficing to supply his woful lack of resources, the inevitable termination at length came, more unexpectedly to him, probably, than to any one else. Paris surrendered on the 30th of March, and the war was over. The Empire of Napoleon had fallen. It only remained for the conquerors to decide what was to become of France and of Napoleon himself.

LECTURE VI.

THE RETURN FROM ELBA.

It is April, 1814. The allied armies are quartered in Paris. Blücher and Schwartzenberg and Barclay de Tolly, generals whose names the Parisians have hitherto connected only with the far-off battlefields of Jéna and Lützen and Dresden and Smolensk and Borodino, may now be seen riding in the Champs Elysées and visiting their camps in the Bois de Boulogne. The good people of France are indignant with the Emperor for having permitted by his reckless conduct such a retribution as this, and no wonder. The allied sovereigns, for the Czar Alexander and the King of Prussia are with their troops, are beset with suggestions and advice from the partisans of the old monarchy. They are assured that France is weary of Napoleon and his endless wars, and desires nothing better than a return to the old, sound, conservative *régime* of the ancient dynasty.

In a certain sense there was a great deal of truth in this. All classes were tired of war. Everybody felt the humiliation of defeat and invasion. There never had been any interest in the Spanish war, and few had ever been hardy enough to justify it. The war with Russia was generally considered as the cause of the present calamities, and the fact that it was, to say the least of it, quite as much the work of Alexander as of Napoleon, was not known; to all appearance it had looked like a wanton invasion of a country with which France might have been and ought to have been at peace. In addition to the condemnation of Napoleon's course in respect to Spain and Russia, there had now come to be felt the most bitter indignation at his recklessness and obstinacy in refusing the honorable and advantageous offers of peace which had been made to him during the year that had passed. In short, there could be no doubt that the country condemned the foreign policy which Napoleon had latterly pursued, which, as people justly thought, had led directly to the humiliation of France.

It was, however, no less true, that, apart from this, the people were content with the existing government. The great body of the middle and lower classes feared and detested a return of the Bourbons and the ancient *noblesse*. The army was still devoted to the Emperor. The upper classes felt that they had more to lose than to gain by a change of dynasty. Only the fanatics in the cause of divine right really demanded Louis XVIII. as the logical sequence of the fall of the usurper and the close of the revolutionary period. But this party was naturally in an hour like this the most jubilant and the most noisy. Moreover, it had the ear of the great personages whose word was to determine what was to be done.

In an evil hour Alexander listened to their suggestions. He decided, and his allies readily acquiesced, that the powers would not treat with Napoleon. It was a most unjust, a most unwarranted, and a most unfortunate decision. What was it to them what should be the government of France? Far better would it have been if they had confined themselves to exacting from Napoleon such a peace as they had a right to exact, and had then left him to settle his accounts as best he might with the French people. He would in that event have had to stand the natural consequences of his mistakes, of his perversity, of his blindness to the true interests of his country, of his wilful and obstinate preference of a military solution of the difficulties which had surrounded him to wiser and more peaceful methods of escape. By thus distinguishing him from the country which he represented, they exhibited their mortal fear lest his genius might some day reassert itself and restore to France some portion at least of her former glory. They forced him to abdicate, thus freeing him at once from the burdens and difficulties, which as a disappointed and defeated monarch he would have had to encounter at every step of the new path of quiet ness and moderation in which alone it was possible at that time for France to walk. But to meet and to bear these difficulties and burdens could not but have been wholesome both for France and her Emperor. The process of readjustment, of reconciliation, would have been doubtless a disagreeable process, but it would have been a normal and necessary one, and there was no reason why the allied powers should have undertaken to prevent its taking place by arbitrarily relieving Napoleon from the cares and duties and responsibilities of continuing to govern a state to which his own folly and obstinacy had brought so many calamities.

Then, if Napoleon was to be ignored, there was nothing else to do but to restore the Bourbons. But what a responsibility was involved in taking this course! It was more than twenty years since the Bourbons had been dethroned, and the king and queen put to death. During that time, the French people had lived under and become profoundly attached to a system of things which was in all respects the opposite of that known as the old *régime*. The differences between the new system and the old, as I have pointed out before, were fundamental. The basis of the one was equality, of the other, privilege. The new system had been accepted by the French people. Embodied in the Code Napoleon, it had connected itself with all the affairs of life, and had regulated and governed the relations of the shop, the factory, the family, and the state for more than twenty years. It is true, no one at this moment proposed to abolish the Code. But if the Bourbons were to be restored, the principle of divine right and of privilege must come back with them. And who could tell what revolutionary catastrophes might not be the result of thus forcibly reintroducing a principle which had been so deliberately and for so long a time rejected?

The allied sovereigns took this responsibility of changing the government of France. One recommendation that this course had was, undoubtedly, that it appeared to terminate the long conflict that, beginning with the French Revolution in 1789, had gone on under Napoleon, between the old and the new order of things, by the definitive, the complete, triumph of the cause of legitimacy and of privilege.

The restoration of the Bourbons necessarily involved the exile of Napoleon. The government never existed that could have put up with Napoleon Bonaparte as a subject, a mere private citizen. For him to remain in France was manifestly impossible. There was nothing left but exile. And it must be admitted that the victorious powers treated their fallen antagonist with consideration when they assigned to him the little island of Elba as the place of his residence. It was, however, as any one might have seen, a very unwise thing to do, for at Elba the fallen

Emperor could receive all the European news as easily as could the Emperor Francis at Vienna or the Czar Alexander at St. Petersburg. And it ought to have been considered, that it was going to prove impossible for the Bourbons fully to satisfy the people of France. How could the exiles of twenty years be expected to become reconciled to the new order of things to which all Frenchmen but the exiles had become irrevocably attached? How were the returning nobility to be treated? Were the lands, which had been forfeited years ago, and which had since passed from purchaser to purchaser and from father to son, to be restored to their original owners? How was the army to be treated? How were the Prince of Condé and the Duke of Berry likely to get on with the Duke of Elchingen and the Prince of Essling? The future of France was full of doubt. Not the least element in this uncertainty consisted in the well-known characteristic of the Bourbon family, that in all its twenty years of exile, it had learned nothing and had forgotten nothing. And in any of the epochs of dissatisfaction which were morally certain to occur, how easy would it be for Napoleon to return from Elba?

Nevertheless, in spite of these ugly probabilities, to Elba was Napoleon sent, and Louis XVIII. commenced his reign. At first, as was natural, everything looked well for the new monarch. The sense of relief from the interminable wars counted, of course, for much in this happy prospect. Then the restoration of peace brought with it in some quarters, at any rate, the restoration of trade, and an influx of foreign travellers. The new monarch was a gracious and well-meaning man. He yielded his own prejudices so far as to give his people a parliamentary constitution. He early saw the impracticability of satisfying the demands of the extreme royalists. Sooner than disturb existing titles, he diminished the state lands by grants to the needy nobility. Doubtless he tried his best.

But the position was one which he never should have been called upon to occupy. It was impossible for any man, no matter what his ability or his good purposes might be, to fill the throne of France at that time with satisfaction to the people of France. It does not make us view the reckless conduct of Napoleon in any more favorable light certainly, when we consider that it was due so largely to his folly that the normal political development of France was thus arrested, and its course turned, to a greater or less extent, into the discarded channels of eighteenth century politics. Yet so it was. The king might try conscientiously to fulfil his duty, but, do what he would, the fact that he and those about him represented ideas and principles which France had long ago rejected, that they were utterly out of sympathy with the views and aims which were so dear to the great mass of the

French people, could not but make it impossible for Louis to obtain a hold upon the national affection and esteem.

Naturally enough, the army was especially dissatisfied with the new government. The royal dukes ranked everybody else, of course; and in addition to the irritation which all Frenchmen felt at distinction of any kind being the perquisite of mere birth was the peculiar grievance always felt by military men when officers who have never seen the face of the enemy are placed above the veterans of many campaigns. Any one in the least acquainted with the standard of feeling on such subjects which prevails among military men the world over can understand that it was impossible that the soldiers of Napoleon should not have felt the transition to the *régime* of the Bourbons irksome and well-nigh insupportable. And this may well have happened without any special fault on the part of Louis or his ministers. In addition, however, to these general causes of dissatisfaction, there were others. The reduction of the army, a measure really unavoidable, could not but render the government unpopular with those officers who were thus summarily discharged from service. Then there was more or less of suspicion of and hostility to the old and tried chiefs, which was fiercely resented not only by them but by the army generally.

During the year 1814, some 200,000 French

soldiers returned to France from foreign fortresses and garrisons. These men could not believe that the Emperor could have been overthrown without the intervention of traitors. They knew nothing of the share which Napoleon's obstinacy and recklessness had had in bringing about the deplorable catastrophe. They were above all things anxious for another trial of strength between France and her enemies.

The new government also made the mistake of interfering with the judiciary. It undertook on various pretexts to get rid of a great many judges, and to fill their places by men belonging to the reactionary party. The suspicions of people were aroused lest the well understood laws of the land should be administered in a sense contrary to their plain meaning.

The returned emigrants, whose services to the royal family had given them a ready access to the throne, were naturally thoroughly distrusted by the nation, and they did not seek to diminish this feeling by their moderation either of language or behavior. They loudly urged the undoing of all the work of the Revolution. They wantonly revived the memory of ancient animosities. Among other pieces of folly, they persuaded the king to ennoble the family of Georges Cadoudal, who had suffered death in 1804 for having conspired against the life of the First Consul. They even undertook to disturb the settlement with the Church effected by the Concordat. They persecuted the bishops who had accepted that wise measure and had for ten years faithfully acted under it. They gave the word to those priests, returned emigrants and others, of whom there were many in France, in whose weak minds the cause of the Church was inextricably confused with the cause of the Bourbons, to preach a crusade against liberal ideas in politics, and to urge upon the government the re-adoption of the discarded system of intolerance in matters of faith and worship. In fact nothing was left undone which could tend to alarm the good people of France in regard to the permanence of the fundamental institutions and reforms, which, acquired at so much expense in the great Revolution, and consolidated by Napoleon, had been the cause and condition of so much prosperity and contentment.

But, I hear some one say, Louis XVIII. was not an absolute monarch, like Napoleon, but a king whose powers were in some sort limited by a constitution. He governed by means of a ministry, and by a ministry which must find its support in a Parliament. Here is a great improvement, certainly, over the government of Napoleon. France ought to have been content.

This criticism, though specious, is in reality not sound. Let us grant at once and freely that the government of Louis XVIII. resembled in its essential features the government of England; and furthermore, that the government of England was a freer government than that of France under Napoleon. But the institutions of Great Britain were based on class distinctions and privileges which were the abhorrence of the French people. The fundamental thing in France was equality before the law. If this be preserved, most Frenchmen cared little then and care little to-day who administers the government. If, on the contrary, this is endangered, France at once becomes agitated, restless, and ripe for revolt. No parliamentary representation is accepted as a compensation for any disturbance of this fundamental principle. The new parliament was all very well, of course, but not having been evolved naturally in the course of the nation's political growth, having in fact been granted as a sort of offset for the infractions of the principle of equality necessarily involved in the return of the Bourbons, it was worth but little either to the royal family as a recommendation of the old *régime*, or to the French people as a means of political education.

The difficulties with which the Bourbon dynasty had to contend were in truth practically insuperable. They were not the ordinary difficulties of all new governments. Changes like those which France passed through from 1789 to the establishment of the Empire in 1804 are, in a certain real sense, the results of a process of evolution. They may, each successive one of them, have their peculiar difficulties, but, for the time being, each fulfils its natural, though perhaps transient, work. But the imposition by force upon an independent nation of a form of government for which its political history has in no wise fitted it, nay even, which in the evolution of its political life it has definitively rejected, is to lay upon the administrators of that government tasks which they cannot accomplish, and to subject the nation to a yoke against which it will inevitably rebel.

Added to these causes which so profoundly disturbed France was the unpopularity to which the government was no doubt undeservedly subjected, arising from the hard terms imposed on France by the allied powers. The ministry had done their best, unquestionably; for it was of course for the interest of the government to obtain for France all the territory and colonies that the allied powers could be induced to concede. But many of their reasonable expectations and demands were disappointed.

Another ground for discontent existed in the unavoidable depression in French manufacturing industries, resulting from throwing open the market to English goods. The declaration of peace operated like a sudden and total change in a tariff, and brought ruin, or at least temporary stagnation, into many hitherto prosperous districts.

Napoleon's exile had, as I have pointed out, exempted him from the task, which by good rights should have fallen upon him, of standing up against these complaints and criticisms, and doing his best to repair these misfortunes. But, influenced partly by fear of his ever active sword, and partly by a desire to terminate the long crusade against the Revolution and Revolutionary principles by restoring the ancient throne of the Bourbons in the spot where the Revolution had its origin, the allied powers committed the mistake of relieving the fallen Emperor from the necessity of facing the obloquy which his recent terrible mistakes had drawn upon him, of going on with the government of the country in spite of his diminished prestige, and of working out for France relief from the evils which his reckless course had brought upon her. As it was, all the complaints were laid at the door of Louis. Napoleon, in exile, driven from his country by his country's foes, became a greater hero than ever. To him all eyes were turned. Not only was the army to a man lamenting its great chief, but the bulk of the people, indignant, amazed, and enraged at the steps which the Bourbon government was taking in the direction of a discarded past, and still more alarmed at the prospect of the future, looked wistfully across the Mediterranean for the return of him who alone had known how both to curb the passions of the Revolution and to give to the people of France the equal, liberal, just, and humane laws which were the dearly bought acquisitions of her great convulsions.

Of all this Napoleon was perfectly cognizant. He had his friends everywhere in France. From the beginning he had seen that he would soon be wanted. He knew that every month would bring greater difficulties to the Bourbon government. The only question was, whether the time for him had come. Whether he hastened his departure by fears of being removed to some distant place, I do not know. Such fears were certainly not without foundation. The allied powers in the Congress of Vienna were debating whether or not to depose Murat, although he had retired from the French alliance some months before the final catastrophe, under a solemn assurance from Austria that his throne should not be disturbed. In all probability, when the Congress had got through with the vexed questions of Saxony and Poland, their disputes about which brought them to the brink of another war, they would take up the question of Napoleon's residence, and it is hardly possible to suppose that he would have been permitted to retain Elba. At any rate, he solved this question for himself, and on the 1st of March, 1815, he landed in the Gulf of Juan near Cannes. He had with him Drouot, Bertrand, Cambronne, and some 1,100 men of the Guard, with four guns.

There is no need that I should tell here the story of that wonderful march : how the peasants brought provisions and transportation for the little army; how the villages welcomed the exile and the cities opened their gates to him; how generals and marshals, feeling themselves bound by their lately given oaths to support the House of Bourbon, vainly endeavored to force the common soldiers to fight with their old commander; how the Emperor, with his customary sagacity and with more than his wonted intrepidity, trusted himself to regiment after regiment, and how he was rewarded for his confidence by their unqualified devotion. Nothing like it has ever been seen in history. Nothing can describe it so well as the words of his own proclamation, written on board the brig which brought him from Elba. "Victory," said he, "victory will advance at the full gallop; the eagle with the national colors will fly from steeple to steeple even to the towers of Notre Dame."

On the 7th of March Napoleon reached Grenoble; on the 10th he was at Lyons; on the 20th he entered Paris. Of the marshals, Masséna had remained at his post at Marseilles; Macdonald had vainly endeavored to get his troops to obey his orders and check the march of the Emperor; Ney, who had foolishly undertaken the task of fighting his former chief, had succumbed partly to the force of circumstances and partly to a natural revulsion of feeling, and had joined him; Soult, who was then minister of war, had kept his faith with the king, but he was no doubt glad to see Napoleon back again. Berthier most unaccountably followed Macdonald into Belgium, where the king had retired. Davout and Mortier, like Soult, remained in France and served the Emperor, as, after his bloodless and successful march, they were fully justified in doing.

Never was a revolution more complete and more unopposed. There was, to be sure, some appearance of trouble in the south of France, where the royalists had many partisans, and specially in Marseilles, the inhabitants of which were bitter against Napoleon for the loss of their commerce during the past twenty years. But these outbreaks were not serious; they do not deserve to be considered as qualifying the statement which may be safely made that France welcomed Napoleon back as the man of her choice.

Wherever Napoleon had spoken on his journey he had announced that his policy would be one of peace and reform. On his establishment at the Tuileries he sent messages of amity and of sincere acceptance of existing treaties to all the courts of Europe. But his couriers were turned back on the frontier. The allied powers then represented at the Congress of Vienna proclaimed that Napoleon, by his escape from Elba, had placed himself beyond the protection of the law of nations. They entered into a solemn league against him, pledging themselves to use their utmost exertions until they should compass his downfall.

Everything that I have said before in reference to the folly and injustice of the conduct of the allies in 1814, in refusing to treat with Napoleon, applies with even greater force to this celebrated declaration. Now, at any rate, there was no room for mistake as to the public feeling of France. Now, it was too plain for controversy that the powers were banding themselves together to force upon France a government which she had positively rejected. Nothing can be alleged in excuse of the course which the allied sovereigns took at this juncture but that they distrusted Napoleon's professions and were afraid of his commencing a course of aggression. To these suggestions it might well have been replied, in the first place, that the extension of the French Empire had been mainly the result of the defeat of the coalitions formed against Napoleon, and not of his ambitious undertakings; in the second place, that Europe, reconstituted as it now was, was certainly able to resist any encroachment of France, should it be made; and thirdly, that the France of to-day was in a very different frame of mind from the France of 1805 or 1806, that Napoleon was likely to have his hands full at home in reconciling her to her altered position among the nations, and in adjusting his own modes of government to the demands of a people rendered exacting by the adversity which had befallen them through his recklessness and folly. But considerations of this kind do not appear to have been urged. The cry was for war, war to the knife.

On his part, Napoleon prepared for the impending struggle with all his usual energy and activity. At the same time he undertook to meet the demands of the leaders of the liberal party, who had long viewed with regret the military despotism which had prevailed during the Empire, and who required at Napoleon's hands the institution of representative assemblies. These demands, reasonable in themselves, it was no doubt wise to grant; at the same time, environed as France then was by her enemies, the realization of them should have been postponed. In time of war, the best government is a military despotism; and if France was going to maintain her right to choose her own form of government in face of the hostility of united Europe, it could only be done by deferring all questions of domestic politics until she had settled the vital question whether she was or was not to be allowed to dispose of her own affairs in her own way. Napoleon, however, proclaimed a new constitution, and convened under it a House of Peers and a Chamber of Deputies.

There can be no question that France in 1815 was prepared for the worst. The people were determined that the Bourbons should not be forced upon them again. Patriotic addresses and offers of assistance were showered upon the Emperor. Public enthusiasm rose to a great height. It was plain that the masses of the people had made up their minds to stand by the tricolored flag no matter what might be the fortune of war. The only quarter where there was any doubt respecting the existence of this determination to resist the threatened invasion to the last was among the leaders of the constitutional party, so called. It is true that these gentlemen had but a small following among the masses of the people, who were by no means sufficiently educated in political matters to care much about parliaments and cabinets; yet the very fact of their being more interested in political matters than other people were made them prominent in the new Parliament which Napoleon had just established. These gentlemen, among whom was our own Lafayette, had practically made their adhesion to their country's cause dependent on Napoleon's granting such parliamentary institutions as they thought France ought to have. It was no secret that, in their eyes, these institutions were the principal things to be considered, to which the right of their country to dispose of herself and her affairs as she saw fit, without dictation from foreign powers, was to be postponed. They had accordingly viewed the restoration of the Bourbons in the preceding year without alarm or hostility, and it was certainly to be feared that they could not be relied upon now to defend the nation to the last against the new invasion. It was a mistake, as it turned out, on Napoleon's part, not to have dissolved the Chambers before he took the field. But that French politicians, whether legitimists or constitutionalists, imperialists or republicans, should prefer the triumph of their own theories to the independence of their country has been a spectacle of such frequent occurrence that it can no longer excite surprise.

The nation, as I have said, had fully made up its mind to the worst; that is, to another invasion of the soil of France. For this invasion, people meant this time to be prepared. The efforts of Napoleon to fortify Paris, Lyons, and other important points were zealously carried out. There was no lack anywhere of energy, activity, patriotism. The thing for Napoleon to do was to conserve all this moral force for the terrible struggle which was now inevitable; to augment his armies, to strengthen his fortifications, to complete his armaments of all kinds, to get all the delay he could, to await the enemy within the territory of France, and then deal him the tremendous blows which no one but he could deal. This course would have given him ample time to bring out the still enormous military resources which France possessed. The opening of the campaign would have been deferred until every fortified town was in condition to resist a prolonged siege. More than this, this course, if undertaken with a deliberate and irrevocable determination never to yield, no matter what might be the odds against him, would have secured the practically unanimous and hearty support of the nation, while a prorogation of the legislature during the period of invasion would have prevented the cause of the country being given away by any weak-kneed political theorists in Parliament.

Unhappily, such a serious grasp of the situation seems to have been beyond Napoleon's capacity. He relied in 1815, as hitherto, mainly upon his own skill and good fortune, and neglected entirely the establishment of that identification of his cause with that of France which alone could give the struggle a reasonable chance of success. France, at this crisis of her fate, needed a Frederic rather than a Napoleon. With a man of the iron temper of the king who carried his country through the Seven Years War, France would have maintained her independence. But Napoleon gave to the struggle the character of a military and political experiment, and the first defeat settled the whole matter. It was another example of the same venturesome reliance on his military combinations which we have observed so often in his history, and which we saw fully exemplified as far back as the campaign of Marengo.

The fall of the French Empire had brought all western Germany and the greater part of Italy under the control of Austria and Prussia. Had any free expression been allowed to the communities which had formed the Confederation of the Rhine and the Kingdom of Italy, they would unquestionably either have declared for France or would have remained neutral. Already had the harsh military rule of Prussia begun to chafe the populations of the late Kingdom of Westphalia. Already had Bavaria and Würtemberg begun to dread the encroachments of the House of Hapsburg. Even now the comparatively free populations of Lombardy and Venice were suffering from the despotic rule of the Austrians. But there was nothing to be done save to submit, and all the resources of these states were placed at the disposal of the three great monarchies.

Austria was far from being in a condition to begin the war immediately. The soldiers of the Czar had arrived home again, and would not be available for service on the Rhine for many weeks. Prussia, however, was ready with a considerable force, and it was arranged that her army, with another to be furnished by England, Holland, Belgium, and some of the smaller German states, should occupy Belgium, defend Holland in case of invasion, and, when the other armies should be ready to move, invade France from the side of the north.

✗ The forces of the Duke of Wellington and Marshal Blücher numbered together about 223,000 men, of whom the Duke could bring into the field about 95,000 men and the marshal about 110,000 men. They were stationed in various towns and villages, extending nearly from Liége on the east to Ostend on the west. Speaking generally, the Prussians were on the east and the English on the west of the great road which runs due north from Charleroi to Brussels. The Prussian base of operations and depots of supplies were on the Rhine, in the direction of Namur and Liége; those of the English were on the sea, at Ostend and neighboring ports. It was plain to Napoleon that if, by a battle fought near this great road from Charleroi to Brussels, he could badly defeat either of these armies the connection between them would in all probability be severed, as the beaten army, if it retired, as it probably would, on its own base, would be obliged to separate itself definitely from the other army, whose base lay in precisely the opposite direction. He would then be able to deal with either army separately; and, as he expected to be able to bring into the field an army decidedly superior to either force taken alone, this plan looked very promising. Moreover, England and Prussia were the two most active powers in the coalition, and any serious misfortune befalling them in the outset of the war could not but tend very much to discourage all the allied powers, and render them, or some of them, willing to listen to reasonable terms of accommodation. I have already expressed my own belief that under the circumstances it would have been wiser for Napoleon to have awaited the invasion of France by the allies: nevertheless, there is a great deal to be said in favor of the policy of taking the offensive which he adopted. It was a policy certainly more in accordance with his character and peculiar genius.

Accordingly he began in the latter part of May gradually concentrating his *corps d'armée* in the neighborhood of the Belgian frontier. Before the middle of June this movement was accomplished. From various causes, which we have not time to recapitulate, he was unable to muster more than 125,000 to 130,000 men for this campaign. These were organized as follows: the first corps under General Drouet d'Erlon; the second under General Reille; the third under General Vandamme; the fourth under General Gérard; the sixth under General the Count de Lobau; and the Imperial Guard. Of these officers it is to be noticed that not one had attained the rank of marshal. They were all gallant and meritorious officers, undoubtedly, but no one among them had made any special mark in his long years of service. Perhaps the Count de Lobau was the most distinguished; he had won his title in the trying days of Aspern and Essling, six years before. Gérard and Vandamme had deserved reputations as hard fighters; d'Erlon and Reille had served a great deal in Spain, and were, perhaps, not so well known as the others to the public.

To Marshal Ney the Emperor assigned command of the left wing of the army, consisting of the first and second corps. But by some inexplicable oversight, Ney had received no orders until he received that to join the army. The consequence was that he knew nothing about the troops he was to command, and that, summoned as he was at the last minute, he was scarcely able to find a horse to ride, and came on from Paris with only a single aide-de-camp. This carelessness of Napoleon's on the eve of a tremendous and exceedingly doubtful struggle it is indeed hard to understand.

To Marshal Grouchy, a new appointment, the Emperor assigned command of the right wing, consisting of the third and fourth corps, reserving the sixth corps and the Guard for his own immediate control. Grouchy was a man of known gallantry and a faithful officer, but he had never made that sort of a reputation which Napoleon in his younger days used to require before he bestowed upon a general the baton of marshal. To entrust a division commander with the command of two corps was taking a very great risk. Nor was there any necessity for it at all. The services of Marshal Davout could have been had, than whom Napoleon never had an abler or more devoted lieutenant. This marshal, whom Napoleon had made Minister of War, and had charged with the defence of Paris, begged the Emperor to allow him to take the field under him; he represented that the defence of Paris, notwithstanding its incontestable importance, was, like all questions of interior defence, a secondary matter, and essentially subordinate to the result of military operations; that when one was about to play a decisive game on the field of battle, it was no time to make trial of new men; that it was necessary, on the contrary, to surround one's self with those who had made proof of their capacity, and had had experience of high command. But to all these representations the Emperor turned a deaf ear. "I cannot," said the Emperor, "entrust Paris to any one else." "Sire," said the marshal, "if you are victorious, Paris will be yours; if you are beaten, neither I nor any one else can help you." There was really no answer to this suggestion. The Emperor undoubtedly was thinking of the unnecessary surrender of Paris the year before; but the circumstances now were wholly different. There was no enemy now threatening Paris, as there was then. It is impossible to imagine any sufficient justification for this refusal of Napoleon's to permit Davout to serve with the active army. It was an error of judgment that probably cost Napoleon his throne.

Deprived of Berthier, his old chief of staff, as we have seen, Napoleon selected Marshal Soult, another singular choice. Soult had for years commanded an army himself, and had had a chief of staff of his own. Such a man is not likely all at once to fall into the careful and methodical habits of a Berthier. There were many younger officers of known capacity, any of whom would have made quite as good a chief of staff as Marshal Soult, and Soult might well have taken command of one of the corps, or of the Guard, which in the absence of Marshal Mortier, who had fallen ill, was without a chief.

The Emperor was about to undertake an offensive campaign with 125,000 men against two armies outnumbering his by about 100,000 men. It goes without saying that he should have made use of all his resources. Had Davout instead of Grouchy commanded the right wing, had Ney been properly forewarned, had Soult commanded the Guard or a corps, and Grouchy the cavalry, the risk would have been great enough; but it would have been much less than the risk actually encountered. In this emergency it was possible for Napoleon to avail himself of the services of the man who had won the battle of Auerstädt; it is absolutely inconceivable why he should have preferred to run the hazard of supplying his place by a general who had never in his life held a separate command.

The Duke of Wellington, after making all deductions for garrisons and so forth, brought into the field somewhat over 90,000 men. Of these only about 35,000 were English troops, however. Of the remaining 55,000, the Duke considered not over 15,000 as perfectly trustworthy. The other troops, being raised in Holland, Belgium, and Nassau, so long under French control, were distrusted by him, as much because of their supposed preference for his antagonist's cause as for their admitted inferiority to his English troops. He had under him Sir Thomas Picton and Lord Hill, two of his best Peninsular officers. The Prince of Orange and the Duke of Brunswick also held high commands in his motley army. The cavalry were under Lord Uxbridge, afterwards the Marquis of Anglesey.

The Prussian army consisted of four strong corps averaging nearly 30,000 men each. Bülow was the only corps commander who had won any European reputation.

On the 12th of June the Emperor left Paris. On the 14th he was with the army, and issued to it one of those stirring proclamations with which he had always aroused the spirits of his soldiers when on the eve of a decisive struggle. He reminded them that it was the anniversary of Marengo and of Friedland; he called to their minds the injustice of the coalition against France; he urged them to conquer or to die.

At noon of the 15th the army, or a large part

of it, was across the Sambre. Its watchfires the night before had given notice of its concentration and near approach. The Prussians on the border were warned, and opposed a resolute countenance to the advancing columns. There was a certain amount of delay here and there in the movements of the troops, such as always happens when an army takes the field after a long period of inaction; but, generally speaking, things went well with the French. Napoleon's plan of campaign was, as I have said, to separate the English and Prussian armies from each other. With his left wing under Ney he undertook to hold the straight road from Charleroi to Brussels; with his right wing and centre he intended to fight the Prussians, who he expected would be able to concentrate sooner than the English, and who he knew would be obliged to fight, if they intended to fight at all, on the east of that road. At night of the 15th, accordingly, Ney was at Frasnes with one division of the second corps and some cavalry, opposite one of Wellington's Dutch brigades,[1] which was holding Quatre Bras; while the greater portion of the third corps was near Fleurus, confronting the Prussian corps of Ziethen. The bulk of the French army was within supporting distance of the heads of the two columns constituting the

---

[1] The commander of this brigade, Prince Bernard of Saxe Weimar, deserves great credit for having, without orders, got his command together at Quatre Bras.

wings, although a considerable part had not yet crossed the river. The progress made had not been what the Emperor had expected it would be, what it would have been had he had as his corps commanders the brilliant men who, brought to the top in the turmoil of the Revolution, had, ten years before, captured Ulm and won Austerlitz; still it had been on the whole a satisfactory day. There was nothing to prevent the whole army being in position at Quatre Bras and at Fleurus by noon of the 16th.

Napoleon has said in his Memoirs that he ordered Ney on the afternoon of the 15th to occupy Quatre Bras that night. That he did give Ney such orders appears certain from the statement in the Official Bulletin, sent off to Paris that evening, that Ney was at that moment at Quatre Bras. But the place ought to have been, and might have been, carried before noon or early in the afternoon of the next day, which would have answered every purpose.

While Napoleon was thus massing his forces, what were the allies doing?

The Prussian corps of Ziethen, as we have seen, had resolutely opposed the French advance during the day of the 15th, and of course Marshal Blücher had had ample warning of the impending storm. He had ordered up the other three corps, though, owing to a blunder, only two of them began their march that day. That evening, while Ziethen was near Ligny, Pirch was at

Mazy, and Thielmann at Namur. Bülow was still at Liége. Notwithstanding the absence of Bülow, which left him only 90,000 men, the brave old marshal meant to fight Napoleon, though he supposed he carried with him 130,000 Frenchmen. He relied to a certain extent, though not probably very definitely, upon help from Wellington. But, as it turned out, the movement of Ney on the Brussels turnpike prevented Wellington from affording his ally any assistance.

The Duke of Wellington was informed of the decision of Marshal Blücher to concentrate his army near Ligny some hours before he was able, from the reports which reached him, to determine with certainty the movements of the French. By some mischance, no news whatever of the advance of the enemy reached Brussels till three P. M. — some twelve hours after the crossing of the Sambre: and then the information was very indefinite. As late as ten P. M., all that the Duke knew was that the French "appeared to menace Charleroi." It was not until between ten and eleven o'clock that it was ascertained that the main body of the French was opposed to the Prussians in the neighborhood of Ligny; and until this was ascertained, the Duke had to take into account the possibility that Napoleon might be carrying the bulk of his army to the westward of Charleroi, by way of Mons, for instance, with the object of breaking the com-

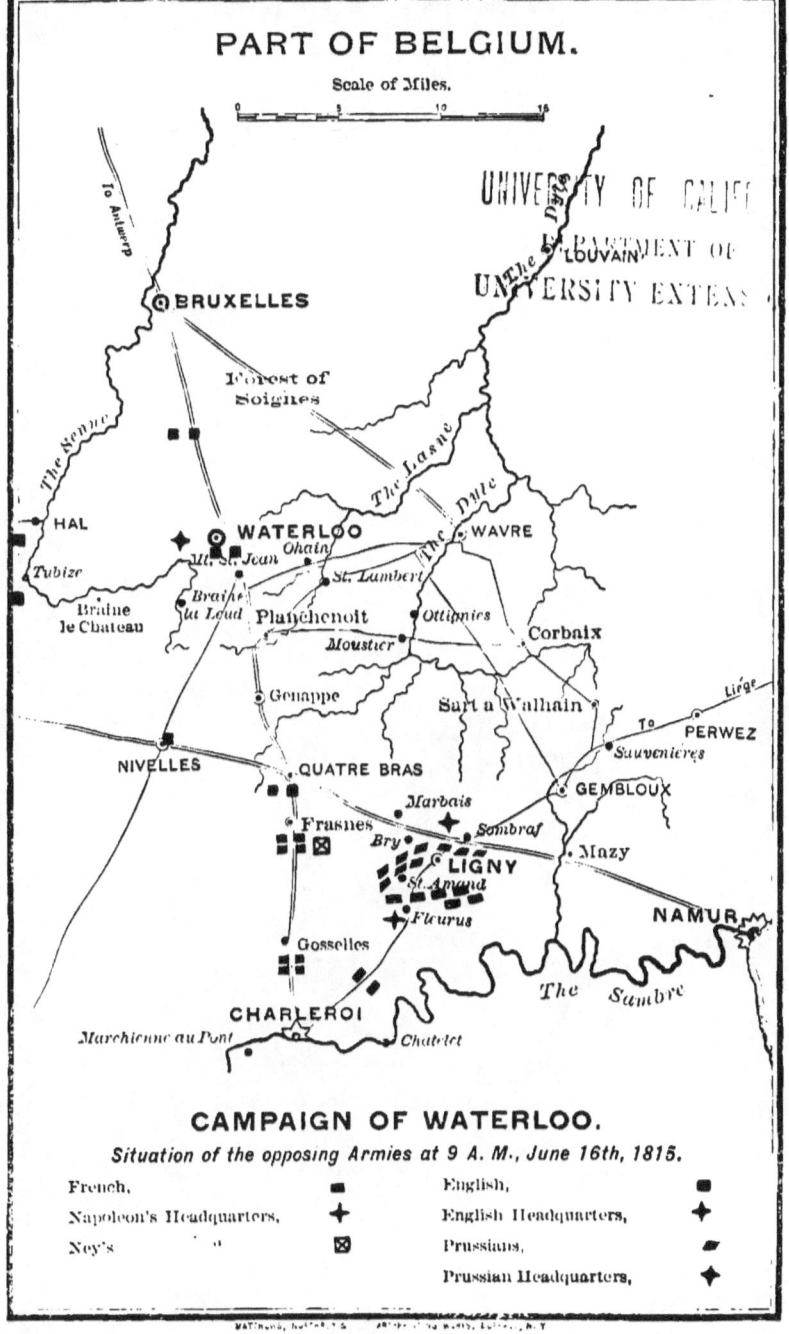

munications of the English with Ostend and Brussels. Hence the Duke's first orders directed the assembling of his divisions at various points on the west of the Brussels turnpike, so that a concentration of his army to meet a French advance by way of Mons, or to the westward of it, might easily be effected; and it was not until he was certain that the main body of the French under Napoleon was in face of the Prussians at Ligny that the Duke felt warranted in issuing orders for his whole army to march to Quatre Bras. Then there seems to have been some delay, either on the Duke's part or on that of his staff, as these orders were not issued till the early morning of the 16th, when there was not time enough for them to be effectually carried out.

But fortune on this occasion, as often before, favored the Duke of Wellington. Not only did Prince Bernard's brigade remain at Quatre Bras, but Perponcher, who commanded the division, brought over to its support from Nivelles the other brigade, Bylandt's. Then, during the forenoon of the 16th, Wellington rode down to Quatre Bras in person, and then rode over to Ligny, where he had a conference with Marshal Blücher.

The French army, in its protracted and laborious march of the day before, had become so much scattered that it took most of the forenoon to get it well in hand. The concentration of the right wing and centre, which took place under Napoleon's own eye, was at last satisfactorily effected, and the third and fourth corps and the Guard were in position near Fleurus by noon, if not before; the sixth corps came up in the course of the afternoon. As regards the left wing of the army, d'Erlon had in the early morning finished crossing the Sambre, and had taken post in rear of Gosselies, where were two divisions of the second corps under Reille. Another division of the second corps was further to the front, at Frasnes. The fourth division under Girard was with the right wing of the army. About nine o'clock the Emperor issued orders for Ney to advance with his entire command and occupy Quatre Bras.

While these movements were being made, the Emperor was studying the situation. It seemed at first as if neither of the allied armies had been able to concentrate in sufficient force to oppose him. The corps of Ziethen was the only Prussian corps which he had yet encountered. The force which had been observed by his advanced posts at Frasnes did not seem like a large one. Could he then safely assume that he was to be allowed to march on Brussels without serious molestation, and that Wellington and Blücher had retired for the time being upon their respective bases?

Before the French army had got itself together, however, it became evident to the experienced eye of Napoleon that the corps of Ziethen was receiving large reinforcements from the eastward, and that the Prussians had no idea of leaving their positions at Saint Amand and Ligny. An attack on them before they should be reinforced by the English became, therefore, imperative. In such an attack he had no doubt whatever of being successful. The Emperor also calculated that Ney, with the 40,000 men assigned to him, would be stronger than any force which the Duke could collect, scattered as he knew the English and Dutch forces to have been. He therefore expected success on both ends of the line.

Accordingly, after making his usual personal reconnoissance on the line of the vedettes, he attacked the Prussians vigorously between two and three o'clock. The corps of Vandamme and Gérard, assisted by the division of Girard from the second corps, threw themselves impetuously into the villages of Saint Amand and Ligny, where the Prussians had taken post. Never was a battle more hotly disputed. The Prussian position was a strong one, and their soldiers made good use of the stone houses in the villages. Saint Amand was captured and recaptured. The contest seemed to gravitate, so to speak, to this village, which was on the Prussian extreme right. It became evident to Napoleon that Marshal Blücher, carried away by his ardor, was actually thinking of turning the French left. It was plain that he was stripping his centre, behind the village of Ligny, of troops. The Emperor ordered the Guard to prepare for action.

Suddenly, about 5.30 p. m., word is brought to him of the appearance of a strong body of troops marching from the direction of the turnpike towards his left. The projected movement of the Guard is at once suspended, until it can be ascertained what these troops are. Meantime a dreadful suspicion runs through the ranks that Ney has met with a disaster, and that it is an English corps which is approaching. But this is of short duration. The Prussian cavalry are seen skirmishing with and then retiring before the strange corps. Every one then assumes that Ney has been successful, and that he has sent this body of troops to assist his master. Suddenly the corps is seen to halt, to face about, and then slowly to disappear to the westward. The battle is resumed as before. The Emperor takes up again his favorite manœuvre of breaking the centre of the enemy's line. The Imperial Guard, preceded by its formidable artillery, and flanked by its equally formidable cavalry, carries everything before it. The Prussian positions in the rear of Ligny are occupied in spite of a spirited resistance, and the safety of the troops in Saint Amand is gravely compromised. Over twenty pieces of cannon are taken. Had the attack been made earlier, as it would have been but for the unexpected delay mentioned above, several thousand prisoners must have been captured. Napoleon had won his last victory.

Let us now return to the left wing, under Marshal Ney. That officer received somewhere between ten and eleven o'clock orders to occupy Quatre Bras. Why they were not sent before is by no means clear, but it was probably because Napoleon had not fully made up his mind what course to take. Ney proceeded at once to execute his instructions. The rest of the second corps, Reille's, was brought up to Frasnes. Orders were immediately sent to d'Erlon to follow Reille. D'Erlon got his orders, he says, at half past eleven; Reille may have received his a little before. As matter of fact they both knew more than an hour before what their orders were to be, as the despatch to Ney had been communicated to Reille as early as ten o'clock by the Emperor's own aide-de-camp on his way to Ney's headquarters, and Reille had at once sent word to d'Erlon. There was no reason in the world why these officers should not have got under way at half past ten, for they ought, of course, to have been ready to move at a moment's warning. In this case they would have reached Frasnes by half past twelve. As it was, Reille, with two divisions of his corps, joined the third division at Frasnes shortly before two. As for d'Erlon, he ordered his corps to Frasnes, and then preceded it, to see what was going on at the front. While there, an aide-de-camp of the Emperor's rode up, showed him a despatch which he was carrying to Marshal Ney, and coolly told d'Erlon that he had ventured, in compliance with this despatch, to order his corps off from the road to Frasnes towards Saint Amand. D'Erlon could of course do nothing else than ride off to rejoin his corps, which he conducted until it appeared as we have seen, heading for the French left, and caused the sensation in the Emperor's army of which we have spoken above.

Meantime Ney, relying on the reinforcement which, as he supposed, d'Erlon would speedily bring him, had attacked Perponcher's Dutch Belgian division under the Prince of Orange with great vigor and with good success. The French troops not only outnumbered their antagonists, but they were much more experienced soldiers. While things were in this state, Wellington returned from Ligny, where he had been to confer with Marshal Blücher. Fortunately for him, Sir Thomas Picton now arrived with his division of British troops. From this time on, the allied forces were continually strengthened by reinforcements.

At last Ney, furious at the non-arrival of the first corps, learned what had taken place, and at once peremptorily ordered its return to Frasnes. But meantime he tried hard to win the day with the troops he had with him. No one could have fought 20,000 men better than Ney did at Quatre Bras. But, as the hours wore on, the

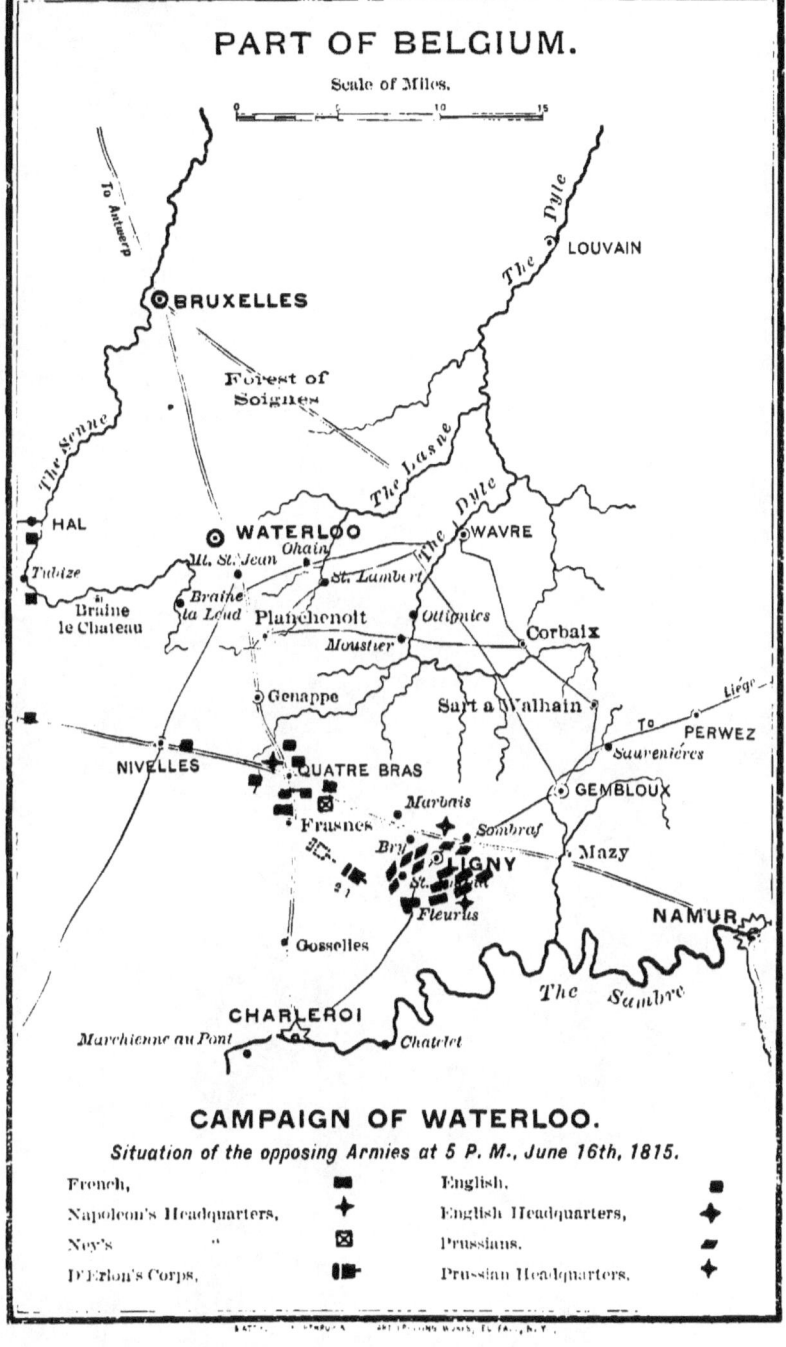

superiority of the allies in numbers, and especially in fresh troops, became painfully manifest. D'Erlon did not return, could not return, in time to take part in the action. Finally Marshal Ney, after a contest most creditable to him, retired to his original position at Frasnes. Wellington had by this time collected in front of him over 30,000 men.

One word in regard to the order which the staff officer showed to the commander of d'Erlon's leading division. It was, in all probability, the order which, dated at two o'clock, directed Ney, after having beaten the troops in front of him, to turn back in the direction of Napoleon, and endeavor to surround the Prussians. The officer carrying the despatch, having to ride about six miles on cross-roads, as far as Gosselies, could hardly have reached the head of d'Erlon's column on the Brussels turnpike before half-past four. It would have taken these troops a good hour to march eastward to the point where their approach was perceived; and they were first seen, as has been stated, about half-past five.

It would be an entire mistake to suppose that the battle of Quatre Bras was a defeat for the French. Tactically, indeed, it may be so considered, as the French undertook to carry the cross-roads, which they were unable to do. But strategically it answered its purpose sufficiently well. That purpose was to prevent the union of the two allied armies, while Napoleon, with the bulk of the French army, was fighting one of them, — the Prussians. The effect of the afternoon's fight at Quatre Bras was that Napoleon had the Prussians all to himself.

In two respects, however, the results of this day were far less than they should have been. The presumption and ignorance of that staff officer who, carrying a despatch to a general commanding an army, — for that was the position of Ney when commanding the isolated left wing, — took upon himself to show it to a division commander *en route* for the headquarters of his corps, before showing it either to the corps commander or to the marshal, altered the whole course of the campaign. Had this not happened, — and I need hardly remind you that for this wretched blunder no one but the staff officer himself is even remotely to blame, — Ney would without question have badly defeated the forces under the Duke of Wellington by four in the afternoon. With 40,000 men he could have inflicted upon them a crushing defeat, and, judging from the vigorous and skilful manner in which he conducted the fight with 20,000 men, he would have done so.

The consequences of this might have been twofold.

First: Whether even the Iron Duke would have risked a battle at Waterloo with his motley army, half of whom he thoroughly distrusted, if he as well as Blücher had been beaten in his first encounter with Napoleon, may well be doubted. But if he had decided not to fight at Waterloo, in all probability the opportunity for a combined operation against Napoleon would have passed away, not to return.

Second: If Ney had so thoroughly beaten the Duke as to have been able to have detached one corps by the Namur road upon the rear of the Prussian army, the result would have been most striking. The Prussians in that event could not have retreated on Wavre, could not have fought at Waterloo. Napoleon would have made as brilliant a campaign as he ever made in his life.

I do not think I am overstating the probabilities of the case at all when I say that, had it not been for the unpardonable blunder of that staff officer, Ney would have routed Wellington at Quatre Bras and Napoleon would have routed Blücher at Ligny. As it was, there were times that afternoon when Ney's 20,000 men came within an ace of beating the motley force which the Duke had managed to collect at Quatre Bras. A glance at any map of Ligny will show how impossible it would have been for the right wing of the Prussian army to have extricated itself from its position at Saint Amand with a force coming up behind it on the Namur road.

The fact is that Blücher and Wellington at the outset of this campaign departed from their proper *rôle* as commanders of allied armies.

Blücher, with his customary obstinacy, fought with a sublime disregard of the possibility of being reinforced by his ally. Wellington, unwilling to order his army to Quatre Bras until he knew that his enemy was concentrating at Fleurus, was obliged to fight for hours against great odds, and nothing but his great tactical skill, practiced eye, cool head, and indomitable pluck carried him through. As Chesney says, the Duke "at dark, thirty hours after his first warning, had only present at Quatre Bras three eighths of his infantry, one third of his guns, and one seventh of his cavalry." That d'Erlon did not come up was no thanks to Wellington. We admire the courage of the Prussian marshal and of the English general, but there can be no reasonable doubt that their arrangements were so faulty that they both would have been beaten save for a pure accident. And if they had both been beaten on the 16th, nothing short of a miracle could ever have united their armies again.

LECTURE VII.

WATERLOO AND ST. HELENA.

It has always been a thing impossible to defend or excuse, that the Emperor and his chief of staff did not take proper measures to ascertain the direction of the Prussian retreat after the battle of Ligny. The Emperor, however, although in a generally sound and robust state of health, and with as clear a head as he ever had in his life, was at this time a sufferer from some local maladies which diminished perceptibly his usually unceasing activity. Soult, as I have said before, was too great a personage for the position of chief of staff; he had been too long an army commander himself. Many a younger man who might have been selected would have had all the requisite information as to the retreat of the Prussians ready for Napoleon in the morning. However we may account for it, the only reconnoissance made was made on the Namur road. Yet there was plenty of cavalry; and had reconnoissances been made to the northward as well as to the eastward, there could have been no room for doubt as to where the Prussians were going. The greater part of the Prussian army bivouacked only a short distance in rear of where they had fought, and only started to leave at daybreak. The ignorance, therefore, which prevailed at Napoleon's headquarters as to the whereabouts of the enemy was utterly without excuse. One Prussian corps was at Gembloux at two in the afternoon of the next day. Whether information of this nature is or is not that which a chief of staff ought to procure without special orders, I shall not undertake to say.

There can be no doubt, too, as to the careless confidence displayed by Napoleon on the morning of the 17th. It is true that he always preferred to give his soldiers a rest after a battle. He never called upon them, when he could help it, for continuous labor and daily exposure. But in the emergency in which he then was, everything depended on knowing where the Prussians had gone, whether to their own base of operations, to Liége or elsewhere to the eastward, or to the north, so as to unite with Wellington and fight another battle. Until this was settled, Napoleon had no right to take a moment's repose.

Napoleon, however, on this occasion did not display the indefatigable activity of his earlier years. Pajol having picked up some cannon and prisoners on the road to Namur, it was hastily assumed, apparently, that the bulk of the Prussian army had retreated in that direction. In this belief, the Emperor was unwilling to march against the English with his whole army; he felt that he ought, and that he could afford, to leave a considerable force to harass and follow up the Prussians, as well as to protect his communications in his march on Brussels, in the event of their rallying.

Hence, near noon, he ordered Grouchy to take the third and fourth corps, which had been previously placed under his command, with one division of the sixth corps, the cavalry of Exelmans, and part of that of Pajol, the whole amounting to upwards of 33,000 men, and to pursue the Prussians. He gave him at first verbal orders; but, having shortly afterwards received news that a Prussian corps had been seen at Gembloux, apparently *en route* for Wavre, he sent Grouchy an order which he dictated to Bertrand, who happened to be with him. This order, the existence of which for many years Marshal Grouchy denied, instructs Grouchy to move to Gembloux, and to explore the Namur road. But, though Napoleon undoubtedly supposed that the Prussians had retreated in this direction, he at the same time recognized the possibility of their having fallen back to the north, so as to join the English. Of this he warned Grouchy in this pregnant sentence, which is unquestionably the gist of the whole order:[1] —

" It is important to find out what the enemy

[1] See Appendix VII.

(Blücher) is intending to do; whether he is separating himself from the English, or whether they are intending still to unite to cover Brussels or¹ [and] Liége in trying the fate of another battle." Liége is coupled with Brussels in this connection simply as an alternative supposition: if Brussels was to be covered, the Prussians must unite with the English; if Liége was to be covered, the English must unite with the Prussians. It might be that the two armies were to be separated; if so, so much the better. If, on the other hand, they were to try to unite, it would be to cover either Brussels or Liége. Any way, it was for Grouchy to ascertain their intentions.

The Emperor had already told Grouchy very explicitly, what he himself was going to do, as Grouchy informs us: "I am going to reunite to the corps of Marshal Ney the troops I carry with me (*i. e.* the sixth corps and the Guard), to march upon the English, and to fight them, if they will stand this side of the Forest of Soignes," *i. e.* anywhere to the south of Brussels.

These dispositions being made, the army at Fleurus breaks up: Grouchy takes the third and fourth corps to Gembloux; the Emperor carries the sixth corps and the Guard towards Quatre Bras, there joining Ney with the first and second corps. The English, slowly and in excellent

---

[1] This order was dictated, not written, by the Emperor; doubtless the "et" should have been "ou."

order, retire through Genappes to their chosen position just to the south of the little village of Mont St. Jean.

The Emperor, many critics have thought, ought to have employed the morning in attacking the Duke's forces at Quatre Bras. It is urged that, on the morning of the 17th, the Prussians were certainly out of reach, and the English could with equal certainty be got at. This criticism seems sound. The Emperor, however, may have thought that his troops were too fatigued for a battle on the 17th; that he would be able to deal the English a much more telling blow on the next day; and that Grouchy's two corps would be abundantly able to stave off any interference by the Prussians, even if they would not be able to join him in an attack on the English. Hence, perhaps, the apparently unnecessary delays of the morning. But I am free to say, the Emperor seems to me to have thrown away a great opportunity.

Napoleon, it must be remembered, would never have divided his army in this way had he learned, as he ought to have done on the morning of the 17th, the direction which the Prussians had taken. Blücher, although badly hurt by having been unhorsed and in fact ridden over in a cavalry charge at the close of the battle of Ligny, was still full of fight; and his able chief of staff, Gneisenau, issued orders for the whole army to retreat north upon Wavre, from whence to march to the assistance of the English, who had agreed to fight at Waterloo, distant some ten miles only. This movement upon Wavre, it is plain, could not be hindered by anything Napoleon could now do, even if he had known it early in the morning. It would have been well enough to have sent a division of cavalry to watch the Prussians; but had he known the facts that morning, he would never have separated his army into two portions, — he would either have attacked the English at Quatre Bras at once, or he would have carried the whole army with him to the position in front of Mont St. Jean. From Napoleon's neglect to ascertain the facts, therefore, arose the wholly unnecessary, and in fact very hazardous, action of dividing his army.

When Marshal Grouchy arrived at Gembloux that evening, he found that a large part of the Prussians had retired on Wavre; and at ten o'clock in the evening he wrote a despatch, which might well have assured the Emperor that his interests on the right would be intelligently taken care of. In this letter he says that he has ordered General Exelmans to push six squadrons on Sart à Walhain, a village to the north of Gembloux, in the direction of Wavre, and three squadrons on Perwez, a village to the east of Gembloux, in the direction of Liége, and then says: —

"If the mass of the Prussians retire on Wavre, I shall follow it in that direction, in order that they may not be able to gain Brussels and to separate them from Wellington.

"If, on the contrary, my information proves that the principal force of the Prussians has marched on Perwez, I shall direct myself by that city in pursuit of the enemy."

When, about midnight of the 17th, the Emperor got this letter, he may well have felt easy in his mind. If the Prussians had gone to Perwez, they were of course going to Liége, and they would not trouble him at all. If, on the other hand, they had gone to Wavre, Grouchy had said that he would follow them in that direction, so as to separate them from Wellington. Now he could not possibly manœuvre with the intention of separating them from Wellington, who was on the Brussels pike, without approaching the main French army under Napoleon; such a manœuvre must be made between Wavre and the main army. To manœuvre in the direction of Wavre, therefore, necessarily implied Grouchy's approaching the main army during the course of the succeeding day; and if he could do anything to separate the Prussians from Wellington, so much the better. As for his preventing them from gaining Brussels, that was plainly impossible; but by operating on the right of the army under Napoleon, he would at any rate prevent their troubling him, and he might even hinder their crossing the river Lasne and joining the Duke.

Before two o'clock in the morning of the 18th Grouchy had ascertained that the Prussians had retired on Wavre, and at that hour he wrote to the Emperor that he was going to Sart à Walhain, which is in the direction of Wavre, and not in that of Perwez. He must therefore have made up his mind that their object was to join forces with the English. Whether this junction would take place to the south of Brussels or not was comparatively immaterial; in any event, it was exceedingly doubtful if it could be prevented; but the course for Grouchy to take was plain enough, — it was to march as quickly as he could towards the main army under the Emperor. His force was the right wing of that army; it was clearly for him to get as speedily as possible between it and the Prussians. The Prussians were at or beyond Wavre, not ten miles from the position where the Emperor had told him he expected to fight the English; he was at Gembloux, more than twenty miles away. There was no time to be lost. Any delay might bring upon Napoleon the pressure of both the allied armies.

All this is very simple; indeed, Grouchy seems at ten o'clock in the evening to have seen it plainly enough. But forgetful, apparently, of his expressed intention contained in his letter of that hour, of manœuvring in the direction of Wavre in such a way as to separate the Prussians from Wellington, he in his two o'clock in the morning despatch announces, as we have seen,

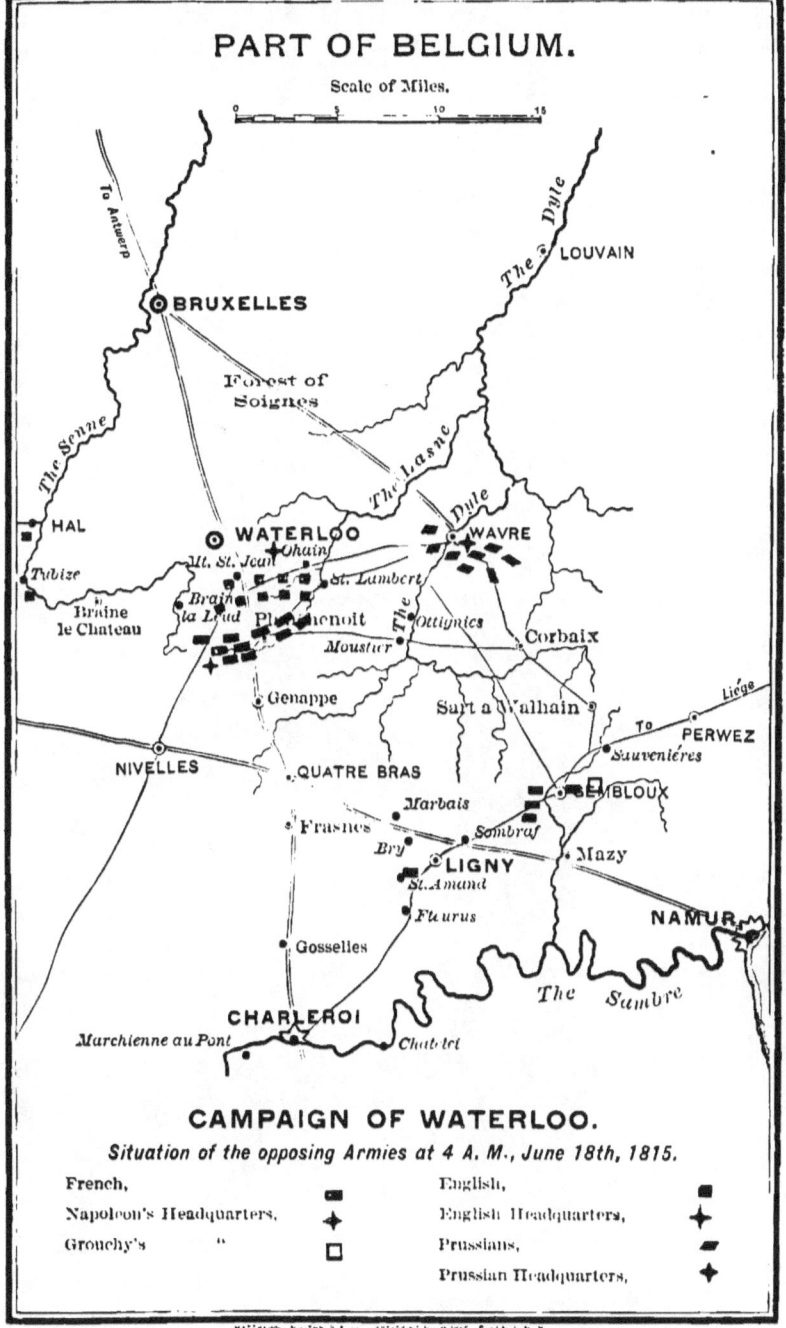

his intention of going to Sart à Walhain, a step which most unnecessarily increased the distance between himself and the turnpike. Grouchy, in fact, instead of marching so as to separate the Prussians from Wellington, proposes to march in such a direction that they will be separating him from Napoleon. Had Grouchy, when, at two o'clock in the morning, he definitely ascertained that Blücher had retired on Wavre, given orders for his troops to march at four o'clock, that is, at sunrise, with all speed, by the country roads, of which there are plenty thereabouts, straight for the bridge of Mousty, he would have crossed the Dyle by twelve or one o'clock at furthest. He would have been able with his two corps to hold the defiles of the Lasne so as in all probability to have prevented the Prussians from taking part in the battle that day. As it was, he did not start till seven or eight o'clock in the morning, and then marched towards Wavre by way of Sart à Walhain, without apparently a thought that this was not the way either to keep the Prussians separated from the English, or, in case that should be found impracticable, to rejoin Napoleon and prevent his being overwhelmed by both armies. He had plenty of cavalry with him, but he never seems to have thought of sending out reconnoitring parties on his left; still less of maintaining frequent communication with the Emperor. Worse than this: while he was taking his breakfast at noon at a gentleman's house near Sart à Walhain, there came across the intervening miles of field and farm the ominous roar which told him that the battle in which Napoleon's fate was to be decided had begun. With the aid of the people of the place, the situation of the contending armies was located with sufficient precision. Gérard, who commanded the fourth corps, urged vehemently that they should march at once to the sound of the cannon. It was the obvious thing to do, and it was a matter wholly in Grouchy's discretion. He had received no orders, as some writers have ignorantly said, to go to Wavre; and the only written order that he had received had warned him in so many words of the possibility of the Prussians uniting with the English to cover Brussels in trying the fate of another battle. That battle he now knew had begun. Could he prevent their uniting with the English by persisting in the course he was now pursuing? On the contrary, if he should succeed in driving them from Wavre it would only be to drive them nearer to the English. The only course to take — and it was, unfortunately, too late in the day to hope that much good would result from it, but still it was the only thing to do — was to march to join the Emperor as fast as his men could go. That, at any rate, might avert a catastrophe; and something more than this, while it could not perhaps be reasonably expected, still might be hoped for. Yet Grouchy, influenced to a certain extent, it is to be feared, by irritation at the temper which Gérard manifested, determined not to yield to his advice, and pursued his useless march northward to Wavre, where he occupied the afternoon in attacking the corps of Thielmann. As I said before, the Emperor's inconceivable recklessness in trusting a man like Grouchy when he might have had Davout, cost him dear.

To return now to the field of Waterloo.

The two armies which found themselves face to face with one another were nearly equal in numbers. But that of Napoleon was not only somewhat stronger than that of his opponent in numbers, but was a far better army, taken as a whole. The Duke, who, still possessed by the notion that Napoleon intended to turn his right, had sent 18,000 men off to Tubize and Hal, had with him not more than 30,000 English troops, including the King's German Legion; of the rest of his 68,000 men, he may have placed confidence in some 15,000 to 20,000 more, but the remainder he rated very low. He had agreed to fight at Waterloo, therefore, only on the assurance which Blücher had solemnly given him that he would send him one or two of his corps by noon at furthest. Had it not been for this assurance, Wellington would not have thought of risking a battle, especially as, for anything that he knew, Napoleon had united his entire force against him. He probably had heard nothing of two corps being sent off under Grouchy to pursue the Prussians.

The Duke, accordingly, prepared for a purely defensive battle. His arrangements were, as they always were, very carefully and skilfully made for such a battle. He did not, to be sure, strengthen his position by field-works, as the Russians did at Borodino, but he did prepare two well-built and solid farmhouses — one on his extreme right, well known to all the world as Hougoumont, and the other just in front of his left centre, on the Brussels turnpike, also well known as La Haye Sainte — for an obstinate resistance. He distributed his English and other trustworthy troops in such a way as to render a serious break in any part of the line improbable. The position he held was an admirable one for defence. The batteries and first line were posted on a crest, from which the ground sloped in front gently down. Behind the crest, his second line and reserves could be to a great extent covered from the fire of the French artillery.

It had rained hard during the night, and the fields over which the French must advance in their attack were thoroughly soaked, and hardly practicable for cavalry and artillery, of both which arms Napoleon always made great use. Hence he delayed commencing the action till half past eleven o'clock. In thus postponing the battle, he relied, of course, on Grouchy's intervening between the main army and the Prussians in case the latter should attempt to assist the English. He supposed that he was going to have the English all to himself, and, in this supposition, he delayed operations until the ground would admit of the free employment of his whole force. He had with him, as we know, the first corps, which had not yet fired a shot, three divisions of the second corps, the fourth having been left at Ligny to guard the wounded and preserve the communications, two divisions of the sixth corps, the Guard, and several fine divisions of cavalry, — in all 72,000 men. In artillery the army was very strong. He entrusted to Ney the handling of the first and second corps, and retained the Guard and the sixth corps in reserve.

At half past eleven the battle was begun by the second corps making a furious assault upon Hougoumont. After an hour or two the orchard and a part of the garden were carried, but the English still held the château, nor could the French drive them out.[1]

This attack, however, was not the one on which the Emperor relied to win the battle. His main operation was a movement to turn the Duke's left. The first corps, massed in deep columns, and accompanied by a heavy force of artillery, advanced from its position to a ridge somewhat in front of it, where the guns were posted. The infantry then advanced rapidly on the allied line.

---

[1] An extension of the French left, which would have secured a position from which artillery could have demolished the orchard wall and even the château, seems to have been deemed impracticable.

The attack was gallantly made, but it was resisted with the admirable steadiness and coolness of British soldiers. While d'Erlon's columns were crossing the valley, they suffered terribly from artillery fire, and on their arrival on the English position they were staggered by a brisk and well kept up musketry fire which hindered their deployment into line. Seeing their unsteadiness and confusion, Sir Thomas Picton, who commanded the English left wing, orders his men to charge them with the bayonet: they are thrown back into the valley, and while endeavoring to straighten themselves out are fiercely charged by the Royal Dragoons, Scots Greys, and Inniskilling Dragoons. Many prisoners are taken, gunners and artillery horses sabred, and several guns rendered useless. The main attack of the first corps has been a complete failure. A gallant attempt to carry La Haye Sainte has also been completely repulsed.

The English, however, had suffered severely. Especially in the death of Picton, a very able and experienced officer, who was killed in this affair, a great loss was sustained. Moreover, the Hanoverian and Dutch Belgian troops on this part of the line had become a good deal demoralized. The English cavalry, also, which had done good service on both sides of the turnpike, had allowed themselves to be carried away in their impetuosity, and had been very badly cut up, when near the main French position; being charged, when their horses were blown, by fresh bodies of French cavalry. The English left, deprived of its gallant commander, and having suffered severely in every way, was open to another and more dangerous attack.

After a while, d'Erlon succeeded in re-forming his corps; his skirmishers in large numbers covered the front of the English position east, and for a short distance also west, of the turnpike. The Emperor was about to make another attack on the English left, in which he intended that the first corps should be supported by the sixth.

Before the attack of the first corps, which we have briefly narrated, was made, the Emperor had perceived, far to the northeast, what appeared to be a column of troops. Cavalry had been at once sent out, and they now reported that it was the Prussian corps of Bülow, approaching from Wavre. Under these circumstances Napoleon detained the sixth corps, and ordered Lobau, its commander, to take position in front of Planchenoit, and protect the right of the army.

Napoleon was now fighting two battles. He was fighting the army under the Duke with the four divisions of the first and three (of the four) divisions of the second corps, containing now not much more than 28,000 infantry. He was fighting the Prussians with two (of the three) divisions of the sixth corps, containing perhaps 7,000 infantry. For the present, at any rate, Lobau could keep the Prussians back. But unless the infantry of the Guard should be put in, it was plain that Ney, who was in general charge of the main attack on the Duke of Wellington's army, which still contained some 40,000 infantry, would not have a sufficient force of infantry to carry the enemy's line at any point. To put in the reserve at this stage of the action was certainly a step to be avoided, if possible, but without more infantry the position could not be carried.

Napoleon, however, decided to allow Ney to try the effect of cavalry. And for some reason, which is not known, that officer directed this attack, not against the already enfeebled left wing of the Duke's army, but against its centre; that is, on that part of the line which is between Hougoumont and the turnpike, where the English infantry, though they had been exposed to the fire of artillery, had not as yet suffered greatly, and were still in perfect order.

Accordingly, the French cuirassiers and lancers advanced gallantly across the plateau upon the English and Dutch squares. But they failed to break one of them. Surrounding them, trying in vain to find or to make an entrance, they were themselves subjected to a heavy musketry fire, and finally, as might have been expected, retired without having made any impression. Again and again was the charge renewed, but when the waves retired, the rock was still there. This series of cavalry attacks lasted some two hours, and greatly exhausted the cavalry engaged in it. In fact, Ney, in his impetuosity and irritation, had even employed without orders the heavy cavalry of the Guard,[1] so that at the close of these attacks the French army was left without any really formidable cavalry force for use in an emergency.

Still, the English infantry lost heavily during this period of the battle; not, to be sure, from the cavalry, but from the artillery and skirmishing fire which was steadily kept up while the French cavalry were not actually riding upon them. It was often impossible to tell when the cavalry charges were impending; the regiments did not dare to break their squares and lie down; they remained hopelessly exposed to the fire of the French skirmishers, to which in this formation they could make no adequate return, while the round shot from the crest of the French position ploughed through their ranks. Thus the effective strength of the centre of the British army was greatly diminished by six in the afternoon.

On the English left, too, the artillery and skirmish fire of the first corps had been very destructive. It is certain that many of the foreign regiments in the Duke's army were pretty well exhausted, not to say demoralized, while many English regiments were fearfully reduced.

Shortly before four o'clock Ney made another

---

[1] See Appendix VIII.

effort to possess himself of the farmhouse of La Haye Sainte. This time he succeeded; the battalion of the King's German Legion, which under Major Baring had heroically defended the post, having exhausted its ammunition. This capture greatly encouraged the French. It carried with it also certain very important advantages. Under cover of the ground thus captured, guns were placed which enfiladed the allied line, and caused destruction among the English batteries on the crest. The French cavalry could be concealed behind the bluffs near La Haye Sainte, ready to throw themselves upon any unlucky regiment which, to free itself from the cloud of skirmishers which were annoying it, might venture to deploy from the square formation into line. Instances of this happened. Everything combined to induce a general feeling of danger and insecurity on this part of the Duke's position. In fact, there was at one time an actual gap in his line, behind La Haye Sainte and a little to the westward of the turnpike, to fill which the Duke brought over from his right portions of his reserves. In spite of this, however, this part of the line was very weak. For an hour and more after the capture of La Haye Sainte, though no organized attack was made on the Duke's army, it was probably suffering more than its antagonist from the causes which have been just pointed out.

Meanwhile Bülow, who, from ignorance on the

part of the French staff, probably, of the nature of the miry and marshy lanes through which he would have to march, had been permitted without molestation to approach the village of Planchenoit, had about half past four o'clock marshalled his corps of 30,000 men and attacked the two divisions of the Count de Lobau. The affair went on with varying success. The village was taken and retaken. Both sides fought obstinately. The Emperor was obliged to reinforce Lobau from time to time from the Young Guard. Finally, about half past six, the Prussians seemed to be definitely driven back; and though the troops which had been used against them could not, of course, be withdrawn for service against the English, still the pressure on the right flank and rear of the French army was for the time being, at any rate, relieved.

In this state of affairs, Napoleon determined to make one more effort to drive the English from the plateau. He still had left just one half of the infantry of the Guard, twelve battalions, say 6,000 men. The remaining twelve battalions had been sent to reinforce Lobau against the Prussians. Orders were sent throughout the whole line to redouble the fire of the artillery, and that the troops of the first and second corps should take part in this general assault on the depleted and, as Napoleon supposed, demoralized line of Wellington's motley army.

Before this attack could be organized, however, it was evident that Prussian troops had joined the English left. The extreme right of the first corps was driven in. Ziethen's corps had in fact arrived. About the same time, also, Bülow was reinforced by the leading division of the corps of Pirch. Nothing was heard or seen of Grouchy and the two corps that were with him. The position of the army thus became, in a moment, critical in the extreme. The French were now outnumbered by at least 50,000 men. It was half past seven o'clock; dusk was coming on. There was, however, still time enough, and there were still troops and guns enough to maintain the right flank of the army against the Prussian attack, which was the real danger, if Napoleon had been willing to accept the situation, to cease taking the offensive, and to dispose his batteries, supported by his reserves, in an attitude of defence. The first and second corps could now be retired in good order behind the guns which faced the English army and commanded the intervening ground. The Guard, which contained at least 12,000 excellent infantry, and the sixth corps ought, properly posted, to have been able to hold the Charleroi road against the Prussians. There were still some thousands of cavalry, a good deal used up, to be sure, but preserving perfectly their organization, and capable of doing good service, if necessary. There was every reason to believe that the army could hold its own against the brief attack, which, at this late hour, was the only thing to be feared. All this would be changed if the proposed attack on the English line should be made and should be unsuccessful. In such an event, not only would the last reserves be sacrificed, but the army would be taken in flank when engaged in making a forward movement, and no well-organized plan of resistance could be formed or executed.

Nevertheless, Napoleon ordered a portion of the Guard to attack the English right centre. He probably selected this point because it would be out of the way of the Prussian troops, which were now coming up on the English left. As we have seen, this attack was to be supported by the infantry of the first and second corps, but the cavalry do not appear to have been expected to support it. Nor was there any general advance of the batteries ordered, as was generally done when Napoleon was making a final charge. It is not easy, in fact I do not know that it is possible, to ascertain precisely what happened in this last charge of the Imperial Guard. There are said to have been two bodies of them, — but this is not probable. Crossing the valley in their usual style, in column, in order to arrive as quickly as possible on the further side, and gallantly receiving the hot fire of artillery which was poured upon them, they were staggered and brought to a halt by a heavy flank fire from the fifty-second and other regiments, which they returned. The English foot-guards opened on the head of the column, which fell back in disorder. Then the fifty-second and other regiments charged them in flank, and the Guard broke in confusion, and was pursued even across the Charleroi road. All this took some time; and, in the interval, the right of the army had felt the full force of the attack of the Prussian corps of Ziethen. Everything was giving way. It needed but for the Guard to retire to convince the common soldiers that the game was up. The men of d'Erlon's corps were the first to break, being taken unawares and in flank. In vain Napoleon disposes the few battalions of the Guard which remain to him in such a way as to form rallying points. It is too late. On the right the Prussians break in like a torrent, and on the left Wellington, seeing the Guard retire, discerns his opportunity with the sure eye of an able soldier, and orders his whole line to advance. His reserve cavalry, — for he had with great judgment retained some fresh brigades, — panting for their share in this glorious day, bear down everything before them. The fifty-second and other veteran English regiments, which had also been husbanded as much as was possible during the fight, drive the isolated battalions of the Guard from place to place, until even these redoubtable veterans are crushed by weight of numbers. The army is in full retreat. Napoleon himself, unwilling for a long while to see the

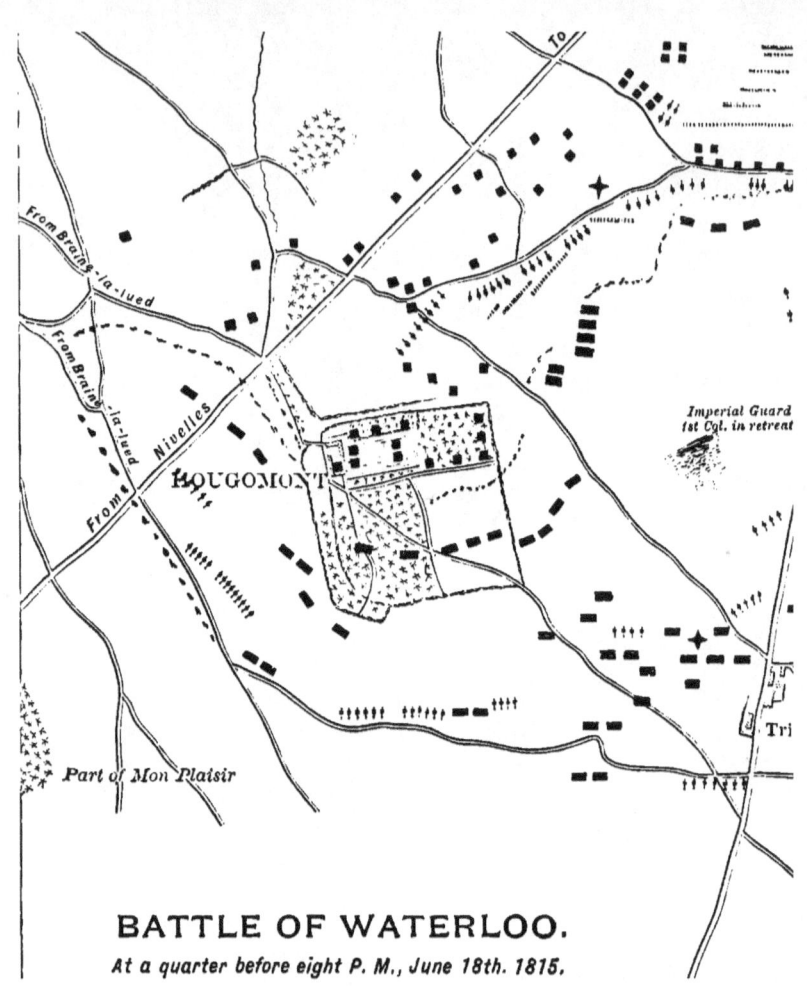

BATTLE OF WATERLOO.
At a quarter before eight P. M., June 18th. 1815.

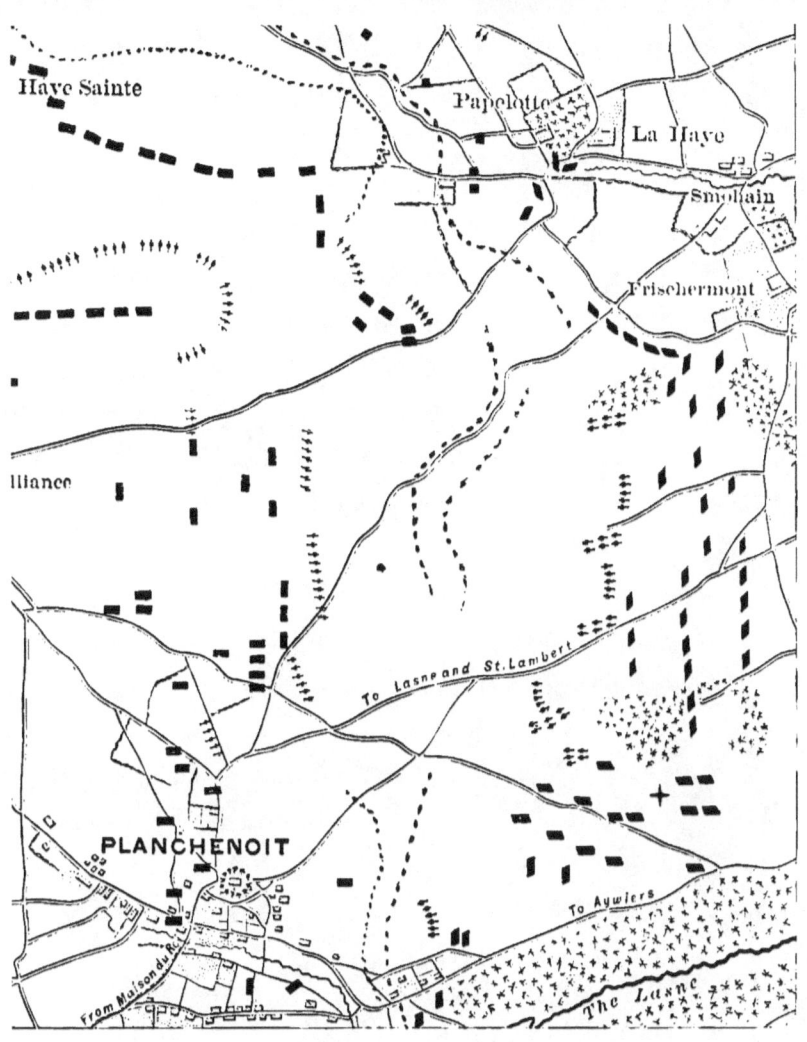

facts as they actually were, after staying in one of the squares of the Guard until his escape becomes very problematical, is persuaded to quit his last field. The pressure of the Prussians on the right flank, resisted so long and so heroically by Lobau and the Young Guard, finally overcomes everything. There is nothing for the army but immediate flight. This is effected in great disorder, according to all the accounts. Nevertheless, not many prisoners were taken besides the wounded; and a large part of the artillery was brought off and carried as far as Genappes. Here the retreating troops had to cross a little bridge over the Dyle. An effort was made to defend the place. But the Prussians were too quick in their pursuit, and most of the guns had to be abandoned. The army had lost at least 30,000 men, and, what was more, it had undoubtedly lost confidence and morale to a great degree.

Such was the famous battle of Waterloo. It has become the synonym for utter defeat. Yet it was lost by the greatest captain of the age. The world has never ceased to wonder how such a terrible catastrophe overtook a soldier of such ability and experience. Volumes upon volumes have been written, explaining, criticising, defending, attacking, Napoleon's management of this campaign. We have followed its course in sufficient detail to be able, I think, to understand these criticisms.

But before we approach them let us pause to admire the loyalty and steadfastness with which Wellington and Blücher stood by each other in the trying days of the 17th and 18th of June, 1815. Wellington, coolly remaining at Quatre Bras until he should ascertain beyond a peradventure what Blücher intended doing; then trusting himself and his army to the issue of a battle in which he knew he should at the outset be outnumbered and outfought by the army which, superior in numbers and *moral*, Napoleon was sure to bring against his miscellaneous command; obliged to wait for the help which had been promised him until nearly the close of that terrible series of assaults; fighting with cool and resolute determination; and, backed up by his own English officers and men, successful in holding his unstable allies to the position he had chosen, receives and deserves all honor. Blücher, defeated at the outset of the campaign; disappointed in not obtaining the expected assistance of his ally, yet determined one way or another to carry out the original plan; unhesitatingly incurring the risk involved in abandoning direct communication with his base of supplies; inspiring his beaten troops with new ardor, and rewarded by a success beyond his hopes, commands the admiration of all who appreciate the real soldier's spirit.

The decision of the two commanders, made on the morning of the 17th, to unite their forces at any risk, involving, as it evidently did, great danger, especially for the Duke's army, but yet justifiable as giving them their best chance of winning the game, has always received and deserved unqualified commendation.

Still there is no justification for Wellington's leaving those 18,000 men at Tubize and Hal during that hard-fought day.

Reviewing now, briefly, the facts: —

Up to the night of the 16th, Napoleon had decidedly the advantage over his antagonists. Though the attack of his left wing under Ney at Quatre Bras had not met with the decided success which would have attended it, had not an unprecedented blunder prevented the coöperation of d'Erlon's corps in the action, yet the English general had been utterly unable to lend a single regiment to his ally, who had been defeated almost under his eyes. Then the battle of Ligny, though it had not been a victory of the first class, yet had been a decided success.

The unaccountable neglect of Napoleon and his staff to ascertain the direction in which the Prussians had retreated, followed, as it was, with a mistaken conjecture on his part as to that direction, and an unpardonable tardiness in taking any measures for pursuit, gravely imperilled the success of his plans. Had the facts been known, as they unquestionably might have been known and ought to have been known, by eight in the morning of the 17th, Napoleon would not have divided his army, — he would have carried it all with him to the field of Waterloo; and, supposing everything else to have happened as it did, he would have been able to hold the crossings of the Lasne with 20,000 men, if necessary, while he threw the rest of his army, which would have numbered 85,000 men, upon Wellington's position. The result, no one can doubt, would have been a complete, an overwhelming victory for Napoleon.

For this neglect in not ascertaining the direction of the Prussian retreat, Napoleon is, of course, directly or indirectly, to blame. Nor did he make up for this neglect by a sagacious divination of his adversary's intentions. On the contrary, he was here utterly at fault. In consequence of this double failure, his not ascertaining the truth and not guessing it, he divided his army. His third mistake was the delay in starting Grouchy. This was wholly his fault, and there is no excuse for it. It added greatly to the chances against success.

But this has nothing to do with Grouchy's responsibility for his own conduct. Had Marshal Grouchy, when, at two or three in the morning of the 18th, he ascertained the northerly direction of the Prussian retreat, acted with common sense and promptitude, the battle of Waterloo might, and probably would, have been won by the Emperor. Had Grouchy been clear-headed enough to see that the all-important thing for him now was to get between the main army and the Prussians; had he marched at daylight, as fast as he could go, for the bridge of Mousty, sending out his cavalry to ascertain what the enemy was doing, I cannot but think that he would have been able to cross the Dyle without serious molestation, and to have established communication with the main army by or soon after twelve o'clock. Had he done this, it is hard to see why, with such a reinforcement, Napoleon could not have been free to employ against Wellington's army the entire force which he had brought with him; and I think that no one who has studied the events of the battle carefully, especially in the extremely valuable narrative of Sir James Shaw-Kennedy, who was in the best position to know the state of the Duke's army during the battle, can doubt that if the 16,000 infantry, whom Napoleon was compelled to withhold from the main attack on the English army and to use against the Prussians, had been employed against Wellington's enfeebled British and demoralized foreign regiments about the time when La Haye Sainte was captured, the Duke would have been defeated.

Before dismissing the subject of Marshal Grouchy's conduct, I must say a few words about the two despatches which Soult sent him during the day. Several writers have maintained that these despatches show that Napoleon himself shared in the mistake which Grouchy made in moving direct to Wavre, and in not marching so as to place himself between the Prussians and the main army under the Emperor.

In the first of these despatches, which is dated on the field of battle, and was written at ten o'clock in the morning, Soult acknowledges the receipt of Grouchy's despatch dated Gembloux at ten o'clock the previous evening. He tells Grouchy that the Emperor is about to attack the English army which has taken position at Waterloo. He then says: "Thus his majesty desires that you will direct your movements on Wavre, in order to approach us, to put yourself in the sphere of our operations, and keep up your communications with us; pushing before you those troops of the Prussian army which have taken this direction and which may have stopped at Wavre, where you ought to arrive as soon as possible."

This first despatch was not received by Grouchy till four o'clock in the afternoon, when he was seriously engaged at Wavre.

The second despatch was dated at one o'clock in the afternoon. It acknowledges the receipt of his despatch of two o'clock in the morning, announcing that he was going to Sart à Walhain. "Your intention, then," says Marshal Soult, "is to go to Corbaix and Wavre. This movement is conformable to his majesty's arrangements which have been communicated to you. Nevertheless, the Emperor orders me to tell you that you ought always to manœuvre in our direction, and to seek to come near to our army, in order that you may join us before any corps can put itself between us. I do not indicate to you," Soult goes on to say, "the direction you should take; it is for you to see the place where we are, to govern yourself accordingly, and to connect our communications, so as to be always prepared to fall upon any of the enemy's troops which may endeavor to annoy our right, and to destroy them. At this moment the battle is in progress on the line of Waterloo in front of the forest of Soignes. The enemy's centre is at Mont St. Jean; manœuvre, therefore, to join our right." A postscript informs Grouchy that Bülow's corps is seen on the heights of St. Lambert. "So," concludes Soult, "lose not an instant in drawing near and joining us, in order to crush Bülow, whom you will take in the very act."

This despatch did not reach Grouchy till after seven o'clock.

Neither of these despatches was received in season to influence Marshal Grouchy's movements. We do not therefore have to change our opinion of the wisdom or folly of those movements by any view we may take of the contents of these despatches. We are simply considering the charge that Napoleon, as a matter of fact, although Grouchy did not at the time know it, approved of Grouchy's movement upon Wavre.

That he did so approve is inferred from the expression in the first despatch, that Grouchy ought to arrive at Wavre as soon as possible, and from the statement in the second, that Grouchy's movement upon Corbaix and Wavre is conformable to the Emperor's intentions.

But these critics leave out of sight entirely the main body of both despatches. It is true that, in the first despatch, Grouchy is ordered "to direct his movements on Wavre;" but why? "So as to approach us; to put yourself in the sphere of our operations, and keep up communications with us," to use the language of the despatch. It is a necessary implication from this language that if, owing to the occupation of Wavre by the Prussians, the movement prescribed would fail to bring Grouchy within the sphere of operations of the main army, it was for Grouchy, as an independent commander, to undertake some other movement. You must remember that Grouchy had, in his letter of the night before, the receipt of which is acknowledged by Soult in this first despatch, stated his intention of marching either in the direction of Wavre or in that of Perwez, according as his information might show the direction of the Prussian retreat. To move in the direction of Perwez was to separate himself from Napoleon; to move in the direction of Wavre was to approach Napoleon. Hence Soult practically says this: "Your taking the Wavre direction instead of the Perwez direction is all right; do so, by all means; direct your movements on Wavre; but remember that the object of your so doing is in order that you may approach us, that you may put yourself in the sphere of our operations, and keep up your communications with us."

Let any one now take the map and put himself in the position of the writer of this despatch on the Brussels turnpike, and he will see that the object of the movement prescribed, namely, Grouchy's coming nearer to the main army, could not be attained, if the Prussians were at Wavre and disposed to make a stand there, unless Grouchy should operate somewhere between the main army and Wavre. No doubt the despatch might have been written more to the point; but when it was written, Napoleon of course could not know the exact whereabouts of the Prussians. That they had gone from Ligny north towards Wavre he had ascertained from his own observation, as well as learned from Grouchy's letter of the evening before. But that was all he knew. He accordingly tells Grouchy to take the direction of Wavre so as to approach him, but he relies on Grouchy's more exact knowledge of the position of the Prussians to take the best course under the circumstances, to carry out the intention and object of the order, which was that Grouchy should approach the main army.

The question for Grouchy to consider, had he got the order in season, would have been, whether, the Prussians being in force at Wavre, as he had ascertained was the fact, in order to obey the order, he would not have to cross the river, and to operate on Wavre on the west bank. He certainly could not have carried out the direction, so explicit, so emphatic, so reiterated, of approaching the main army and putting himself within the sphere of its operations, without so doing.

The second order contains such precise directions to join the main army that its meaning can hardly be mistaken. But the approval of Grouchy's expressed intention to go to Sart à Walhain, and thence to Corbaix and Wavre, it is not perfectly easy to explain. Probably Soult supposed that that was the best route for Grouchy to take to come near the main army. That Grouchy, instead of approaching the main army, should go through Corbaix to Wavre, to attack a Prussian force posted there, is a course which it probably never occurred to Soult that Grouchy would adopt.

The remaining incidents of the campaign need not detain us long. Grouchy, who finally succeeded in driving the Prussian corps of Thielmann from Wavre, heard the next morning of the defeat of the Emperor, and by skilful management effected his retreat, finally joining the wreck of the main army.

Napoleon left at once for Paris, leaving Soult in command. He doubtless felt that his reign was over. He had chosen, as I said in my last lecture, to give to this war the character of an experiment, instead of the character of a serious and determined struggle, and now the experiment had failed. Of course, he may have thought that all that France was willing to attempt at that time was one brief campaign, that she would not support him in a costly and bloody war carried on in her own territory. But whether it was with this idea that he risked the Belgian campaign, or whether it was that he thought that he saw in the position of the English and Prussian armies a good opportunity for one of his crushing strokes, we do not know. All we know is that the whole struggle seemed to turn in great measure on the success of this one operation.

He found at once, on arriving in Paris, that he could not count on any support by the new legislature. The constitutional party were much more anxious to try their experiments than to defend their country. The people probably would have stood by him, although the apparently rash invasion of Belgium revived memories of other risks taken and other armies lost. By beginning the war by a brilliant offensive operation which totally failed, Napoleon had lost not only prestige, but moral support. Had such a defeat occurred to him when fighting on the soil of France, it would have intensified the patriotism of the people. As it was, it was impossible not to see in the campaign of Waterloo the old and familiar characteristics of Marengo and Aspern, so entirely at variance with the sober and resolute attitude with which a nation encompassed by its foes determines to fight to the last rather than surrender its independence.

It is but just to Napoleon to admit that he frankly accepted the situation. He saw that although he could, by his still great influence among the people and his control over the army, prolong the war indefinitely, there was no reasonable chance of ultimate success. It was no part of his plan to engage France in a bloody and purposeless struggle. He was, very likely, disappointed not to see the representatives of the nation rally around him, press upon him offers of help, and urge him again to take the field. But when he found that people generally had made up their minds that it was useless to continue the contest, he allowed no egotism or vain confidence to obscure his perception of the duty of the hour. That duty was to give France immediate peace. He accordingly abdicated. A provisional government was established, which tried to avoid the necessity of a second restoration of the Bourbons. But the liberal members of Parliament who were engaged in this hopeful project soon found that Wellington and Blücher, now that Napoleon was gone, were not disposed to have anything to do with them, or to listen to any proposals of this nature. Paris, where the army had been concentrated under Marshal Davout, was surrendered by a convention dated the 3d of July, and the army retired behind the Loire. Before long, the whole matter was settled. On the 8th of July Louis XVIII. resumed his throne; and on the 15th of July Napoleon surrendered himself to the British government on board of the man-of-war Bellerophon.

I am not disposed to blame the British ministry for exiling their illustrious prisoner to St. Helena. It certainly would not have been easy to suggest any other disposition of the fallen Emperor. The situation was one of those for which there are no precedents and no laws. Napoleon was in the prime of life. He was a man of inextinguishable energy. He still had, without any possibility of doubt, a great hold on the people of France. Had he been allowed to retain his throne in 1814, as he ought to have been, the question of his exile would never have arisen. But the allies, having most unwarrantably taken upon themselves to force upon France a government other than that of the man she preferred, were obliged, when they had succeeded in their object, to dispose of Napoleon. And there was really nothing else to do with him than to consign him to some distant spot from which he would be unable to escape. For this purpose St. Helena was no doubt as good as any other island.

Napoleon's life at St. Helena is not an agreeable study. No man not a philosopher, and a philosopher too of the most placid and amiable disposition, could possibly have undergone such a sudden and tremendous change in his surroundings and manner of life without showing its bad effects in an irritability, moroseness, despondency, never seen before. In Napoleon all these traits were developed to a greater or less extent, for he was by no means a philosopher. Yet he made many fast friends at Longwood. Those about him became devotedly attached to him. He numbered among his admirers not a few of the good people among the English garrison and residents. He resolutely and with a laudable industry undertook writing commentaries on his own wars. In Gourgaud and Montholon he found most intelligent secretaries; in Las Casas he had a valued and wise friend; with the Bertrands his intercourse was most familiar and intimate. There is after all much in his St. Helena life that it is pleasant to look at.

His treatment by the English government would have been well enough, had it not begun with the exasperating and gratuitous humiliation of denying him his proper title of Emperor.[1] For this unnecessary and indefensible course no apology, even, can be made. Except in this respect, Napoleon's treatment by the English was that accorded to a prisoner of war, who was al-

[1] See Appendix IX.

lowed a good degree of liberty. The expenses of his maintenance and that of his friends were borne by the English government, and while no extravagance was permitted, there was no parsimony shown. As a rule, the English officers treated the prisoner with courtesy and respect. I do not know how it may have been with Sir Hudson Lowe; I have never thought it worth my while to get at the facts of that disagreeable and interminable controversy. There was probably fault on both sides.

Fortunately for the world, the sayings and writings of Napoleon at St. Helena have been in great part preserved. The narratives of his campaigns are always lucid, forcible, and most interesting. As for the mistakes that are to be found in them, and they are many, I am well aware that it is the fashion to call them wilful perversions of the truth. But when we take into account the innumerable multitude of facts which these narratives comprise, and the confessed inability of Napoleon at St. Helena to refresh and correct his memory by official and other papers and by the recollections of his officers, the charge of mendacity has precious little to rest upon. Those of us who have ever made a study of any of our own campaigns, who have endeavored to reconcile the conflicting statements of living actors and the opposing narratives of official reports, will be much more inclined to marvel at the accuracy of Napoleon's narratives than to suspect him of wilful omissions or misstatements. Assuredly, never were accounts so generally correct composed under such serious disadvantages. But the idea of going to such narratives as these, which do not profess to be anything but the recollections of one of the chief actors, which do not pretend to be carefully made up from official and other papers, with the expectation of finding minute accuracy in dates and numbers, is the idea either of a fool or an enemy. No man of sense would be so silly as to expect this accuracy; and he who, on returning from such a quest, parades before the public his discovery of a mistake here or an error there, is a partisan so bigoted that it is not worth our while to spend any powder on him. The St. Helena narratives give us in the main, undoubtedly, the key to Napoleon's plans, the views he entertained, the projects he contemplated. Whenever it is necessary to obtain strict accuracy in details, a historical student will of course consult contemporary documents, instead of any man's recollections.

After a few years of this uneventful and restricted life his health gave way, and on the 5th of May, 1821, he died. On his body were found several scars, showing that he had more than once concealed the fact of a slight wound or contusion from the knowledge of the army. It was, in truth, impossible that he should have entirely escaped the perils of so many battle-fields.

He was buried with military honors, rendered

to him by the British garrison of St. Helena. The spot selected for his grave was a quiet valley. The tomb itself was sheltered by a weeping willow. Shoots of this famous tree have since been planted throughout the world.

Returning now to Europe. The second downfall of Napoleon intensified the reaction against liberal ideas which had been for the preceding two years increasing in violence. In France, the Bourbons returned in a vindictive temper. The leading officers of the army were at once proceeded against. Soult and Grouchy saved themselves by flight. The convention of Paris of the 3d of July, the twelfth article of which provided that no one should be called to account for his conduct during the hundred days, was disregarded, and Ney, though claiming its protection, was tried for treason and executed. It is not to the credit of Wellington that he did not insist upon the king's respecting the terms which had been granted by this convention, the consideration for which was the peaceable evacuation of the capital by a powerful French army. Far otherwise did General Grant act when it was proposed to try the Confederate officers for high treason. By his energetic remonstrances made to his government, he maintained the inviolability of the paroles he had granted. Wellington, on the other hand, pretended that it was not the intention of the article to restrain the French government from acting as it might deem fit, but only to restrain himself and Marshal Blücher from perpetrating any atrocities! Had such a construction been given to the convention at the time, it stands to reason that Davout and Ney and the rest would never have accepted it. They were all in the same boat, and as for the army, it would have stood by them to a man. Paris would have been defended to the last, and thousands of lives would have been sacrificed before it could have been taken. But the position taken by the Duke is obviously absurd. What danger was there that the English and Prussian generals would punish anybody for his conduct during the hundred days? Clearly none whatever. The only danger apprehended — the danger to meet which the article in question was inserted — was that of retribution being inflicted by Louis XVIII. for the support given to Napoleon. The Duke's contention as to the import of the article renders it absolutely nugatory. It is in fact very hard to believe Wellington sincere in the view which he puts forth. Certain it is that he left Ney to his fate, without making even an effort to save him. We are irresistibly impelled to recall Nelson's action towards the Neapolitan prisoners in 1798, when he set the capitulation aside, and had Caraccioli hanged from the yard-arm of an English frigate. But though Wellington would never have touched a hair of Ney's head himself, he nevertheless stood still and saw with complete indifference the articles of the convention brutally violated. Had he chosen to interfere, a word from him would have sufficed. The conqueror of Waterloo could not have been ignored by the restored king, especially when insisting upon the proper effect being given to the terms of a military convention to which he had been one of the principal parties. There is no excuse for Wellington's course in this matter.

On the continent generally there came after the battle of Waterloo a revival of all the old-fashioned notions about legitimacy and privilege. The normal development of liberal ideas in government and legislation in France, Italy, and western Germany was forcibly checked. The influence of St. Petersburg, Berlin, Vienna, was for the time being dominant. In fact, it was not very long before the attitude of the three great reactionary powers became too pronounced even for the English Tories and the French Bourbons. Except, however, in England and France, the reaction (or the "Liberation of Europe," as some good people prefer to call it) had full swing. The series of insurrections and atrocities in Spain, culminating in the armed intervention of France in 1823 to reseat the Bourbons on the throne; the Austrian oppression in Lombardy and Venice; the terrible misgovernment of Naples; the bloody suppression of the Polish struggle for independence, and of the Hungarian contest for ancient rights; the Holy Alliance, — these and many other features of the period which succeeded the fall of Napoleon show what a retrogression had taken place. During all this time Napoleon's fame was steadily gaining. People in western Europe looked back upon the early years of the century, and saw that they had mistaken the transitory repression, the military dictatorship, incident to a state of war, for systematic tyranny, and had been deluded by the war-cries of 1813 into exchanging the fundamentally equal and liberal government of France and the Confederation for the fundamentally unequal and aristocratic government of Austria and Prussia, supported and backed up by the unblushing absolutism of the Russian Czar. They saw that in spite of his faults, in spite of his defects, Napoleon had been the man of the time; that he had understood the needs and the capacity of the people in his day and generation. It was in fact owing solely to the wise and liberal laws which he introduced at so much pains into the countries which had composed the French Empire, that the reaction of 1814 and 1815 did not work a permanent injury to the cause of European liberty.

The just credit due to Napoleon in this great struggle has always been withheld from him by liberal writers. They dwell on his seizure of the supreme power in France on the 18th of Brumaire, on his assumption of imperial dignity, on his despotic and military rule, on his well-known dislike of representative bodies. They fail to see that France at the beginning of this century was wholly unfit for a republican form of government, that her people at that time were, and necessarily must have been, utterly unable to govern themselves; that the only thing that anybody could do for them was to secure to them in permanent institutions the benefit of the immense reforms and changes of the Revolution. This Napoleon did, and this was his great work. To defend France, thus reconstituted, against her foes, both foreign and domestic, it was necessary to consolidate the administrative functions of the government. But this was not to enslave her, but merely to postpone to a more peaceful time her entrance upon the long and difficult course which her people needed for their education in popular government.

What, however, has been refused to Napoleon by liberal writers and historians has always been cheerfully given to him by the people. For, in spite of all the open hostility and the bitter and venomous hate of which Napoleon has been and still is the object, the mass of mankind have always recognized that he was in the main on the right side, and that in him the good cause of our common humanity had a powerful helper. There never was a country over which he ruled, either mediately or immediately, which he did not make a freer and happier country than it was when he took charge of it. Fighting as he was, all his life long, coalition after coalition of the nations of legitimist Europe, he did not neglect to consolidate the newly gained liberties of his country in his Code. It is true that he could not in the turmoil and danger of constant war do much towards even a beginning of representative government. But the important thing was precisely that which he did attend to. Whether all the adult males of a country, or only some of them, and if only some, which, shall exercise the franchise, are questions the answers to which may be exceedingly various, without much affecting people's rights to life, liberty, and the pursuit of happiness. Certain it is that France was deprived by Napoleon of no liberties which her people had ever enjoyed, of no rights which they had ever exercised. Moreover, it was due to his strong arm and wise direction that the fundamental changes which had been brought about by the Revolution were not swept away by an earlier return of the Bourbons.

I do not claim for Napoleon the praise due to a great philanthropist. The honor we pay to a clear-headed, intelligent, enterprising business man, who, being largely interested in manufactures, let us say, undertakes the improvement of a factory-town, who cleans out the filthy dens where the operatives have been wont to lodge, who repairs the defective sewerage, who builds new and convenient houses, who introduces practical reforms into every department of the life of that town, is certainly not the honor which we give to a John Howard or an Elizabeth Fry; yet it is a real tribute of honor nevertheless. If we see such a man opposed and thwarted at every turn by blind conservatism, his efforts at enlightenment and sanitary reform and the elevation of the poor people derided, and attributed to mere selfish greed of money, our sympathies and our good wishes are with that man. We see that he is on the right side in the universal contest of human life and work. Nor do we wonder greatly if we find in him the faults and defects that are peculiar to men of his stamp; if we see with sorrow that in him enterprise sometimes becomes rashness, and resolution verges upon obstinacy; that in his determination to carry through his reforms he is sometimes careless of the rights of others and intolerant of their weakness and folly. Nay more, even if we find him so wilful and so rash that in the end his enterprises fail, and his narrow-minded opponents are able to triumph over him, not even then do we forget that, after all, this man has been the best friend and helper that that town ever had. Our sympathies and our judgment are still with him, and not with his bigoted though more fortunate enemies.

"*Render therefore unto Cæsar the things which are Cæsar's.*" While we do not hesitate to speak with proper severity of Napoleon's reckless course in 1813 and 1814, of his obstinate adherence to a military solution of the difficulties which encompassed his Empire, of his indifference as a soldier to the evils of war, of his forgetfulness as a soldier of his duties as a sovereign, — while we recognize these defects and faults, let us be equally frank in acknowledging his great qualities, — his untiring industry, his devotion to the public service, his enlightened views of government and legislation, his humanity.

I know that there is a short and easy way of disposing of this evidence. It is only necessary to believe that in all his labors he was impelled solely by selfish motives, and all his wise measures, his laborious tasks, his consistent furtherance of humane and liberal legislation, go for nothing in the minds of some people. But I cannot think that such a wholesale mode of disposing of a man's life-work as throwing light on his character and motives, requires any serious refutation. People who accept such a theory as this have made up their minds, and no amount of testimony can convince them. Undoubtedly, Napoleon, in common with us all, had his own interest and advancement in view all through his career. That goes without saying. But if he is to be found guilty of the charge of selfishness in the opprobrious sense of that word, his accusers should be able to point to some instances at least where he preferred his own pleasures or gains or fame to the public welfare. As for his pleasures or his gains, they, as is admitted, never interfered with his public duties. And it would be a task well-nigh impracticable to point out how he could have preferred his own fame to the public good, since it was only in the successful conduct of public affairs that he could make his reputation.

Other unfriendly critics have derived great comfort and support by comparing Napoleon with those distinguished public servants who, like Washington and Wellington, had their well defined duties to perform towards a recognized political superior, and performed those duties faithfully. But this is to commit the blunder of trying the head of a great concern, who is his own master, by the standard applicable to his clerk. The well-marked and intelligible round of duty prescribed to an inferior furnishes no criterion by which we can determine whether his superior fully recognizes his responsibility for the talents committed to his charge, and for the improvement of which he is accountable to no one on earth.

The fact is, the character of Napoleon must to a certain extent be left undetermined. It is not probable, as it seems to me, that it was a strong or deep character; that in him there existed any very definite and solemn recognition of his responsibilities; that his life was a struggle to come up to the requirements of an educated and vigilant conscience. Be it so. Nevertheless, it remains true, that his powers were always at the service of the public; that his efforts as a whole were on the right side; that he was the unsparing foe of tyranny and injustice; and that he did more than any man of his time to relieve the masses of the people of Europe from the burdens which oppression and intolerance had laid upon them, and to open to them the prospects and hopes which under a liberal and enlightened government give to life so much of its enjoyment and value. He must be classed among the friends and helpers of the race.

APPENDIX I.

LECTURE I.

ON NAPOLEON'S OCCASIONAL SEVERITIES.

It is not inconsistent with the views here presented of the character of Napoleon, that we should find him occasionally resorting to measures of extreme severity. Where it seemed to him to be necessary, in order to preserve his army, to suppress dangerous insurrections, or the like, he rarely hesitated to employ what seemed to him the most sure mode of accomplishing his object. It is in this way that we must account for the wholesale execution of the prisoners at Jaffa, most of whom, having been recently released on parole, were found again in arms against the French. In a similar light we should regard the severities which accompanied the final extinction of the insurrections in La Vendée, and those which he recommended his brother Joseph to employ against the fierce and obstinate resistance of the Neapolitan lazzaroni. In this unhesitating employment of force on occasions of this nature, Napoleon much resembled Cromwell.

But this sort of thing does not constitute a man a tyrant, or even a harsh ruler. The stability of society, the welfare of well-disposed citizens, the interests of progress and of liberal government even, may well, in times of turmoil and revolution, be more secure when entrusted to the hands of such a man, than if committed to the charge of one less practical and less inflexible.

APPENDIX II.

LECTURE I.

ON NAPOLEON'S HOLD ON HIS SOLDIERS.

A FEW illustrations of the wonderful hold upon his troops that Napoleon possessed may be not without interest in this connection. Sir Robert Wilson, who served in the Russian army in 1812, in his account of the retreat from Russia says: —

"The atmosphere seemed to be rarefied till it became quite crisp and brittle.

"The enemy, already afflicted by hunger, fatigue, sickness, and wounds, were ill prepared for this new, though always certain calamity. From this time a state of feeling prevailed that denaturalized humanity — a general recklessness pervaded all — a callousness to every consideration but selfish momentary relief, with one honorable exception in favor of the French, who, when captive, could not be induced by any temptation, by any threats, by any privations, to cast reproach on their Emperor as the cause of their misfortunes and sufferings. It was 'the chance of war,' 'unavoidable difficulties,' and 'destiny,' but 'not the fault of Napoleon.'

"The famished, dying of hunger, refused food rather than utter an injurious word against their chief to indulge and humor vindictive inquirers." [1]

[1] *Narrative of Events during the Invasion of Russia by Napoleon Bonaparte, and the Retreat of the French Army,* 1812. By General Sir Robert Wilson, K. M. T. Second edition: London: John Murray, Albemarle Street, 1860, page 254.

To the same effect I cite a touching story from rather an out of the way source: —

"The next morning, after breakfast" [Napoleon had fallen and the allied armies had entered France in 1814], "Dame Prieure, with another Sister, accompanied their guests over the wards of the hospital [at Boulogne]. They stopped at the bedsides of some of the soldiers, many of whom were disabled from old wounds; others, the survivors of the Russian campaign, were still suffering intensely from frost-bites and the amputation of their limbs. Most of them appeared miserably weak and dejected from the pain they had endured and all the hardships they had undergone. Mr. Sidney's daughter observed to one of them,

"'Are you not glad we now have peace? You must be rejoiced to hear that Buonaparte, who had drawn you all from your homes and families, is safe out of the way at last.'

"'Madame,' replied a mere boy of a soldier, who had lost both his feet, 'de qui parlez vous? de notre Empereur?'

"'What,' said the lady, 'do you still call him so?'

"'Certainly,' he replied; 'we would all willingly die for him!' and at the top of his feeble voice, he suddenly shouted out, 'Vive l'Empereur!'

"All the rest in the ward, which was exclusively for soldiers, joined at once in the same cry, and the effect became almost deafening, as those in the adjoining wards united with their comrades in the same hearty demonstration. It was even taken up by the soldiers occupying a higher story, and 'Vive l'Empereur!' resounded through the whole building with wonderful energy by all who were capable of making themselves heard. The poor nuns ran away, stopping their ears, and saying, 'Oh méchants, méchants enfans! Stop your cries; this cannot be allowed.' At last the noise subsided, and quiet being restored, the good Sisters proceeded with their guests to other departments of the hospice."[1]

[1] From *A Hundred Years Ago; or, A Narrative of Events*

A little volume entitled, "Reminiscences of Army Life under Napoleon Bonaparte," by Adelbert J. Doisy De Villargennes, former vice-consul of Italy at Cincinnati (Cincinnati, Robert Clarke & Co., 1884), has recently appeared, from which I make the following citation (pp. 12-18) : —

"After the battles of Eckmühl and Ratisbon, a magnificent avenue leading to the latter city had been totally ruined by the passage of upwards of two hundred thousand men. The Emperor ordered it to be repaired, and a company of infantry was posted at each extremity, with the express command not to allow any one to enter it on horseback. General Vandamme, as well known for his bravery as for the extreme rudeness of his manners, presented himself on his horse at the entrance of the avenue, and was proceeding further, when the sentry on duty, a raw young recruit, came forward and stated the orders he had received. 'General Vandamme passes anywhere,' exclaimed Vandamme; 'get out of the way.' On the soldier's appearing to insist, the general gave him a blow of his whip across the face, cursing his impudence. The young lad, intimidated, was about to yield, when the captain who commanded at the post, and who, walking about, had witnessed the scene, rushed toward the sentry, snatched the musket violently out of his hands, and, running in front of the general, levelled the piece at him, exclaiming, 'General, if you advance one step more I will shoot you like a dog for daring to treat my sentry as you have done.' Vandamme, seeing at once whom he had to deal with, thought it best to comply, and withdrew, muttering a threat to revenge himself on the bold captain.

"An opportunity soon presented itself. General Vandamme, being the temporary governor of Ratisbon, on visiting the different posts, recognized in the officer on duty at

leading to the Marriage and Conversion to the Catholic Faith of Mr. and Mrs. Marlow Sidney, of Cowper Hall, Northumberland, London, 1877, 12mo.

the main guard on the great square of the city, the unlucky
captain who had checkmated him at the avenue. The square
was then swarming with lounging officers of all ranks. Vandamme took no apparent notice of his adversary, but having
fully recognized him, went away without addressing him a
word. Soon, however, profiting by the vicinity of a small
crooked street, such as are almost all streets in Ratisbon, he
suddenly reappeared before the post. The sentry immediately called out the guard, according to regulations when
the commanding general presents himself. The captain
instantly rushed out with the guard, but so sudden and unexpected had been the second visit of the general that a few
minutes elapsed before the ranks were formed and arms
presented. Meanwhile the general, standing motionless, had
waited for this moment; then, giving vent to his brutal disposition, he assailed the unfortunate captain in the most
opprobrious terms, telling him that he was fitter to drive a
herd of hogs than to command soldiers, etc. By this time
a crowd of officers had collected round the spot. The captain, during this painful scene, had sufficient control over
himself to refrain from answering a single word. But, as
soon as his post was relieved, he called on Marshal Oudinot,
the commander of the staff, and, after relating the facts of
the affair, demanded permission to challenge General Vandamme. The marshal, in rather severe tones, refused the
request. On this, the captain (his name was, I believe,
Jollivet, 14th light infantry) did not hesitate a moment, but
aware, as was all the army, how easy of access the Emperor
was, he at once determined on having direct recourse to his
majesty. He accordingly repaired to the pavilion occupied
by Napoleon, demanded and obtained an immediate audience, related in the fullest details both his interviews with
General Vandamme, and concluded with a request for the
same favor which he had vainly solicited from Oudinot.
Napoleon, with his usual affability toward his inferiors, answered: 'Sir, I sympathize with your feelings on this occasion; but you must feel that your demand is inadmissible.

The general officers of the army are to be here to-morrow at twelve o'clock; come at the same hour. Meanwhile, I shall have strict inquiry made; and if, as I do not doubt, your version of the affair is quite correct, I shall require a suitable apology from General Vandamme to you.'

"Punctual to the hour, the captain attended the meeting; and modestly, from the inferiority of his rank, remained behind the circle formed round the Emperor. The conversation, as on such ceremonious occasions, was confined to trivial subjects, and the company seemed preparing to take their leave, when our bold captain, elbowing his way through marshals and generals, stepped into the centre of the circle, and fearlessly addressing the Emperor, said: 'Sire, you vouchsafed to promise me you would demand from General Vandamme, here present, some apology for the undeserved insults which he offered me. I come here in consequence of this promise.'

"Napoleon, without answering the captain, turned to Vandamme, saying: 'General, I have inquired into the facts of this disagreeable affair, and I find that you have most unwarrantably and outrageously insulted an officer who enjoys in his corps the highest character. You owe him a suitable apology, as public as your insult has been, and I insist on your making it here.' 'Sire,' answered Vandamme, 'I must regret having been carried away by passion in my addressing Captain Jollivet; but these gentlemen'— 'That's enough,' exclaimed the captain. 'I am satisfied. Sire, I owe you more than my life. I thank your majesty.' He could say no more; emotion had stifled his voice; he bowed and retired. I have not heard what his subsequent career may have been.

"It frequently happened that sudden acclamations of 'Vive l'Empereur!' stirred the humors of our bivouac fires. This often occurred from the enthusiasm of the soldiers at the recital of some trait in the life of their idolized chief. The first outpouring of such a feeling witnessed by me was occasioned by the animated account of the foregoing incident by a sergeant to a large concourse of soldiers. The strict sense of justice; the generosity of Napoleon toward those who had served well, or toward the families of those who had fallen; his paternal attention to those in hospitals; his severe surveillance over the conduct of contractors for the supply of the troops; the commanding influence which he unaffectedly exerted over his most distinguished generals — all these aroused the enthusiasm of our soldiers at the mere recital of some agreeable trait in the acts of their idol."

Nor can I omit the hearty and enthusiastic tribute from his German soldiers to Napoleon to be found in Niklas Müller's " Liederbuch für die Veteranen der grossen Napoleonarmee von 1803 bis 1814." I quote from Rambaud's " L'Allemagne sous Napoléon Ier," Paris, 1874, pp. 182, 183.

" ' Le guerrier qui a suivi Napoléon sous tous les climats de l'univers,' s'écrie l'auteur dans sa préface, ' le guerrier qui a combattu sous ses ordres en tant de royaumes, qui tant de fois a pris sa part de la gloire et du triomphe, qui a mené cette vie tourmentée, pleine de privations, de souffrances, de fatigues et de dangers mortels, ne peut pas, ne doit pas oublier son grand général. Transfiguré, il continue à illuminer nos heures de joie ; nous lui dédions, ainsi qu'à nos victoires immortelles, de bienfaisantes fêtes commémoratives. Le vétéran s'y rajeunit ; il recherche ses compagnons d'armes, ses fidèles camarades, pour jouir dans leur société de ces douces joies qui surgissent du sein du passé, comme la pierre précieuse des mines de diamants. — Quel souverain pourrait prendre ombrage de voir une telle association fêter les anciennes victoires, jeter un regard ému sur les aigles brisées de Leipzig et de Waterloo, laisser tomber une larme de douleur dans les flots de la Bérésina ? "

" Napoléon, sur le théâtre du monde, a été l'image classique du héros ; mais il était aussi le père des soldats, le fort bouclier de l'honneur. — Le camp, la misère, le danger, la fatigue, il partageait tout en camarade ; il partageait la faim ou la mauvaise soupe et guérissait nos esprits malades. — Quel Charlemagne, quel Otton, quel Alexandre, a fait autant que lui? Tout le monde les nomme grands ; mais *lui* est encore audessus d'eux. — Sous ses étendards victorieux nous avons servi fidèles, intrépides. Son nom ne peut nous rappeler que des sentiments, que des souvenirs, sans cesse nouveaux d'héroisme."

I cannot close this appendix without quoting for my readers the touching poems of Heine and Von Zedlitz. Heine's "Two Grenadiers" is particularly *apropos* of the subject we have been considering. I give it in the translation of the Rev. Dr. Furness of Philadelphia.

THE TWO GRENADIERS.

To France were travelling two grenadiers
    From prison in Russia returning ;
And when they came to the German frontiers,
    They hung down their heads in mourning.

There came the heart-breaking news to their ears
    That France was by fortune forsaken ;
Scattered and slain were her brave grenadiers,
    And Napoleon, Napoleon, was taken.

Then wept together those two grenadiers
    O'er their country's departed glory ;
"Woe's me!" said one, in the midst of his tears,
    "My old wound, how it burns at the story!"

The other said, "The end has come ;
    What avails any longer living?
Yet have I a wife and a child at home,
    For an absent father grieving.

"Who cares for wife? Who cares for child?
    Dearer thoughts in my bosom awaken;
Go beg, wife and child, when with hunger wild,
    For Napoleon, Napoleon, is taken.

"Oh grant me, brother, my only prayer,
    When in death my eyes are closing, —
Take me to France and bury me there,
    In France be my ashes reposing.

"This cross of the Legion of Honor bright
    Let lie, near my heart, upon me;
Give me my musket in my hand,
    And buckle my sabre on me.

"So will I lie, and arise no more,
    My watch like a sentinel keeping,
Till I hear the cannon's thundering roar,
    And the squadrons above me sweeping.

"Then the Emperor comes! And his banners wave
    With their eagles o'er him bending;
And I will come forth, all in arms, from my grave,
    Napoleon, Napoleon, attending."

THE MIDNIGHT REVIEW.

FROM THE GERMAN OF VON ZEDLITZ.

At midnight from his grave
    The drummer woke and rose,
And, beating loud the drum,
    Forth on his errand goes.

Stirred by his fleshless arms,
  The drumsticks rise and fall;
He beats the loud retreat,
  Reveillé and roll-call.

So strangely rolls that drum,
  So deep it echoes round,
Old soldiers in their graves
  To life start at the sound;

Both they in farthest North,
  Stiff in the ice that lay,
And they who warm repose
  Beneath Italian clay;

Below the mud of Nile,
  And 'neath Arabian sand,
Their burial place they quit,
  And soon to arms they stand.

And at midnight from his grave,
  The trumpeter arose,
And, mounted on his horse,
  A loud, shrill blast he blows.

On airy coursers then
  The cavalry are seen,
Old squadrons, erst renowned,
  Gory and gashed, I ween.

Beneath the casque, their skulls
  Smile grim, and proud their air.
As in their bony hands
  Their long sharp swords they bare.

And at midnight from his tomb
  The chief awoke and rose;

And, followed by his staff,
  With slow steps on he goes.

A little hat he wears,
  A coat quite plain has he,
A little sword for arms
  At his left side hangs free.

O'er the vast plain the moon
  A paly lustre threw;
The man with the little hat
  The troops goes to review.

The ranks present their arms,
  Deep rolls the drum the while;
Recovering then, the troops
  Before the chief defile.

Captains and generals round
  In circles formed appear;
The chief to the first a word
  Now whispered in his ear.

The word goes round the ranks,
  Resounds along the line;
That word they give is, — France!
  The answer, — Saint Hélène!

'T is there, at midnight hour,
  The grand review they say
Is by dead Cæsar held,
  In the Champs Elysées!

APPENDIX III.

LECTURE III.

ON MR. HERBERT SPENCER'S USE OF THE "GREAT MAN THEORY OF HISTORY" IN REFERENCE TO NAPOLEON.

THAT the statement in the text is not an exaggerated representation, as some might suppose, of the views of the influential classes in England, may be seen from a passage in a work of Mr. Herbert Spencer's, entitled "The Study of Sociology." (London: Henry S. King & Co., 1874, pp. 156 *et seq.*) In his chapter on "Subjective Difficulties-Emotional," we find all the accusations against Napoleon enumerated, accepted without an instant's hesitation, and dressed out in the most lurid colors. We are told (p. 157) that "it was natural, too, that, in addition to countless treacheries and breaches of faith in his dealings with foreign powers, such a man should play the traitor to his own nation by stamping out its newly gained free institutions and substituting his own military despotism. . . . Year after year he went on sacrificing by tens of thousands and hundreds of thousands the French people and the people of Europe at large, to gratify his lust of power and his hatred of opponents. To feed his insatiable ambition and to crush those who resisted his efforts after universal dominion, he went on seizing the young men of France, forming army after army, that were destroyed in destroying like armies raised by neighboring nations. . . . And all this slaughter, all this suffering, all this devastation, was gone through because one man had a restless desire to be despot over all men."

It would be difficult to find a more striking example of the "great man theory of History," as Mr. Spencer himself in the second chapter of this very book calls it, than in this truly extraordinary passage. All the social, political and legal conditions which made the era of Napoleon an era of conflict, which made such a military career as his possible, are here utterly ignored. All the European powers are quietly assumed to be the inoffensive and peaceful victims of one brutal and ambitious soldier. As Mr. Spencer says in his second chapter (p. 33), in speaking of this "great man theory of History," "the interpretation of things thus given is so beautifully simple, seems so easy to comprehend. Providing you are content with conceptions that are out of focus, as most people's conceptions are, the solutions it yields appear quite satisfactory." No one could make a better criticism than this on Mr. Spencer's simple and forcible presentation of the domestic and foreign policy of Napoleon, which I have quoted above, and I am quite content to leave the matter here, without adding a word of my own.

APPENDIX IV.

LECTURE IV.

THE POLISH QUESTION AND THE RUSSIAN WAR.

The Czar of Russia felt himself to be the representative on the Continent of the old order of things. He had in this capacity unhesitatingly joined the coalitions. He had, to be sure, at last made peace with France at

Tilsit, and had, in fact, entered into alliance with her. But the French alliance was detested by the Russian nobility, and Alexander himself had no heart in it. He had made it because he saw that nothing more could be attempted at that time against Napoleon, — the three Eastern powers being too much exhausted. Besides, he wanted to purchase Napoleon's permission to embark on a career of conquest. And he obtained it. Since the treaty he had attacked the Turks and had annexed Moldavia and Wallachia: he had attacked the Swedes and had annexed Finland. He now coveted Warsaw, and the surrounding territory, formerly Prussian Poland, but now organized as the Grand Duchy of Warsaw. It had greatly annoyed him to see the Duchy enlarged by the greater part of Austrian Galicia, as a result of the Austrian war of 1809. He knew that Czartoriski and other Polish patriots were looking forward to the entire reëstablishment of Poland with the help of France. This he cordially dreaded. The effect of it would be to push the boundary of Russia back to the Dneiper, and to destroy the greater part of her influence in European affairs. At the same time, there was no special reason to suppose that a restoration of Poland was one of Napoleon's schemes. Napoleon, when questioned on the subject, always denied that he had any plan of the kind.

Thus, in front of Alexander stood the Grand Duchy of Warsaw, composed of the Prussian and Austrian shares in the partitions, which might, perhaps, if affairs were skilfully managed, be annexed to Russia; or, on the other hand, if things went wrong, might form the nucleus to which might be added the much larger territory of Russian Poland. The Polish question occupied the chief place in Alexander's thoughts from the beginning of 1810 to the breaking out of the war with France. Various solutions occurred to him. Early in 1810 [1] he consulted Prince Czartoriski on the possibility of organizing Russian Poland as a separate state, of which the Czar of Russia should be the head. But the Prince said that a half measure of this sort would utterly fail to satisfy the national feeling.

In December, 1810,[2] Alexander suggested to Czartoriski the union of the Grand Duchy of Warsaw and the Russian provinces of Poland into a kingdom, having a regular government of its own, but of which the Czar should be the king. This, of course, meant war with Napoleon, for the Grand Duchy was a member of the Confederation of the Rhine. The scheme was, in effect, to annex forcibly the Grand Duchy to Russia, giving the Poles, however, what we now call home-rule. In his letter to the Count, Alexander desires him to ascertain the state of feeling in Warsaw and throughout the Duchy by personal observation. Appended to this letter is an estimate of the forces which the contending powers could bring into the field.

Czartoriski [3] made his investigations, and reported to the Czar that the Poles would not think of such a proposition; that they expected sooner or later to obtain their restoration at the hands of Napoleon.

To this Alexander replied [1] in January, 1811, reiterating the feasibility of the scheme; stating that he intended to offer Austria the Danubian principalities in exchange for Galicia, and should offer some compensation to the King of Saxony, who was the Grand Duke of Warsaw, if he took his side in the war. He also goes over his estimate of his available forces.

[1] *Life and Times of Alexander I.*, Joyneville, vol. ii. pp. 96, 97.

[2] Id. pp. 108 *et seq.*   [3] Id. p. 113.   [4] Id. p. 114.

The most important thing in this letter is the light it throws on the way in which the Czar regarded his relations to France. To attack Napoleon was a mere question of expediency. Alexander says: "It would be a mistake to be the aggressor in present circumstances, — and I shall not make that mistake. But everything changes if the Poles join me. Reinforced by the 50,000 men I should owe to them, by the 50,000 Prussians who might, without risk, also join me, and by the moral revolution which would be the unfailing result in Europe, I might advance to the Oder without striking a blow." Further on he says: "*Till I can be sure of the coöperation of the Poles I have decided not to begin the war with France.*" [1]

Among the results of the war would be, he says, "a complete revolution in the opinion of Europe" and "deliverance from the yoke under which the Continent languishes."

Now observe. The Czar does not pretend to have a *casus belli* of any kind. The Grand Duchy of Warsaw, which he proposes to annex, never belonged to Russia. But if he can settle the Polish question by uniting all the scattered portions of the ancient monarchy under the rule of Russia, and can thereby also assail the Empire of Napoleon with a fair chance of success, and bring about the triumph of the legitimist side in this weary contest, — which is what he means by delivering the Continent from the yoke under which it languishes, — he will not hesitate to commence a war of aggression.

[1] The italics are mine. Id. p. 117.

APPENDIX V.

LECTURE IV.

ON MARMONT'S CRITICISM ON NAPOLEON'S TACTICS IN HIS LATER CAMPAIGNS.

MARSHAL Marmont, in his valuable work entitled "The Spirit of Military Institutions," after speaking of the earlier successes of Napoleon, says: "In 1812, it depended upon his own will to give to the great battle which he fought upon the Moskwa the character of his preceding victories. A simple flank movement would have permitted him to fight the Russian army with much greater advantages. But a decided taste for direct attacks already began to manifest itself in him, a taste for the pleasure of employing force, and a kind of disdain for the concurrence of art and skilful combinations." (Am. Ed., Part III., chapter vii., page 186.)

I doubt this statement. In the first place Napoleon did organize a movement, under Davout and Poniatowski, having for its object to turn the Russian left. It is true the movement was only measurably successful, but that was not the fault of the plan. Very possibly the Russian army might by some other movement have been compelled to evacuate their position at Borodino. But it was the policy of the French at that stage of the campaign to fight a great battle, not to compel a further retreat of the Russians into the interior. As regards Napoleon's alleged taste for direct attacks, the employment of main force, and so forth, it should be recollected that at this period of his career his adversaries did not make the blunders, either strategical or tactical, which were so common in his earlier experience. Battles like Wagram and Borodino are not to be classed with Austerlitz and Friedland. Besides, there was never any falling off in Napoleon's quickness in availing himself of any mistake of his enemy's: witness, for instance, Dresden and Ligny.

APPENDIX VI.

LECTURE V.

ON THE NUMBERS ENGAGED AND ON THE LOSSES IN THE WAR WITH RUSSIA.

CHAMBRAY, in his "Campagne de Russie," in a table annexed to the second volume, gives the following figures, which are taken, Chambray says, from the returns sent to the war department of the strength of each corps at the moment of its passage into the territory of Russia.

Field and Staff	3,983
First Corps, Davout	72,051
Second Corps, Oudinot	37,139
Third Corps, Ney	39,342
Fourth Corps, Eugène	44,798
Fifth Corps, Poniatowski	36,311
Sixth Corps, St. Cyr	25,134
Seventh Corps, Reynier	17,189
Eighth Corps Junot, afterwards Vandamme	17,935
Ninth Corps, Victor, entered Russia in September	33,567
Tenth Corps, Macdonald	32,497
Schwartzenberg	34,148
Guard	47,373
Forward	441,467

APPENDIX VI.

Brought over		441,467	
Cavalry:—			
Nansouty	12,077		
Montbrun	10,436		
Grouchy	9,676		
Latour Maubourg	7,994	40,183	481,650 [1]

Durutte's Division entered Russia in November 13,592
Loison's Division entered Russia in November 13,290

Total as from official returns . . . 508,532
Chambray adds to this total an estimate of troops who, during the campaign, rejoined their regiments 80,000
And for men connected with the grand parks of artillery, engineer corps, etc., an estimate of 21,526

. . . . 610,058 [2]

I think that a deduction of probably ten per cent. should be made from the official total of 508,532
Say 50,853
Thus reducing the official total to . . . 457,679

---

[1] From this total of . . . 481,650
Deduct the Field and Staff . 3,983 477,667
Deduct also an estimate of 10 per cent. for excess of estimate . . . 47,766
Leaving 429,901
Which is slightly below the Duc de Fezensac's total of 447,000
De Fezensac adds for recruits and fresh troops . 53,000
Making a total of 500,000
See Fezensac's *Journal de la Campagne de Russie*, p. 4, note; p. 191.

[2] To this Chambray adds 37,100 for those absent from the ranks, — an estimate to get at what the French call *l'effectif*, which is the total, present and absent. His total, therefore, reaches the enormous figure of 617,158

Brought over	457,679
And as for the estimates, I should think the first altogether too large, probably by one half; let us then add for recruits	40,000
And for extra-duty men, as above	21,526
Making a total of	519,205

In Bourtourlin's Atlas, Tableau No. 1, he puts the total allied force at the opening of the campaign at 525,800 men, but this includes the whole corps of Augereau, of 60,000 men, most of which did not enter Russia. In Tableau No. 20 he puts the actual number that entered Russia during the whole campaign at 554,000 men.

The Russian estimate of the fate of the armies of the French and their allies does not differ materially from this figure. In Bourtourlin's History, vol. ii., pp. 445, 446, it is thus given:—

Killed in battle or died of wounds	125,000
Died of disease, cold, exhaustion, etc.	132,000
Taken prisoners	193,000
Returned	80,000
Total	530,000

General Gourgaud in his Examen Critique of the work of the Count de Ségur, Book XII., chapter iv., gives a higher estimate of those who returned, viz:—

Troops which repassed the Niemen to Kowno on the 15th of December	36,000
Tenth Corps, Macdonald	30,000
Fifth Corps, Poniatowski	20,000
Seventh Corps, Reynier	15,000
Schwartzenberg's	26,000
Total	127,000

I think his estimate of the strength of the Fifth Corps is very wide of the mark. It should be observed that the troops of Macdonald, Reynier and Schwartzenberg had not penetrated far into the country.

Charras, in his "Guerre de 1813," chapter i., gives the numbers as follows: —

P. 5. Repassed the Niemen — 35,000 or 40,000 men, of whom about 26,000 or 27,000 were in good condition.

P. 9-13 — Macdonald — 22,000 to 25,000 men, Schwartzenberg, Reynier, etc., 45,000 to 50,000 men.

Taking the smaller figures, we have: —

Grand army, main column	35,000
Macdonald	22,000
Schwartzenberg	45,000
Total	102,000

APPENDIX VII.

LECTURE VII.

ON THE BERTRAND ORDER.

I HAVE related the history of this Bertrand order in an article published in the "Atlantic Monthly" in June, 1881, entitled "Who Lost Waterloo?" It is certainly a very curious story.

As to the effect to be given to this despatch in any critical estimate of the campaign, it seems to me that it cannot well be exaggerated. In it, the Emperor in effect says to Grouchy that, even although it looks now as if the Prussians had fallen back in the direction of Namur, still it may be that they have not really done so at all, but that they are intending to unite with the English and fight a battle for the defence of Brussels. Yet, in face of this, Chesney[1] says that this letter " serves to show *two things only*,[2] (1), that Napoleon was now uncertain of the line of Blücher's retreat, and (2) that he judged Gembloux a good point to move Grouchy on, in any case."

Nor is Chesney the only English critic who seems to me to underestimate the importance of the warning contained in this despatch. Kennedy, Hooper, Hamley seem to me to be open to this criticism. Hamley, in fact, in his elaborate critique on the campaign in his "Operations of War," does not even allude to the order.

In the first place, they all of them consider the despatch chiefly in reference to Napoleon's conduct of the campaign. Very likely they are right in holding that Napoleon's omissions and delays that morning of the 17th are not redeemed even by the sagacity which warned Grouchy of a possible union of the Prussian army with the English. But they do not stop here. They are so much impressed by the delays and the omissions that they entirely fail to do justice to the Emperor's sagacity in predicting the operation which actually was effected. In the second place, it is quite evident that they have not considered the Bertrand order with reference to Grouchy's conduct, which is a matter with which our praise or blame of Napoleon has, of course, nothing to do. Grouchy at Gembloux during the night of the 17th and 18th, in fact by three A. M. of the 18th, had ascertained that the Prussians had retreated on Wavre, in other words had fallen back upon their allies. He had no specific instruc-

---

[1] *Waterloo Lectures. A Study of the Campaign of* 1815. By Colonel Charles C. Chesney, R. E. Third Edition. London: Longmans. 1874. P. 152.

[2] The italics are mine.

tions, nothing whatever to hamper him in any way. He had no orders to go to Wavre, or anywhere else. The only order which he had, warned him in so many words that the Prussians might perhaps be intending to unite with the English to try the fate of another battle for the defence of Brussels. He had with him two fine corps, between 33,000 and 34,000 men. That under these circumstances he should have marched towards the main army under the Emperor, should have drawn near to it, so that he might have received his orders directly from the Emperor, I submit is too plain for argument.

To judge fairly of the question, whether Marshal Grouchy's movements were what they should have been or not, one must consider it by itself, and not allow one's mind to be confused by dwelling on any previous shortcomings of Napoleon. Stated briefly, then, the case is this: Early on the morning of the 18th of June, Grouchy at Gembloux knows that Napoleon is on the Brussels turnpike expecting to fight the Duke, and that Blücher has retired on Wavre so as to support the Duke. The danger to Napoleon is therefore evident, and pressing. To manœuvre in his direction, keeping the Prussians always on his right, using the large force of cavalry which he had with him to secure the roads and bridges, and, above all, to start at daybreak and to lose no time, was clearly the dictate of common sense.

Whether, if he had done this, he would have interposed his force between the Emperor's army and the Prussians, may perhaps admit of some difference of opinion. I have not time to discuss the question here. I have given my own opinion in the text. Certain it is, that to stop Grouchy in such a march would have necessitated such a complete change in the Prussian programme for the day that the chance of Napoleon's beating the Duke before any considerable force of the Prussians could arrive, would have been very greatly increased, to say the least of it. Probably all will allow that the catastrophe would have been avoided. I am not now speaking of the effect which would have been produced by Grouchy's marching at noon, when he heard the guns, from Sart à Walhain: that is a very different question. I am speaking of Grouchy's marching at daybreak from Gembloux.

A criticism on Napoleon which is made by the distinguished English general, Sir James Shaw-Kennedy, which is adopted by Chesney in his Lectures, and is there said to have been first suggested by Clausewitz, seems to require a brief consideration. I quote from General Kennedy's work: —

"The idea that Grouchy was entirely wrong, that the fault was entirely his, that his bungling or treason caused the loss of the action, cannot be admitted as a portion of authentic history: it has soothed French susceptibilities, and has been employed to give a more favorable view of Napoleon's combinations. In respect to the latter it utterly fails, which may be shown by the following view, which, so far as I know, has not hitherto been brought forward; but which, when stated, must, as I conceive, be a self-evident proposition. The allegation is, that, when at noon Grouchy heard such a cannonade as to indicate that a general action was in progress, he ought to have marched directly to the field of battle. Now, even admitting this to be true, it implies that Napoleon committed the same error in a far stronger and more inexcusable degree. If Grouchy's proper place was on the field of battle at Waterloo, then Napoleon should have sent for him at daylight on the morning of the 18th, when he saw the Anglo-Allied army in position, and determined to attack it. Napoleon knew with positive certainty that a general action was taking place: if, then, the principle was correct that Grouchy should take part in it, why did not Napoleon order him to march upon Planchenoit? Napoleon had positive and certain knowledge of the existence of a general action, and was free to give to Grouchy what orders he chose: Grouchy, on the contrary, only could guess as to the existence of a general action, and, in acting upon a probable supposition, would have done so contrary to his instructions. Now Napoleon not only failed to send any order to Grouchy to march upon Waterloo, when he knew positively that he was about to engage in a general action with the Anglo-Allied army, but even when the action was actually commencing, he caused Soult to write to him, approving of his marching upon Wavre. If then Grouchy violated a principle in not marching to the field of battle, Napoleon violated the same principle, and in an aggravated degree, by not ordering his march upon Waterloo early on the morning of the 18th, and in going the length of approving his march upon Wavre when the battle of Waterloo was actually commencing." [1]

The answer to this is very simple. "Early on the morning of the 18th" Napoleon did not know where the Prussians were, but supposed that Grouchy was looking out for them. Why then should he send for him? Napoleon did not need Grouchy to help him fight the Duke: he knew perfectly well what sort of an army the Duke had, and how small a force of English troops the Duke had with him. The Emperor would beyond a reasonable doubt have beaten that army had he been able to employ his whole force against it. Nor did the Duke himself ever dispute this view. Everybody knows that Wellington took up his position relying on the assurance of Blücher that he should be largely reinforced. If Grouchy ought to have

[1] *Notes on the Battle of Waterloo.* By the late General Sir Sir James Shaw-Kennedy, K. C. B London: John Murray. 1865. Pp. 159-161.

marched to the field of Waterloo, as indeed he ought, it was not because he might suppose his master to be in peril from the army under Wellington, but because he would fear that that army would be strengthened by a large part of the force under Blücher. Had Grouchy been where he should have been, between Napoleon and the Prussians, he would never have thought of marching to the field of Waterloo; for not only would his presence there not be needed, but only by remaining where he was would he be fulfilling his appointed rôle of preventing the Prussians from taking a hand in that fray. For Napoleon, then, to have sent for Grouchy early on the morning of the 18th to help him fight Wellington, when, for anything that Napoleon knew, Grouchy might be ably and skilfully playing his part of keeping the Prussians off, would have been unwise indeed.

As for Soult's order, "approving Grouchy's march upon Wavre, when the battle of Waterloo was actually commencing," I have fully explained in the text that it was written when it was evident to Napoleon that the Prussians were approaching, and that it was, in effect, an order to Grouchy to join the main army at once.

In conclusion, let me say a word on the very unfortunate effect which the political *animus* of Charras, Quinet, and other writers had on their discussions of the subject. These men were not historians at all, properly so called. They wrote for a present political purpose. They were the enemies of the Second French Empire, and they were, in these books of theirs, trying to break down the prestige of the First Napoleon, which, as they supposed, had much to do with the establishment and success of the Second Empire. They were endeavoring to destroy "la légende Napoléonienne." It is true that we owe much to their indefatigable researches, but we must always remember that their object was not the truth of history, but such a version of this campaign as could be made to tell against the Imperialist side in the political controversies of their own day and generation. The worst of it is, that their captious, suspicious, and unfair spirit has to a certain extent infected certain English writers. In fact Captain Siborne, whose exhaustive work on the campaign was written in 1844, in the days of Louis Philippe, is beyond question the most impartial and reasonable English writer on the subject.

A good illustration of this disposition towards faultfinding may be found in Chesney's Waterloo Lectures, (3d ed. pp. 118, 119,) where he is accusing Napoleon of negligence in his management of the left wing of the army : —

"Did he direct that at daylight (of the 16th) d'Erlon should close up his long column on Reille's rear at Gosselies, and be ready for the marching order forward? Were there any signs of pressure or hurry in Ney's morning instructions, or any notion then of a great pitched battle which that marshal was by a flank movement to win for his master? We are enabled to answer all these questions in the direct negative from Napoleon's own authority. The only letter from the latter to Ney, written before the five orders already mentioned [the orders given on the 16th, beginning with the one which assigned him to the command of the First and Second Corps], was merely a formal one, assigning Kellerman's cavalry to the marshal, and inquiring if d'Erlon had completed his movement of the day before and 'what are the exact positions of his corps and Reille's.' Not a word of any urgency, or of preparing to advance by closing d'Erlon's divisions on to the *chaussée* at Gosselies."

Why Colonel Chesney should have approached the

subject, as he evidently did, with the notion that he would find Napoleon's management of the campaign characterized by the carelessness which he attributes to him, I will not pause to inquire. But the fact is, that the movement which Chesney charges the Emperor with having omitted to order, "that at daylight [of the 16th] d'Erlon should close up his long column on Reille's rear at Gosselies, and be ready for the marching order forward," was actually prescribed, — only, instead of its being an order to close up and reach Gosselies at daylight of the 16th, the order was sent at three P. M. of the 15th, and was to be executed at once. The order is to be found in the very valuable work published by the son of Marshal Ney, and entitled "Documents inédits sur la Campagne de 1815." (Paris, 1840, p. 25.) It reads as follows: —

"A M. LE COMTE D'ERLON.
Extrait du registre du major général.
EN AVANT DE CHARLEROI,
A 3 *heures du soir*, 15 *Juin*, 1815.

Monsieur le comte d'Erlon, l'Empereur ordonne à M. le comte Reille de marcher sur Gosselies, et d'y attaquer un corps ennemi qui paraissait s'y arrêter. L'intention de l'empereur est que vous marchiez aussi sur Gosselies, pour appuyer le comte Reille et le seconder dans ses opérations."

This order was not sent to Ney, for he only joined the army about five o'clock in the afternoon on the 15th, but it was sent to the Count d'Erlon, and it completely relieves Napoleon of the charges which Chesney so vehemently urges. Colonel Chesney, beyond a question, intended to be impartial in his treatment of the conduct of all the actors in this campaign, but he seems somehow to have been infected with the then prevailing disposition to disparage the capacity of Napoleon. Napoleon, having sent orders to d'Erlon, on the afternoon of the 15th, to close up on Reille at Gosselies, and to support him in his attack on the enemy there, naturally enough inquires of Ney,[1] the first thing in the morning of the 16th, if the First Corps has finished its movement, and what was the exact position of the two corps. There is no carelessness here, not a trace of it. Why Chesney should call this letter to Ney "merely a formal one" is not very clear, until we see that Chesney did not know what the orders of the afternoon before had been.

The truth is, there has been altogether too much temper shown by most of the historians of this campaign. This is true of both sides, and is especially shown in dealing with the conduct of Napoleon. The best English writers now frankly admit Wellington's mistakes in not concentrating more promptly at Quatre Bras, and in leaving such a large force at Hal during the battle of Waterloo. It is generally conceded that it was unwise for Blücher to risk a battle alone and unsupported. But it seems to be well-nigh impossible for one and the same writer to admit that both Napoleon and Grouchy made mistakes; to point out how Napoleon's carelessness in not ascertaining the direction of the Prussian retreat after Ligny, his mistaken guess as to its direction, and his delay in sending out Grouchy, gravely imperilled the success of the campaign; but that nevertheless he did foresee the possibility of the union of the allied armies, and warned Grouchy of it; and that, had this warning been sufficiently heeded, the campaign might have had a very different termination. Let us hope, that, as time goes on, this impossibility will cease to exist, and that the historical spirit will fully supplant the controversial.

[1] *Documents inédits,* pp. 26, 27.

APPENDIX VIII.

LECTURE VII.

ON NEY'S EMPLOYMENT OF THE CAVALRY OF THE GUARD AT WATERLOO.

How Ney was permitted thus to engage troops not under his orders has never been satisfactorily explained. But it was one of the natural results of Napoleon's mode of fighting this battle, which was entirely different from his usual practice. By giving to Ney the general direction of the battle against the English army, it resulted that there were, so to speak, two generals on the field, Ney and himself. That Ney on a detached operation should command two corps might well have been a judicious arrangement; but that such an arrangement should be persisted in during a great battle where the Emperor was present in person, strikes one at first as uncalled for and unwise. It is, however, undoubtedly, to be attributed to the necessity under which the Emperor labored of conducting also the other battle against the Prussians near Planchenoit.

APPENDIX IX.

LECTURE VII.

ON DR. EDWARD A. FREEMAN'S CONTINUING TO USE THE NAME "BUONAPARTE" IN HIS HISTORIES.

It is curious and not a little amusing to see the persistency with which some English writers of to-day retain the petty prejudices of a former time. Dr. Edward A. Freeman, to whose historical researches in many fields the world is much indebted, evidently enjoys speaking of Napoleon by his family surname. In fact, he will not even allow his victim to decide for himself how that name ought to be spelled. In the "General Sketch of European History" (London: Macmillan & Co., 1874; pp. 329 *et seq.*), Buonaparte (*sic*) is spoken of as "calling himself" Consul, Emperor of the French, and King of Italy. Whether he ever was the First Consul of France; whether it is or is not correct to speak of him as Emperor of the French and King of Italy, are questions which do not seem in the least to trouble Dr. Freeman. To him, an Englishman, this objectionable foreigner, having started in life as a private citizen possessing the family name of Buonaparte, Buonaparte he shall remain, so Dr. Freeman wills, no matter what may have been the world's recognition of the titles he assumed, or the posts he filled. I had at one time thought that this extraordinary refusal to give to the ruler of France the rank which was accorded to him by all the states of Continental Europe might be accounted for by the fact that the English government never recognized Napoleon the First as Emperor of the French. But this theory I find is untenable; for when Dr. Freeman comes to speak of the Third Napoleon, whose title was not only recognized by England as by the other powers, but who was the ally of England in the Crimean war, was received at Windsor Castle and received the Queen at the Tuileries, he gives him no more decent treatment than he gave to his uncle. It is Buonaparte (*sic*) who becomes a prisoner at Sedan (p. 351). I recall nothing quite so good as this, except the conduct of the jacobins in calling Louis XVI. and Marie Antoinette Citoyen and Citoyenne Capet.

INDEX.

Abensberg, action at, 142.
Abercromby, Sir Ralph, 49.
Alexander I., of Russia, tries to induce Prussia to join the coalition, 124; loses his army at Friedland, 129; makes peace with Napoleon, 129; aspires to "the deliverance of Europe," 198; in Paris, 220; decides that the powers will not treat with Napoleon, 222; an unfortunate decision, 222; a representative of the old order of things, 321; in alliance with France, 322; had no heart in the French alliance, 322; his conquests, 322; attitude on the Polish question, 322, 323; to attack Napoleon a question of expediency, 324; decides not to begin the war, 324; what he hoped to do in 1811, 324.
Alison, Sir Archibald, 1.
Alps, passes of, 52; Napoleon crosses, into Italy, 53.
Alvinzi, general, 24.
Amiens, peace of, broken by England, 108.
Arcola, bridge of, 24.
Aspern, battle of, 143.
Auerstädt, battle of, 127.
Augereau, marshal, 28.
Austerlitz, battle of, 114-117; Napoleon's greatest battle, 115, 116; character of the French army, 115; blunder of the allies, 116; a decisive success, 117.
Austria, in 1789, 3; war with France, 21-25; Napoleon's brilliant campaign against, in Italy, 23-25; peace preliminaries signed at Leoben, 25; treaty of Campo Formio, 25; war breaks out again (1799), 38; aided by Russia, 38; Moreau's able campaign against, 50, 51; the campaign in Italy, 51-57; peace concluded at Lunéville, 62; results of the war, 99; joins England and Russia against France, 108; invades Bavaria, 111; rejects peace offers, 112; loses the Tyrol and Venice, 117; opens the campaign of 1809, 141; defeated at Wagram, 149; peace concluded at Vienna, 149; ally of France in the Russian campaign, 163; demands a price for neutrality, 211; joins the coalition against Napoleon, 214; course in Italy, after Waterloo, 301.
Bagratiou, Prince, 164-167.
Barclay de Tolly, general, 164-167.
Bautzen, battle of, 210.
Bavaria, refuses to join the coalition, 111; the Tyrol annexed to, 117.
Beauharnais, Eugene, Viceroy of Italy, 108; defeats the Austrians in the Tyrol, 144; in the retreat from Moscow, 185.
Beauharnais, Josephine, marries Napoleon, 20; character, 20; influence over Napoleon, 21; divorce, 155.
Beaulieu, general, 24.
Belgium, preparations for the campaign in, 241; the allied forces, 242; Napoleon's plans, 242, 248; crosses the Sambre, 248; movements of the allies, 249-252; Saint Amand and Ligny, 253, 254; Quatre Bras, 255-257; the Prussian retreat after Ligny, 261, 262; Waterloo, 271-283; review of the campaign, 285-292.
Benningsen, general, 129.
Beresina, passage of the, 187-191.
Bernadotte, marshal, 115, 127.
Bernard, Prince, of Saxe-Weimar, 248.
Bertrand order, the, 263, 329-337.
Blücher, marshal, urges the Saxons to revolt, 204; his army in Belgium defeated, 242; at Ligny, 253; unhorsed at Ligny, 265; retires to Wavre, 268; promises Wellington assistance, 271; joins Wellington, 280; shows the real soldier spirit, 284.
Bonaparte, Jerome, made King of Westphalia, 130; Napoleon's letter to, 132.
Bonaparte, Joseph, King of Naples, 136; King of Spain, 137.
Bonaparte, Napoleon, at Brienne, 12; military enthusiasm, 12; an accurate student, 13; love of detail and exactness, 13; at Toulon, 14; appointed general of brigade, 15; not a harsh man, 16; quells insurrection of the Sections of Paris, 19; marriage, 20; in command of the army of Italy, 21; plan of the Italian campaigns, 22, 23; at the Bridge of Lodi, 24, 27; enters Milan, 24; defeats Wurmser, 24; mili

342 INDEX.

tary reputation, 26; at Arcola, 27; idol of the army, 27; departure for Egypt, 31; return, 41; his popularity, 42; overturns the Directory, 43; not a destroyer of French liberties, 46; chosen First Consul, 47; reorganization of the government, 47; desires peace, 48; war resumed with Austria, 49; his plan, 51; his army, 52; crosses the Alps, 53; enters Milan, 54; at Marengo, 56; a characteristic campaign, 57; audacity, 58; incurred unnecessary hazard in Marengo campaign, 59; compared with Moreau, 59; Lanfrey's criticism, 60; opposed by jacobins and royalists, 62; plots against his life, 65; Georges' scheme, 66-70; orders seizure of the Duc d'Enghien, 71, 72; did Napoleon commit a counter-assassination? 73-87; kindness to Moreau, 88; share in forming the Code Napoleon, 91-94; domestic policy, 89-98; the Concordat, 94; blamed for his part in reorganizing Germany, 100; Emperor of the French and King of Italy, 107; projected invasion of England, 108-110; campaign of 1805, 111; captures Ulm, 112; enters Vienna, 112; peace offers, 112; the Prussian envoy, 114; Austerlitz, 114-117; peace of Presburg, 117; his success a gain for European progress, 119; establishes Confederation of the Rhine, 120; Protector of the Confederation, 120; war with Prussia, 126; Jena, 126-128; conquest of Prussia, 128; winterquarters at Warsaw, 129; Eylau, 129; peace of Tilsit, 129; introduces the Code into Westphalia, 131; letter to Jerome, 133; better government the need of Europe, 133; desires a consolidation of the German states, 134; not justified in dethroning the Spanish Bourbons, 136; did not understand the Spanish people, 137; proper course toward Spain, 140; invasion of Spain, 140; departure for Paris, 140; war with Austria, 141; enters Vienna, 142; at the island of Lobau, 143, 144; Wagram, 145-149; peace of Vienna, 149; the succession, 152-154; divorces Josephine, 155; marriage to Maria Louisa, and birth of a son, 155; prospects of the Empire, 155; accepts the Russian challenge, 162; preparations for the campaign, 163; welcome at Wilna, 163; Smolensk, 168-170; Borodino, 172, 173; refuses to put in the Guard, 173; a terrible mistake, 174; arrival at Moscow, 175; burning of the city, 177; retreat unavoidable, 178; weakness shown in delaying the retreat, 180; discipline of the army impaired, 182; Malo-Jaroslawetz, 183; the retreat commenced, 184; terrible losses, 184; Krasnoi, 185; "a day of honor," 186; passage of the Beresina, 187-191; arrival at Paris, 192; machinations of the powers against, in 1813, 200-202; prepares for the campaign, 202, 208, 209; Spanish policy, 206, 207; Lützen, 210; Bautzen, 210; the Austrian demands, 211-214; his scattered army, 215, 216; regards the war as a game, 217; France invaded, 218; fall of the Empire, 219; his policy condemned, 221; abdication, 222; exiled to Elba, 224; the mistake of the allies, 232; a hero in exile, 232; the return from Elba, 233; his welcome, 234; enters Paris, 234; reception by his marshals, 234, 235; policy of peace and reform, 235; messages of amity to the powers, 235; declared against by the Congress of Vienna, 235; combinations against, 236; undertakes to meet the demands of the liberal party, 237; proclaims a new constitution, 237; attitude of the Chambers, 238, 239; neglects to identify his cause with that of France, 240; plan for invading Belgium, 242, 248; his army, 243; his officers, 243-246; refuses Davout permission to take the field, 245; proclamation to the army, 247; crosses the Sambre, 248; Ligny, 253, 254; his last victory, 255; neglect to ascertain the direction of the Prussian retreat, 261, 262, 285; his careless confidence, 262; orders Grouchy to pursue the Prussians, 263; ought to have attacked Wellington at Quatre Bras, 265; Grouchy's despatch, 266, 267; the consequence of trusting Grouchy, 271; had a better army than his opponent at Waterloo, 271; delay in commencing the action, 272; reliance on Grouchy, 272; assault on Hougoumont, 273; tries to turn Wellington's left, 273; failure, 274; fighting a double battle, 275; should have acted on the defensive, 280; the last charge of the Guard, 281; the flight of the army, 282; he quits the field, 283; his fatal mistakes, 285, 286; arrival in Paris, 293; abdication, 294; surrenders himself to the British government, 295; exiled to St. Helena, 295; his life there, 296; treatment by the English government, 296; his narratives of his campaigns, 297, 298; death, 298; burial, 299; erroneous view of, by liberal writers, 302; estimate of, 304, 305; charge of selfishness, 306; his character and his acts, 307; his occasional severities, 309; his hold on his soldiers, 310; anecdotes, 311-315; tribute from his German soldiers, 315; his tactics in his later campaigns criticised by Marmont, 325.

Borodino, battle of, 171-173.
Bourbon plots against Napoleon, 67-71.
Bourbons, the, restoration of, 225; after Waterloo, 299.
Bourtourlin, colonel, 174.
Brunswick, Duke of, 126, 128, 247.
Bülow, general, 247, 249.
Buonaparte, on Freeman's use of the name, 338.

INDEX. 343

Cambacérès, consul, 47.
Campo Formio, treaty of, 25.
Caraccioli, admiral, executed by Nelson, 37, 300.
Chamber of Deputies, convened by Napoleon, 237.
Chambray's statistics of the war with Russia, 326.
Charles, Archduke, 25; at Wagram, 145-149.
Charles IV. of Spain, 137.
Chesney, C. C., quoted, 330, 332, 335-337.
Cisalpine Republic, 26.
Coalition of 1805, causes of, 108.
Code Napoleon, 46; Napoleon's share in forming, 91-93; its utility, 94; introduced into the German states, 120; into Westphalia, 131; into Naples, 134.
Confederation of the Rhine, 120.
Congress of Vienna, declares against Napoleon, 235; the allied sovereigns' distrust of Napoleon, 236.
Constitutional party in France, 237, 238.
Consulate, the, 47; the beginning of the Empire, 62; jacobin and royalist opposition to, 62-65; English attacks on, 69; reforms of the Consular government, 89; Lanfrey's criticism, 89; the Code Napoleon its most important measure, 91.
Continental System, the, 151.
Convention of Paris, 295; Wellington allows it to be violated by the king, 299.
Czartoriski, Count, 322, 323.

Danube, passage of, 142-144.
D'Artois, Comte, favors Georges' scheme, 67.
Davout, marshal, 115; at Auerstädt, 127, 128; made Duke of Auerstädt, 128; entry into Berlin, 128; at Smolensk, 166; Minister of War, 245; wishes to take the field, 245; Napoleon refuses to permit him to serve, 245; surrenders Paris, 295.
Defeat, Waterloo a synonym for, 283.
D'Erlon, general, 243, 244; at Quatre Bras, 255, 256, 335, 336.
Desaix, general, at Marengo, 56.
Directory, the, established, 19; *coup d'état* of 1797, 29; despotic rule of, 30, 40; unpopularity, 39; quarrels with the United States, 39; a transitory phase of the Revolution, 39; its singular position in 1799, 39; composed of insignificant men, 40; existing on sufferance, 42; overturned by Napoleon, 43.
Divine right of kings, 2.

Eckmühl, action at, 142.
Elba, Napoleon's exile to, 224; an unwise thing, 224; his return from, 233.
Egypt, expedition to, projected, 30; object, 31; an act of folly, 31; sailing of the expedition, 31; return, 49.
Empire, the, the Consulate its beginning, 62; demanded by the people, 96; its meaning, 98; its aggrandizement a cause of alarm, 156, 157; its extension a result of the defeat of the coalitions, 236; effect of its fall, 241.
England, assists French royalists, 64; supports Bourbon schemes against Napoleon's life, 68-71; breaks the peace of Amiens, 108; Napoleon's projected invasion of, 108-110; in alliance with Russia, 108; continues the war after peace of Presburg, 121; motives in opposing Napoleon, 121; effect of the continental wars on, 151; unintermitted hostility to France, 207; Napoleon's mistake, 207; part in the Waterloo campaign, 241; Napoleon surrenders to the British government, 295; treatment of Napoleon at St. Helena, 296.
Enghien, Duc d', suspected of complicity in the plot against Napoleon, 69; arrest at Ettenheim in Baden, 72; trial and execution, 72; charges against Napoleon, 72; the arrest justifiable, 74; proceedings of the court-martial, 75-77; who composed the court, 75; the official records stolen, 75; the duke's avowals, 76, 77; the court had no choice but to condemn him, 77; why was he tried? 78; the evidence in his papers, 78-84; Napoleon examines them, 80; questions based on their contents, 80; their contents, 81; Count Miot de Melito's statement, 82; the duke desires an interview with the First Consul, 83; his hurried trial and execution, 84; the First Consul astounded, 85; who was responsible, 86.
Essling, battle of, 143.
Europe, prior to the French Revolution, 2-6; ruled in the interest of privileged classes, 2; improvement in the condition of the people, 5; government by the people impracticable, 5; the need of, 5; nature of the contest in, 32; shown by the Revolution of Naples, 34; benefited by war of 1805, 119; condition in 1809, 150; grievances against Napoleon in 1813, 199-207; after Waterloo, 299-302.
Eylau, battle of, 129.

Ferdinand IV., of Naples, declares war against France, 33; is defeated, 34; breach of faith toward France, 135; banishment, 135.
Finland, annexed to Russia, 322.
Fleurus, action at, 252.
France, before the Revolution, 4; during the Revolution, 7-11; volunteer and regular army of, 12; the 9th of Thermidor, 1794, 18; change in public opinion, 18; constitution of 1795, 19; provisions ensuring republican rule, 19; rising of the Sections, 1795, 19; war with Austria, 21-25; the 18th of Fructidor, 1797, 30; a deliverer from Middle Age barbarism, 33; on the side of progress, 34; French reverses, 38; the 18th of Brumaire, 1799, 43; work of the Revolution, 44,

INDEX.

danger of the return of the Bourbons, 45; the *coup d'etat* hailed with joy, 46; the three Consuls, 47; war with Austria resumed, 49; French peasants' regard for the republic, 63; in a state of administrative disorder, 90; work of the Consulate, 90; the Code Napoleon, 91; the Concordat, 94; the Empire established, 96; peace of Lunéville, 99; territorial acquisitions, 99; influence in reorganizing Germany, 99, 100; the coalition of 1805, 108; cause of the coalition, 108; German allies, 111; peace of Presburg, 117, 121; war with Prussia, 126; peace of Vienna, 149; war with Russia impending, 158; peace negotiations, 160; expected to act on the defensive in the Russian campaign, 162; fall of the Empire, 219; the allied army in Paris, 220; weary of Napoleon, 220; his policy condemned, 221; restoration of the Bourbons, 224; a doubtful future, 225; Louis XVIII., 225; a dissatisfied people, 226, 227; the returned emigrants, 228, 229; difficulties of the new kingdom, 230; grounds for discontent, 231; Napoleon's return, 233; a complete revolution, 235; right to choose her own form of government, 236; prepares to maintain the right, 237, 239; public enthusiasm, 238; the constitutional party, 238; the need of France, 240; after Waterloo, 293; Napoleon's abdication, 294; a provisional government established, 294; but does not obtain recognition, 294; the convention of Paris, 295; Louis XVIII. resumes the throne, 295; vindictive action of the Bourbons, 299; the convention violated by the king, 299–301.
Francis I., of Austria, unsatisfactory answer to Napoleon's peace overtures, 48.
Frasnes, 248.
Freeman, E. A., criticism on his use of the name "Buonaparte," 338.
French Revolution; see *Revolution*.
Friedland, battle of, 129.
Fyffe's "Modern Europe" quoted, 101, 102.

Genoa, Masséna besieged in, 51.
George III., of England, reply to Napoleon's peace overtures, 48.
Georges Cadoudal's scheme to murder the First Consul, 66; the conspirators aided by the Bourbon princes, 68; and by the British government, 68; arrest of the conspirators, 68; execution, 88.
Gérard, general, 243, 270.
Germany, Moreau's campaign in, 50, 51; French influence in reorganizing, 99, 100, 102; Rhenish provinces annexed to France, 99; a popular measure, 103; the wisdom of the measure, 107; campaign of 1805 in, 111; state of western Germany in 1815, 241;

Waterloo a check to liberal ideas in, 301.
Great man theory of history, 320, 321.
Great St. Bernard pass, 52.
Grouchy, marshal, 244; ordered to pursue the Prussians after Ligny, 263; at Gembloux, 266; despatch to Napoleon, 266, 267; learns that the Prussians are at Wavre, 268; proposes going to Sart à Walhain, 268; his true course, 268, 269; delay in starting, 269; refuses to march to the sound of the cannon, 269; his useless march, 270; Napoleon's reliance on, 272; responsibility for his own conduct, 286; Soult's despatches to, 287–291; did not influence his movements, 289; learns of the Emperor's defeat, 292; joins the wreck of the main army, 292; controversy on Grouchy's responsibility for the loss of Waterloo, 329–337.

Hamilton, Lady, 36, 37.
Hamilton, Sir William, 36.
Haugwitz, Prussian envoy, 124.
Hill, Lord, 274.
Hohenlinden, battle of, 51.
Hohenlohe, Prince, 126, 128.
Holy Alliance, the, 301.
Hougoumont, Wellington's position at, 272; attack on, 273.
House of Peers, convened by Napoleon, 237.
Hulin, brigadier-general, 75.

Italy, prior to the French Revolution, 4; Napoleon's campaigns in, 22–25; what the advent of the French meant to, 25; campaign of the First Consul, 51; the Austrian situation in, 55; becomes a kingdom, 107; Venice annexed to, 117; state of, in 1815, 241.

Jacobin opposition to Napoleon, 62.
Jaffa, execution of prisoners at, 309.
Jéna, battle of, 127, 128.
John, Archduke, 51, 145.
Jomini, general, 187.
Junot's inaction at Valoutina, 169.

Knights of the Empire, 101.
Königsberg, fall of, 129.
Koutousof, Prince, 171; at Borodino, 173; his mistake as to the crossing of the Beresina, 187; proclaims the "deliverance of Europe," 198; and the dissolution of the Confederation of the Rhine, 204.
Krasnoi, Napoleon's conduct at, 185.
Kray, marshal, 49, 50.

Lafayette, a leader of the constitutional party, 238.
La Haye Sainte, Wellington's position at, 272; French repulse at, 274; capture of, by Ney, 278.
Lanfrey, 1, 62, 89, 96, 97, 98.
Lannes, marshal, 28; defeats the Austrians at Montebello, 54; at Marengo, 56; at Austerlitz, 115.

INDEX. 345

La Vendée, 64.
Lebrun, consul, 47.
Legitimacy, the cause of Europe in 1813, 202.
Leipsic, battle of, 215.
Leoben, 25.
Liberal ideas, France stands for, 34.
Ligny, battle of, 253, 254; a decided success for Napoleon, 285.
Lobau, Count de, 243; attacked at Planchenoit, 279; defeated, 283.
Lobau, island of, 142–144.
Lodi, bridge of, 24.
Losses in the Russian campaign, 193, 194, 326–329.
Louis XVIII., on the throne of France, 225; efforts to satisfy the people, 226; hostility of the army to, 227; unwise measures of, 228, 229; retires to Belgium, 235; resumes the throne, 295.
Lunéville, peace of, 62, 99.
Lützen, battle of, 210.

Macdonald, marshal, 196–198.
Mack, general, surrenders Ulm, 112.
Malo-Jaroslawetz, action at, 183.
Marengo, battle of, 56; moral effect, 57; dramatic character of the campaign, 57; its completeness of design, 57; its audacity, 58.
Maria Louisa, of Austria, marriage to Napoleon, 155.
Marmont, marshal, criticism on Napoleon's tactics in his later campaigns, 325.
Masséna, marshal, 28; defeats Souvorof near Lake of Zurich, 38; besieged in Genoa, 53; at the island of Lobau, 143, 144; created Prince of Essling, 144; at Wagram, 146–148.
Mélas, general, 49, 52–56.
Melito, Count Miot de, 82.
Metternich, Prince, 211.
"Midnight Review, The," by Von Zedlitz, 317.
Military despotism, the best government in time of war, 237.
Moldavia, annexed to Russia, 322.
Mollendorf, general, 126, 128.
Mont Cenis pass, 52.
Mont St. Gothard pass, 52.
Montebello, battle of, 54.
Moore, Sir John, 140.
Moravia, 112, 113.
Moreau, general, commands Army of the Rhine, 49; able campaign in Germany, 50, 51; routs Archduke John at Hohenlinden, 51; character and abilities, 51; exile, 51, 88; and death, 51; compared with Napoleon, 59; kindness of Napoleon to, 88.
Moscow, Napoleon's arrival at, 175, 176; condition of the army, 176; abandoned by the inhabitants, 177; burning of, 177; an appalling catastrophe, 177; reasons for the retreat, 177, 178; Napoleon's delay, 178–181; activity of the Russians, 181; lack of discipline in the French army, 182; the retreat, 183.

Müller, Niklas, his eulogium on Napoleon's military character, 315.
Murat, marshal, responsibility in Duc d'Enghien's case, 85; at Austerlitz, 114.

Naples, misgoverned by the Bourbons, 33; French sympathizers in, 33; British aid to the court party, 33; the French army welcomed by the better classes, 34; abandoned by the French, 36; Nelson sets aside the capitulation, 36; remonstrances of the English captains, 37; Bourbon breach of faith, 135; the Bourbons banished, 135; Joseph Bonaparte made king, 136; effect of his rule, 136.
National Convention, 18.
Nelson, Lord, at Naples, 36, 37.
Ney, marshal, at Borodino, 172; joins the army in Belgium, 244; at Frasnes, 248; ordered to occupy Quatre Bras, 252; battle of Quatre Bras, 255–257; why he did not occupy Quatre Bras, 256–258; captures La Haye Sainte, 278; trial and execution, 299; on his employment of the cavalry of the Guard at Waterloo, 338.
Nile, battle of the, 38.

Orange, Prince of, 247.
Orcha, 186.
Ott, general, 55.
Oudinot, general, 182, 187, 188, 190.

Paris, surrender of, 219; Davout charged with its defence, 245; situation in, after the battle of Waterloo, 293; surrendered by Davout, 295.
Parthenopæan Republic, 36.
Picton, Sir Thomas, 247; death, 274.
Piedmont annexed to France, 99.
Pitt, William, and the coalition of 1805, 123.
Planchenoit, action at, 279.
Polish question and the Russian war, 321–324.
Political theorists, 104.
Presburg, peace of, 117.
Privileged classes in Europe, 2.
Prussia, in 1789, 3; the campaign of 1805, 113, 123, 124; reasons for not joining the coalition, 123; alliance with Russia, 124; hostile feeling toward France, 124, 125; position among the nations, 125; declares war, 126; suffers defeat at Jéna, 128; conquest of, 128; territorial changes, 130; ally of France in the Russian campaign, 163; hopes to profit by French disasters, 195; grievances against France, 199; duplicity, 203; war preparations, 203; takes part in campaign of 1815, 241.

Quatre Bras, Wellington concentrates his troops at, 251; Ney's attack on, 255–257; a staff officer's blunder, 256–260; battle of, not a French defeat, 257; effect of the fight, 258.

Réal, councillor, 80, 81, 84, 85.
Reign of Terror, 8, 18.
Reille, general, 243, 244.
Revolution, French, Europe prior to, 2–6; based on the rights of man, 7; despotism in, 7; an anomaly, 8; its necessity, 8; did not give the people political power, 9; their gain in liberty and equality, 9; not a rose-water revolution, 9; losses of the privileged classes by, 10; their hostility, 10; beginning of a new order, 10; "an irrepressible conflict," 11; work of, 44.
Rivoli, action of, 25.
Robespierre, 15; downfall, 18.
Roman Catholic Church in France, 94–96.
Rostopchin, Count, governor of Moscow, 177.
Royalist opposition to Napoleon, 62, 64, 65.
Ruffo, Cardinal, 36.
Russia, prior to the French Revolution, 3; aids Austria in 1799, 38; joins England against France, 108; seeks a pretext for war (1810), 159; preparations, 159; Napoleon welcomed at Wilna, 163; the Russian armies, 164; military manœuvres, 165-168; Smolensk, 166; Borodino, 171-173; burning of Moscow, 177; Napoleon's retreat from Moscow, 183-193; end of the campaign, 193; losses in the campaign, 193, 195; Koutousof's proclamation, 198; Polish question and the Russian war, 321-324.

Saint Amand, action at, 253, 254.
St. Helena, Napoleon's exile to, 295; his life there, 296.
Sardinia absorbed by Austria, 51
Sart à Walhain, Grouchy's useless march to, 269, 270, 332.
Savary, colonel, commanding at castle of Vincennes, 75; report of Duc d'Enghien's reply to the court, 76, 77; not responsible for the prompt execution of d'Enghien, 86.
Schmettau, general, 128.
Schwartzenberg, Prince, 181, 198.
Scott, Sir Walter, 1; "Life of Napoleon" cited, 69.
Sections of Paris insurrection put down by Bonaparte, 19. 29.
Shaw-Kennedy, Sir James, on Grouchy's responsibility for loss of Waterloo, 333, 334.
Smith, Spencer, intrigues of, 71.
Smolensk, 168, 169, 184.
Soult, marshal, 114, 115; chief of staff in Waterloo campaign, 246, 261.
Souvorof, general, in Italy, 38; defeated by Masséna, 38.
Spain, backwardness of, 5; under Bourbon rule, 134; Napoleon's treatment of the Spanish Bourbons, 135; his mistaken view of the people, 136; his reforms not welcomed, 137; the patriotic feeling in, 138; Joseph Bonaparte's ill-success in governing, 138;

the new system rejected, 130; invaded by Napoleon, 140; history since 1814, 139; the Spanish war, 206, 207.
Spencer, Herbert, the "Great-Man-Theory of History," 309-311.
Stein, Baron, 101.

Tchitchagoff, admiral, 181, 187, 188, 190.
Thiers, L. A., 1.
Tilsit, Peace of, 129, 130.
Toulon, siege of, 14.
Trafalgar, battle of, 110.
"Two Grenadiers, The," by Heine, 316.
Tyrol, ceded to Bavaria, 117.

Ulm, capture of, 111, 112.
United States, the Directory quarrels with, 39.
Uxbridge, Lord, 247.

Vandamme, general, 243; and the captain, 312-314.
Venice, ceded to Kingdom of Italy, 117.
Victor, marshal, at Marengo, 56; in the retreat from Moscow, 188, 190.
Vienna, Congress of, declares against Napoleon, 235.

Wagram, battle of, 145-149.
Wallachia, annexed to Russia, 322.
War, a game of hazard, 60.
War, causes for, in 1810, 156-158.
Warsaw, Grand Duchy of, created, 130; evacuated by the French, 198; occupied by the Russians, 198; the Russian designs on, in 1810-11, 322, 323.
Wartensleben, general, 128.
Waterloo, battle of, 271; the two armies, 271; Wellington's position, 272; Napoleon's delay in commencing the action, 272; attack on Hougoumont, 273; the attack a failure, 274; French repulse at La Haye Sainte, 274; approach of the Prussians, 275; a double battle, 275; failure of the cavalry attacks, 275; losses of the English, 277; capture of La Haye Sainte, 278; arrival of the Prussians, 280; the French outnumbered, 280; Napoleon should have taken the defensive, 280; the Guard attacks the English right centre, 281; and is driven back, 282; Wellington's advance, 282; rout of the French army, 283; Napoleon quits the field, 283; a synonym for utter defeat, 283; discussion of the campaign, 329-337.
Wavre, Blücher retires to, 268; Grouchy's march on, 269, 270, 329-337.
Wellington, Duke of, in Spain, 206; his army in Belgium, 242. 247; his officers, 247; at the Duchess of Richmond's ball, 250; his idea of Napoleon's movements, 250; favored by fortune, 251; concentrates his troops at Quatre Bras, 251; saved by a blunder, 259; agrees to fight at Waterloo, 266; his army, 271; assistance prom-

ised by Blücher, 271; acts on the defensive, 272; his position, 272; Napoleon tries to turn his left, 273; his critical situation, 277; loses La Haye Sainte, 278; reinforced by Blücher, 280; forces the Guard to retire, 281; orders his whole line to advance, 282; puts the French to rout, 282; honor due to, 284; allows the convention of Paris to be violated, 299–301; and Ney to be shot, 299; comparison of his conduct with that of General Grant, 299.
Westphalia, Kingdom of, created, 130; its constitution, 131.

"Who Lost Waterloo?" 329.
Wilna, 163–167, 191–193.
Wilson, Sir Robert, quoted, 186, 188, 192.
Wittgenstein, Count, 181, 187, 204.
Wurmser, general, 24.
Würtemberg, ally of France in 1805, 111.

Yorck, Prussian general, surrender of, 196; an indefensible transaction, 196–198.

Ziethen, Prussian general, 248, 249.

www.ingramcontent.com/pod-product-compliance
Lightning Source LLC
Chambersburg PA
CBHW032015220426
43664CB00006B/253